Mary
Christmas.
1984.

Peter & Susan

The Little White Schoolhouse

(Volume 1)

Bryant School as it looked (above) when the author taught there in 1929 and as it looked (below) in 1967, forlorn but full of fond memories of bygone years.

The Little White Schoolhouse

(Volume 1)

JOHN C. CHARYK

WESTERN PRODUCER PRAIRIE BOOKS
SASKATOON, SASKATCHEWAN

Cover painting by Don Frache
Cover design by Warren Clark, GDL

Printed and bound in Canada by Modern Press ⟶1
Saskatoon, Saskatchewan

Western Producer Prairie Books publications are produced and manufactured in the middle of western Canada by a unique publishing venture owned by a group of prairie farmers who are members of Saskatchewan Wheat Pool. From the firs book in 1954, a reprint of a serial originally carried in the weekly newspaper, Th *Western Producer*, to the book before you now, the tradition of providing enjoyable and informative reading for all Canadians is continued.

To
My Mother (Anna) and Father (John)
and all the pioneers across Canada who, in one way or another,
contributed their precious time and energy
towards making the rural schools of our land
a truly proud moment in the growth of a great Canadian nation.

Canadian Cataloguing in Publication Data

Charyk, John C., 1908-
     The little white schoolhouse

     Includes index.
     ISBN 0-88833-140

     1. Rural schools — Prairie Provinces.
I. Title.
LB1568.C2C46   372.9'712

TABLE OF CONTENTS

LIST OF ILLUSTRATIONS

PREFACE

After taking a teachers' training course at the Calgary Normal School in 1929 I accepted a position in the Bryant School District No. 2533 some eleven miles north of the village of Bindloss in southeastern Alberta. After three years I found the experience of teaching in a rural school satisfying and rewarding. I boarded with the John Young family who took me in as one of them. They introduced me to every aspect of farm life. Alton, their second son and a grade ten student in my school, probably did more than anyone else in giving me, a railroader's son and completely ignorant of farm life, a feeling and a love for rural Alberta. It was with a heavy heart that I said farewell to Bryant School when I left to continue my education at the Mount Royal College in Calgary.

I did not return to the district until thirty years later. What a shock! My former rural school had been sacrificed in the name of progress. Perhaps it would have been much better had I never gone back. The schoolhouse, which had meant so much to me, had been converted into a mere granary. Not a single family that I used to know lived in the district any more. The familiar homes that formerly housed these friendly people were forlorn, deserted and quiet. Where was everybody? I stood near the dilapidated schoolhouse and pondered. Disturbing memories came out of the past. Had my three years at Bryant accomplished anything in the scheme of things? From what I could see around and about me I might never have existed. I felt distraught, humble and disappointed. I eventually consoled myself by realizing that the results of education are not always evident in material things but are of the mind and spirit. A teacher affects eternity— one can never tell where his influence stops.

As I drove back home to Hanna I had a feeling—a call—that I must do something to bring "my" rural school back to life. Why not all rural schools? Yes! I knew what I would do. I would write a book so that future generations could learn what the country schools were like. I would portray the life and spirit of these once notable and respected institutions. After all, the Canada of today owes much to the one-room schools of yesterday. Only an educated democracy can be a real democracy. It was what transpired in these country schools during the past three-quarters of a century that was largely instrumental in consummating this precious way of life for Canadians. Canada's future was written on the blackboards of the Little White Schoolhouses.

Yes, I would ask the oldtimers across Canada through advertisements in the press to assist me in this historical venture by sending their reminiscences of school days to me. Certainly their first-hand knowledge would help round out an interesting and informative account of the one-room country schools.

What title should I give the book? At this moment the phrase "The Little White Schoolhouse" began to hound me like the refrain of a popular ditty. There and then I decided to use it.

That very night I mulled over plans for writing the book and doing the necessary research work as the preliminary steps towards making *The Little White Schoolhouse* a reality.

Today, some nine years later, my labor of love is over and anyone who wishes may relive the heydays of the rural school vicariously by reading the book.

The results of this study of rural schools in Western Canada disclosed that in nature and history they differed little from their counterparts in other parts of Canada and the United States. This was found to be particularly evident in the Maritime provinces of Canada and the Mid-western states of the U.S. Hence this narrative could well apply to the one-room schools that used to dot the countryside in most parts of the North American continent.

So much material on the country school has come to light that it is impossible to include the entire story in a single volume so a second volume follows. It includes, chapters on. Recesses; Discipline; School Pony; Blizzards; School Fairs and Music Festivals; Christmas Concerts; Rural Schools as Community Centres; Humor in the Rural School; School Boards; The Inspector; What Oldtimers Remember; The Decline and Fall.

I wish to express my sincere thanks to the more than one thousand individuals who responded so readily to my requests for information. This manuscript could not have been possible without such splendid co-operation. I wish to extend a special thanks to the following for their more than generous assistance. These people took the time, the interest and the trouble to supply memoirs that frequently extended to theses in themselves.

Armstrong, E. Vernette
Bach, Mrs. I. J.
Beierbach, Mrs. Kay
Bell, Mrs. E. J.
Birdsall, J. E.
Bishop, Mrs. C. A.
Bolton, Margaret
Boose, Edith
Branton, H. F.
Braun, John J.

Breuning, Mrs. A. J.
Burns, Mrs. C.
Campbell, Alice A.
Campbell, Mrs. M. J.
Cay, Maurice
Christie, Mrs. R.
Clark, Mrs. George A.
Collins, Ruth
Colwell, Kathleen
Cossar, Mrs. M. E.

Davis, Mrs. W. H.
Denny, C. D.
Dickson, D. B.
Donaldson, Mrs. Lucille O.
Douglas, Mrs. H.
Duncan, Mrs. H. D.
Edmundson, Edith Cecilia
Erickson, Merril
Everatt, Mrs. A.
Farrer, B.
Farwell, Mrs. M. C.
Fenske, Melvin
Fines, Mrs. C. E.
Florkewich, Mrs. Peter
French, C. K.
Garriott, Mrs. Clarence
Glendinning, Mrs. J. A.
Glenn, Mrs. H.
Graham, Jean
Green, Cecil
Gunnarsson, Caroline
Hambly, Stan
Harris, Maude
Hedberg, Mrs. G.
Helmer, Larry E.
Hemphill, Leona G.
Hodgins, Mrs. M. A.
Hodgson, W. Eric
Hoff, Raymond A.
Hoffs, Dorothy
Holden, F. M.
Hosie, Mrs. I.
Ironside, Judy
James, Ferg
Johnson, D. F.
Johnston, Stella F.
Jones, M. W.
Knauft, Mrs. Louis
Kyforuk, Mrs. Sofia
Lalor, Bert
Lamb, Bruce
Lee, Mrs. Gina
Lee, G. W.

Liddell, Ken
Loat, Mrs. Allen
Lowrey, C. W.
Lyle, E. B.
Macdonald, R. H.
MacGregor, J.
McCrea, G. R.
Mills, Mrs. Louise
Mitchell, Mrs. D. R.
Moules, John W.
Mitchell, Mrs. J. P.
Nesbitt, J. L.
Parkes, Mrs. J.
Perrick, Vladimer
Plunkett, William
Primrose, Tom
Rault, Ethel
Relf, Mrs. Norman C.
Robertson, George
Roddick, Dorothy
Runyan, Mrs. Carl
Ryan, Mrs. A. T.
Sabey, Ralph
Schaefer, Mrs. D. E.
Shipley, Mrs. H. R.
Smith, Mrs. Joseph
Smith, S. B.
Sutherland, Mrs. J. S.
Talmage, Mrs. G. C.
Thompson, Mrs. Glenn
Thomson, Georgina H.
Toews, Henry
Tower, C.
Trudeau, Mrs. O. J.
Unsworth, Mrs. O. J.
Viste, Mrs. Freda
Van Blaricom, Earl
Webb, Alice
Wiggins, F. W.
Wigmore, George
Willner, Dorothy W.
Wilson, Mrs. R. A.
Winter, Ken

February 13, 1968.

John Constantine Charyk
Hanna, Alberta

Publisher's Note: The second volume that John Charyk alludes to in his Preface was published in 1970 as *PULSE OF THE COMMUNITY*.

THE BEGINNING OF THE
LITTLE WHITE SCHOOLHOUSE

The problem of education in the early days in Canada was especially pressing because an increasing proportion of the later immigrants were of foreign extraction and spoke foreign languages. The pioneers of the West had come from eastern Canada, Great Britain and the United States; they were resolved that their tradition of combined order and freedom should not be lost and they knew that one of the best means of instilling the immigrant with these objectives was to teach him the English language. Fortunately the majority of immigrants were equally keen to learn it, knowing that without it they would be at a disadvantage. Yet many of them loved their mother tongues and desired to retain them. The problem was further complicated by the presence of a number of French who felt that the history of their ancestors in Canada put their language in a different light from those of the other non-English-speaking peoples. In spite of these difficulties the majority of immigrants planned to provide their children with an education, hoping that their decision would give the youngsters a better chance in life than they had themselves. Therefore as soon as the rudiments of a home were established they turned their attention to the task of establishing a school for their children. The attainment of such a goal was not without its share of hardship, sacrifice, or discouragement but eventually a school district would be formed and a building of some sort erected. It mattered little whether it was of log, stone, sod, mud or boards so long as it could be called a school. Yet with all its shortcomings and lack of qualified teachers it was able to educate.

The idea of a schoolhouse was so new that one day in 1896 Miss McCullough, the teacher in the Heather Brae S.D. (O'Haton, Alta.) looked up to see the swarthy figure of an Indian at the window. With a hand at each side of his face he was directing his curious gaze inward. The children froze in fear but the lone figure, having acquainted himself with the wonders of education, melted silently into the woods. Little did that Indian realize that out of thousands of such little schoolhouses, scattered across Canada, would crystallize the backbone of a great country.

—Photo provided by Mrs. D. J. Mathieu
"A tiny dot on the harvest lands." Cessford S.D., Hanna, Alta., 1916.

The late Canadian writer, Nellie McClung, who spent many years teaching in rural schools near Brandon, Manitoba, envisaged the important role that one-room schools were to play in the development of the country:

> "Weather-beaten and gray it stands,
> A tiny dot on the harvest lands.
> Not very much to see!
> Porch at the end where the gophers play;
> Smelling of crumbs on a summer day.
> Row of windows, two or three
> Inside walls of smoky gray
> Hung with torn and crooked maps.
> A broken blind that taps and taps.
> 'Not an attractive spot', you say?
> No! but here in this lowly station,
> Slowly is working an ancient law.
> And a temple is rising, that we call a nation,
> Without the sound of hammer or saw."

The Little White Schoolhouse was the bulwark of civilization in a new and primitive land. Under its roof devoted and knowledgeable men and women, steeped in the traditions and cultures of the old world, passed on to the children the fundamentals of an education that had taken mankind centuries to garner and learn. It was the cradle of a nation that was to be, a nation that in a scant one hundred years has grown up to be respected and recognized throughout the world by both large and small powers alike. If we as Canadians are to acknowledge ourselves as a nation we cannot ignore the part that the one-room school had in shaping this destiny.

Forming a school district was not difficult. The settlers who had children of school age collaborated in petitioning the provincial government to organize a school district in the area and to provide the necessary school facilities. They in turn received a copy of the government ordinance providing them with the official procedure to follow in accomplishing this objective. All they had to do was to carry out the instructions step by step as if they were following a recipe out of a cookbook.

The first requisite was the selection of a school committee. Any three residents of the proposed district could constitute this committee or, if they preferred, a meeting could be called to appoint the necessary personnel. The only qualification required of members making up this administrative body was that they actually reside in the proposed district.

The initial duty of the school committee was to apply to the Deputy Minister of Education for the forms and instructions prescribed by the Department of Education relative to the formation of new districts. Not only did they receive all this official material but also a map showing the boundaries of the schools already existing in the vicinity of the proposed district.

A careful examination of the ordinance led promoters to conclude that the government was very helpful and fair in its objective to facilitate the organization of school districts throughout the province. The district could not exceed five miles in length or breadth exclusive of road allowances. It had to include at least four persons who actually resided therein and who, on the formation of the district, would be liable to assessment of taxes for school purposes. The potential district was to contain at least eight children not younger than five nor older than sixteen years. The boundaries of the new area were to correspond as far as possible with those of neighboring districts. In other words, narrow strips of territory could not be left between the proposed district and existing districts. Large lakes, impassable streams and other natural barriers were not to separate portions of a district unless facilities had been provided whereby children could cross these to reach the school. Whenever possible the district had to be so formed as to include a road allowance at its centre. The school committees were instructed not to establish large districts as these were usually the cause of much dissatisfaction since some of the ratepayers would of necessity be at an inconvenient distance from the school. The committees were accordingly advised to petition for the formation of districts either four miles square or at the most four miles by five. In all cases where it was found necessary to petition for a district situated at some distance from existing districts it was recommended that sufficient territory be left for the convenient formation of other districts when they would be required.

In case the local school committee desired to include in their proposed district lands which had been already assimilated in established districts they were advised to follow certain procedures in order to avoid delay in the formation of the new district. First, the committee were asked to consult the trustees of the district or districts to be affected and to obtain from them written statements setting forth their views respecting the proposed alterations in the boundaries of their district. Secondly, they were asked to obtain from the residents on the lands proposed to be withdrawn from the existing districts and included in the new district a statement of their willingness or unwillingness to join the district. Opposite the signature of each resident there was to be given a description of his land and the number of children of school age living thereon. These statements were to be sent to the Department of Education along with the petition for the formation of the district.

The Department of Education, realizing the embarrassment and difficulties that could accrue from inaccurate or incomplete data, time and again emphasized the fact that in drafting the petition for the formation of a new district care should be exercised that all the information called for be given. The lands to be incorporated in the new district were to be precisely defined as to the sections, parts of sections, townships, ranges and meridian. In case quarter sections or half sections were to be included the particular quarter sections or half sections had to be specified.

The petition could not be trifled with as it carried legal status. The Department of Education required a declaration signed by a member of the local committee and declared before a commissioner, a notary public or a justice of the peace, to accompany the request. A map of the proposed district had to be provided and in order to prevent any blunders the committee were asked to number the sections and mark the townships and range not only on the map itself but in the margins as well. Yet in spite of all these safeguards, errors were still made that resulted in delay after delay or precipitated one local incident after another.

As each district was identified by an official name and number it was the school committee's responsibility to select a suitable name and include it with the original petition. As there was always the possibility that the name chosen may have already been assigned to some other district the local authorities were asked to submit four or five names.

In due course the committee received a report from the Department of Education that the limits of the proposed district had been approved and that the notices calling for the first school meeting could now be displayed. The regulation governing their posting left little to chance, for they had to be set out as prominently as possible in widely-separated places in the district and at least fourteen days before the scheduled date of the meeting. As a declaration had to be made to the effect that the notices were displayed as required by the ordinance, the work was done by one person who would note carefully the time and place of each posting. The Department of Education also cautioned the school committee to exercise diligence in recording the lands to be included in the proposed district on every notice.

The first school meeting was required by law to commence at one o'clock sharp on the afternoon of the day appointed in the notices posted. It was at this time that the potential ratepayers present elected from among themselves a chairman and a secretary. The chairman, as soon as duly elected, signed a declaration. Then before any other business could be transacted it was also necessary for each resident ratepayer to do the same if he desired to vote or take an active part in the meeting to follow. The signature or mark of each person signing the declaration was witnessed by both the chairman and secretary. To make sure that only resident ratepayers of the proposed district appended their names to the document the ordinance clearly stated that if unqualified persons signed it they were liable to a fine of ten dollars. Eligible individuals even if they arrived late at the meeting were still permitted to sign the declaration.

Once every signature had been secured the chairman announced that the poll would be open for exactly one hour for recording the votes of those in favor of and those opposed to the formation of the district. Each certified individual then presented himself in turn to the chairman who asked each voter the following questions, the answers to which were recorded by the secretary in the poll book or sheet:

1. What is your name?
2. Do you vote for or against the formation of the proposed . . . School District?

At the conclusion of one hour the chairman declared the poll closed and then announced the results. In the case of a tie the chairman was required to cast the deciding vote.

If the vote supported the formation of a school district the chairman next called for nominations of candidates to serve as trustees. On the other hand if the vote was not favorable the meeting would be adjourned. The ratepayers were allotted thirty minutes in which to propose nominees for election to the school board. Each such candidate had to be nominated by a mover and a seconder. In cases where only three persons had been nominated the chairman declared their election by acclamation, while if there were more than three, he declared a poll to elect the necessary trustees. Again each voter presented himself to the chairman who asked him the following two questions:

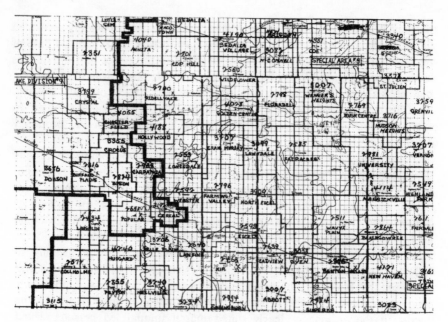

A patchwork of rural school districts in southeastern Alberta.

1. What is your name?
2. Which of the candidates nominated do you vote for?

Each resident was entitled to vote for any three nominees but he could not vote more than once for the same individual. The secretary recorded each person's replies in the official poll book. At the end of an hour the chairman was required to sum up the results of the voting and announce them. This concluded the business of the first school meeting.

The Commissioner of Education upon receipt from the local chairman of all the necessary forms pertaining to the organizational meeting that was held and being satisfied that all proceedings had been properly followed, had the prerogative of establishing the district. The official notice of the formation of the district appeared in the provincial gazette, a copy of which was sent to the trustee who had received the highest number of votes. The school board was instructed to study carefully the notice establishing the district to make sure that its composition was the same as was proposed in the original petition. If any errors or omissions were discovered they were to be reported to the Department of Education immediately.

Ultimately the trustees received the much-anticipated letter from the Minister of Education indicating that the district had been officially promulgated. The news was received with mixed feelings. The parents were elated and thankful while the children and the bachelors accepted the announcement with some reservation. For the school board it was a signal for increased activity. They were required to meet within ten days of receiving the notice of establishment to elect a chairman and secretary-treasurer.

The first school board meeting was of some significance locally. It implied that the district had accepted the responsibility of providing the very best education possible for every child within its borders and that it was now taking the initial step towards attaining this objective.

The problem of where to build the proposed school confronted the newly-constituted board right from the start. They usually agreed that the centre of the district was the ideal building site but soon discovered that it was easier said than done. The topography of the land, the nature of the soil, the presence of a slough, the lack of easy access, the difficulty of obtaining a clear title to the required land, or the violent opposition of some ratepayers, often militated against the decision to erect the school building in the geometric centre of the district.

The regulations of the Department of Education were quite helpful in providing the school board with directions in this important matter:

"In rural districts the site selected for the schoolhouse shall be at the centre of the district. If for any reason the central site is unsuitable the written sanction of the Minister of Education shall be secured before any other site is obtained.

The site selected should as far as possible meet the following conditions:
(a) It should be easily accessible to all the children of the district.
(b) It should be in a dry, elevated position admitting of easy drainage.
(c) It should be removed from stagnant water or any noisy surroundings.

The school grounds in rural districts shall comprise an area of at least one acre. In shape the grounds should be about twice as long as they are wide. They should be levelled and kept clear of all underbrush, weeds, rubbish, etc. The grounds should be surrounded by a suitable fence (not barbed wire) which should be kept in good repair. The fuel supply should be kept in a woodshed or suitable box, or it may be neatly piled near the schoolhouse."

A perusal of the minute books of any school district will indicate that the school boards of old were seriously concerned with the problem of selecting and acquiring a good building site. Take for example the following three entries taken from the minute book of the Dundee S.D. 4326 (Hanna, Alta.).

January 13, 1928: Moved by Mr. Greenway and seconded by Mr. Rehill that the school site be as near to the centre of the district as possible as a suitable parcel of land could be obtained from Mr. Wickson. Carried."

"*March 15, 1928:* Moved by Mr. Crowe and seconded by Mr. Hemstock that the secretary write Mr. Wickson in regard to obtaining a school site on his quarter section of land, namely, N.W. ¼ of 34-32-13. Carried."

"*April 6, 1928:* Moved by Mr. Hemstock and seconded by Mr. Crowe that Mr. Wickson's donation of two acres for a school site to the district be accepted and that the District purchase another acre from him at $20, making a total of three acres. Carried. Moved by Mr. Rehill and seconded by Mr. Hemstock that the secretary write to Mr. Wickson indicating that a vote of thanks had been passed for his kindness in donating two acres of his land for a school site.   Carried."

"*April 29, 1928:* Moved by Mr. Crowe and seconded by Mr. Hemstock that the secretary proceed to get the school-site title transferred from its present owner to that of the District.   Carried."

It was difficult to explain why with all the official and unofficial concern over the selection of a suitable building site obvious blunders still occurred. If the school was located near a slough the children were pestered by swarms of mosquitoes and flies during the spring and summer seasons, while the decomposition of the organic matter in the stagnant water often saturated the air with foul odors. The slough, like a magnet, irresistibly drew the children from the schoolyard and seemed to invite them to play on the surface of the thin ice, the muddy banks, or even to test their skill as sailors. All too often these escapades ended in some of the children receiving a ducking or, more tragically, a drowning.

When cultivated fields bordered the north or the northwest limits of the schoolyard the prevailing westerlies enshrouded the Little White Schoolhouse with clouds of whirling topsoil. It was impossible to maintain a semblance of cleanliness anywhere in the school with this perpetual bombardment of dirt. The best-fitting doors or windows were no match for such persistent black blizzards.

The location of the school on low-lying land turned the schoolyard into a catch-basin for any snow or moisture that fell in the district. Playground activities always suffered as a consequence. On the other hand if the site was spotted on higher ground the drainage was so rapid that it left the school corner without sufficient moisture for grass or shrubs. The ground, denuded of most of its vegetation, had the appearance of a miniature desert, bare and forbidding. If the trustees attempted to make up for nature's deficiencies by planting a hedge, it was usually able to survive for only a short time. Low-lying or high grounds had the added disadvantage of being difficult to reach from the road, particularly in wet weather or after a heavy snowfall.

Why should a schoolyard adjoin a graveyard? To the present generation it might appear to be a lack of foresight or even a sacrilege on the part of the early ratepayers to allow this to happen. Such was not the case. The country school was more than just a school. It was, among other things, the religious centre of the community. Every faith whether Catholic, Methodist, Presbyterian, Lutheran, Baptist or Anglican, found it convenient to worship in the Little White Schoolhouse. When a member

Not many school districts are as venerable as the Netherby S.D. 2348 near Hanna, Alta. The original plan that called for the schoolyard and the cemetery to be adjacent to each other continues to be in the forethought of the ratepayers today.

of the community died it was only fit and proper to have the last rites performed in the school. Under the conditions that prevailed during the pioneer era the land contiguous to the school property was the right place to bury the dead. This practice varied little from the age-old custom of setting aside a part of the churchyard for a cemetery.

The preliminary surveys of parcels of land to discover whether they would make suitable school sites were often done all too casually. For instance, when a well was dug to supply fresh drinking water for the school it was sometimes found that water was non-existent in the area, or if water was reached within a reasonable depth in some cases it contained such a high concentration of various salts that it tasted like a potent medicine—with similar results! This all-too-late discovery made it necessary to cart drinking water from the nearest or the most convenient farmyard for the entire period during which the school operated, be it five or fifty years. Very few soil studies were conducted so the schoolyard frequently blossomed forth as a potential rockpile, a mudhole or a sandpile. Generation upon generation of school children played on these dangerous or otherwise unsuitable grounds all because of the lack of a little foresight on the part of the early school boards. However in being critical it must be realized that the technology of surveying was in its infancy and that the need for a school was often so urgent that many elementary steps leading up to its construction had to be overlooked.

All too frequently it was found that the part of the district where the school had been located was subject to many oppressive whims of the weather. It could be wind-swept, cold, damp and prone to sudden storms. Certainly a most undesirable environment for the children when the area a quarter of a mile west turned out to be the "banana belt" of the region.

Once the school site had been selected it did not mean that the problem was solved. It had the habit of recurring again and again throughout the lifetime of the Little White Schoolhouse. A pronounced shift of the school population to the extreme limits of the district, or the consolidation of two or more districts, often left the school in anything but a convenient place for the youngsters using it, so it was moved to a more central location. A few years later it might be found expedient to backtrack and relocate the school on its original site. The whole process could be compared to chasing a will-o'-the-wisp. The school board members attempted to keep up with the problem but they never quite succeeded. No one could predict with certainty the number of families that would take up residence in the district, the number that would depart, or the increase in population of the families already living in the district. Marriages, birthrates, and a shifting population always have and always will upset the projected plans of school boards and statisticians. Thus one can realize why there was continual dissatisfaction and disagreement as to where the school should be located in the district.

The government regulations pertaining to the formation of a school district were so cold and matter-of-fact that one wonders whether the pioneers followed the prescribed routine in automatic fashion as well. In actual practice such was not the case. Behind each effort to form a school district lies a story pulsating with human foibles and emotions. There was intrigue, pathos, humor and courage.

When plans for a school were being considered in the Elkart S.D. (Smeaton, Sask.), every family in the district wanted it built in a different location depending on where they lived. Travelling conditions were extremely poor in that part of Saskatchewan in 1930 so everyone wanted the school as close to his homestead as possible. By the time the school was finally erected many former good friends had become bitter enemies. The feuds that erupted took several years to subside and were generally carried on through the children at school. Ill feeling prevailed in the school to such a degree that fighting among the pupils was a common occurrence. Bruce Lamb describes what happened to him at this school:

> "One particular irate father came into school during a noon intermission when the teacher was away and called me all sorts of names and actually threatened me. I had only one mile to go to school while his children had three. I was eight years old at the time but I still remember the incident clearly."

A Fordville S.D. 1908 (Midnapore, Alta.) ratepayer asked at a school meeting to have his land transferred to the Priddis S.D. The trustees, fearful of the loss of even one taxpayer, argued that it was two and a-half miles to Fordville as the crow flies and three and a-half miles to Priddis. They also maintained that by a good usable route it was four miles and nine gates to open to Priddis and only three miles and two gates to open to Fordville. The request was not granted.

The education committee of the Ensleaf S.D. (Buffalo, Alta.) encountered considerable difficulty in their first efforts to line up support for the formation of a school district. The many bachelors living in the area feared that the move would raise their taxes and so opposed the plan. The next time Mr. Stone and his sole supporter presented the proposition to the homesteaders it was for the erection of a "community hall". The new idea received the necessary support to warrant the formation of a school district.

The site of the Bally Hamage School (Priddis, Alta.) was one that did not come up to the expectations demanded by the Department of Education. The schoolhouse was located on one side of the road allowance and the playing field on the other. A number of sloughs surrounded the site from three sides and a grove of trees completed the encirclement from the playground area. A number of these large trees had been cut off well above the ground to make room for a ball diamond. As school children go in for descriptive nicknames the Bally Hamageites were always called the Stump Jumpers by the opposing teams. The comedy of errors was made complete when it was discovered that due to a blunder in locating fence lines the school had been built smack on the road allowance.

The School Act requirement respecting the minimum number of children between the ages of five and sixteen living in an area before a school district could be formed, was the signal for more than one rural community to come up with ingenious schemes of realizing this statutory number.

On counting the youthful noses in the Stanley S.D. in 1889 the settlers discovered that they were one short of the minimum. What was to be done? At this critical moment someone remembered that Rachael Kilpatrick, who had married a Mr. Dimmick, was within the age limit. Why not register her with the rest of the school children and so make the organization of the district possible? No sooner said than done! The school district came into being on February 7, 1889. It is interesting to note that the young married lady who was kind enough to lend her name to make the formation of the district possible did not have to attend as a Mr. James Young had moved into the community in the meantime, bringing with him two children of school age.

The trustees of the Concord S.D. 658 (Ponoka, Alta.) thought that they had picked out an ideal locale for their school but later events proved them to be wrong. One parcel of land belonging to the district was on the south bank of Chain Lake. Sixty years later children from that area still could not get to the Concord School. Since 1901 had been a very wet year the school board picked a high, gravel and stone hill for the site which turned out to be a very poor place to play ball and other sports. The building itself was set on a two-foot foundation that made the windows five feet off the ground. Sitting up on that high concrete support on top of a hill the school received more than its share of wind.

The New Haven S.D. 1925 (Sibbald, Alta.) built in 1922 had as handy a site as any mother could wish for. It was located on a hill on E. C. Green's land where the parents could all see their children arrive at and leave school.

Selecting a building site near a public thoroughfare had its disadvantages as well as advantages. The Cuthbert S.D. (Winnipeg, Man.) erected its school on the old Melita Trail. Hence it was often used as a halfway stopping house by travellers passing through the area. They would bring their blankets and camping equipment into the school and spend the night there. The teacher's desk was used as a table and the old pot-bellied stove enabled them to do some cooking. A sign was posted inside the school with the words, "Please Clean Up Before You Leave". Many a new settler and his family made good use of the Cuthbert School in this way.

Mrs. Florkewich of the Manly S.D. 1744 (Carvel, Alta.) wrote a poem entitled "Manly", in which she catches much of the color of the days when country schools were first formed:

MANLY

Charlie Hollings built the school way back in nineteen seven,
To serve the needs of pioneers who thought that it was heaven.
There were windows on both sides and a dais for the teacher,
But when each Sunday rolled around it also served the preacher.

A table stood on the dais so bright and shining new
With an armchair beside it to serve the long years through.
There were double desks for the children and a big pot-bellied stove,
And at the back of the yard stood a little barn for the horses which they
    drove.

The trustees did the best they could with funds so very low,
When the district first was organized in years of long ago.
A picture of our King and Queen was hung upon the wall,
And near the road on a pole so high the flag waved over all.

We'll remember "Windy" Miller in the years that are to be,
For he was the "roadhouse" keeper and the district's first trustee,
He hired and fired the teachers, in those years so long ago,
But his thoughts were for the people as he watched the district grow.

The school had many teachers; there were some who would not stay
In a lonely, rural outpost, with friends so far away.
Until Miss Knox came out to teach; she loved the wilderness,
And soon at nearby Carvel, she found life's happiness.

Among the early pioneers, for some are long since gone,
I'll mention just a few, perhaps, before this tale is done.
Beside the school was a little store to serve the settlers' needs,
And some folks will remember, the owner, Charlie Reid.

The kids were lucky in those days, as I have oft' been told,
For to them, an egg was as precious as a little bag of gold;
They gathered them most carefully, and if a spare was handy,
They carried it to Charlie Reid, for a barber-pole stick of candy.

Included among those pioneers, were Turlucks, Best and Florkewich,
Comchi, Capp and Tyrkalo, along with Danilowich.
There were Pettyls and Kocherofskys and the families of Hollings and
    Miller;
Krashowskys, Reid and McLaughlin, and the two families of Mastaller.

There were Stecyks, Smith and Pawlyk; Smigelski and Wasylyshyn,
Schooley, Marsom and Matthews, Pawlow and Andrushchshyn,
Thus the district was established, by oldtimers, long since gone,
Each one receives his true award, and memories linger on.

Late in the nineteen-thirties, a new schoolhouse was built,
With books and modern fixtures, bright as polished gilt.
In the fall of fifty-seven, the teacher closed forever the schoolhouse door,
Knowing that in Stony Plain, the children would profit more.

Now the little schoolhouse, has become a community centre,
A place where all the neighbors find a welcome when they enter,
For the members of the Goodwill Club, gather now and then,
And as they talk and frolic, they all feel young again.

THE NAMING
OF SCHOOL DISTRICTS

The various ways in which school district names originated make for an interesting study. Since the authorities provided very little assistance in the matter of selecting appropriate designations it was amazing how aptly and expeditiously the majority of the district christened themselves. Some names blossomed out of history, both local and national; others recorded minor tragedies, discoveries or personal experiences; a number were named after places the pioneers had left behind in other parts of the world; still others characterized the geographical features of the district that set it apart from all other areas; and then there were always those that did not appear to have any rhyme or reason behind their derivation. Many choices reflected ingenuity on the part of their originators while others showed that the easiest way out had been employed.

The government ordinance requested the local educational committees to submit a list of four or five suitable names. The Department of Education in turn made the final selection. The pioneers discovered that originality and haste were the two attributes required to bring about success in this naming ordeal. All too frequently the title selected was rejected as some other district in the province had a prior claim. Common names like Buffalo, Badger, Crocus, Prairie Rose, Meadowlark, Gopher and Wolf Willow had to be turned down scores of times. Then on the other hand if the local citizens were too slow in coming forward with a designation, the authorities in the capital had the habit of saddling the district with a choice of their own. Most districts resented such interference with local autonomy but realized that they were at fault in not showing some degree of compliance with the instructions issued. The first page or two of the minute book of most school districts invariably contains some reference to this problem. Here is such an entry from the minute book of Spondon S.D. (Hanna, Alta.) March 25, 1916:

"It was proposed that the district be called 'Maypole' but on being informed by the Minister of Education that there was a district in the province already called 'Maypole' a number of other names were submitted including 'Spondon'. The Department of Education selected Spondon."

In the majority of districts the naming routine followed democratic procedure. Notices were sent to all the settlers in the community asking for suitable names for the school district. Then at a special public meeting four of the names were selected and sent to the Department of Education for a final decision. Where dogmatic methods prevailed some influential and/or learned individual submitted names of his own choosing without consulting any other settler in the district. A good number of people in a newly-opened part of the country, ignorant of the official techniques to be followed, blindly accepted such dictatorial tactics.

Mossdale S.D. 3101 (Star City, Sask.) was quite representative of the routine employed by most school boards in order to obtain an acceptable name for their district. Each board member was asked to submit a name. The Scotch trustee suggested "Abernethy" which was not only his own name but that of a town in Scotland. His American counterpart selected "Flint", a famous manufacturing city in Michigan. Mr. Bottomley, the secretary and the third member of the board, put forward the designation "Mossdale" which was the name of his father's summer cottage in the Lake District of England. After some consideration the Department of Education in Regina notified the school board that they had authorized the name "Mossdale" for the district. In due course an official announcement appeared in the Saskatchewan Gazette, 1912 issue, to the effect that Mossdale School District Number 3101 had come into existence.

Just as soon as a Department of Education approved the formation and the name of a particular school within its borders it also assigned a number to the district to further identify it. These consecutive numbers were doled out in sequence as district after district came into being, somewhat similar to the modern practice of issuing automobile licences. The annual reports of the Department of Education of any American state or Canadian province meticulously recorded these inclusions. Below is an abstract from the 1912 report of the Department of Education of Alberta:

School District Erected During Year 1912

Name	Number	Date of Entry	Gen. Location Tp.	Rg.	M.	Senior Trustee
COTTONWOOD	2624	Jan. 10	41	6	4	Walter Brooks, Czar
COOKING LAKE	2625	Jan. 10	51	21	4	H. A. Kidney, Deville
CLANSMAN	2626	Jan. 10	39	5	4	Jas. Shurmer, Cairns
GREEN BUSH	2627	Jan. 10	53	10	4	Otto Larsen, Myrnam
GLEN FALLOCH	2628	Jan. 10	44	27	4	G. H. Clark, Ferry Bank
FOUR WAYS	2629	Jan. 10	6	7	4	J. H. Peck, Glen Banner
HOLMBERG	2630	Jan. 10	4	10	4	A. P. Holmberg, Lucky Strike
POPULAR	2631	Jan. 10	28	7	4	Percy J. Barnes, Cereal

Name	Number	Entry	Tp.	Rg.	M.	Senior Tustee
TEETERS	2632	Jan. 10	39	6	4	E. Hedblorn, Czar
SUNNY CREST	2633	Jan. 25	41	27	4	A. E. Drader, Lacombe
SLEEPY HOLLOW	2634	Jan. 25	2	14	4	A. M. Sinclair, Milk River
BUFFALO VIEW	2635	Jan. 25	41	6	4	John Wiggins, Hughenden
GLEN WILLOW	2636	Jan. 25	9	26	4	R. V. Grier, Ft. MacLeod
LAHAIEVILLE	2637	Jan. 25	67	23	4	G. Castonguay, Athabasca
FUNNELL	2638	Jan. 25	48	4	5	Harry Allen, Stones Corner
FEADVIEW	2639	Jan. 25	28	4	4	W. Ostrander, Excel
GLEN AVON	2640	Jan. 25	28	6	4	W. H. Burrows, Excel
IDEAL VALLEY	2641	Jan. 25	35	16	4	Hugh Wallace, Cornucopia
ISLAND HILL	2642	Jan. 25	51	5	4	H. B. Evans, Vermillion
LOVE VALE	2643	Jan. 25	29	3	4	John Love, Fairacres
MIZPAH	2644	Jan. 25	28	10	4	H. A. Wiertz, Stoppington

Valuable as this information may have been the stories of the derivations of the names of these districts were much more animated and interesting. They retold in a dramatic way a part of the history of the Little White Schoolhouse which has been lived once and which will never be relived except in memory.

Many school district names described some distinguishing geographical feature of their particular area.

Chain Lakes S.D. 2323 (Hanna, Alta.) characterized the endless chain of sloughs, dry most of the year, weaving through the district.

The Indians who used to inhabit the area along the Red Deer Valley in Alberta made good use of the high hills as vantage points from which to spot the buffalo or antelope grazing on the plains below. When the white man entered the area and formed school districts it was only natural for him to pick names like Hunting Hill, Antelope Hill, Deer Hill.

The schoolhouse in the Mountain Chase S.D. 1373 had been built on the lee side of the Last Mountain. The latter was a range of hills in Township 25, Range 20, West of the Second Meridian in Saskatchewan, stretching for six miles in a northerly direction. The inclined or hunched position of each of these so-called mountains and the fact that they seemed to tail each other in rapid succession gave one the impression of runners sprinting across the prairie, hence the appropriate title, "Mountain Chase."

Prairie dwellers were especially mindful of the seemingly endless plains that here and there were punctuated by hills. It required no stretch of the imagination for these people to adopt such names as Lonebutte, Twin Butte, Picture Butte, or Redcliff. One district went so far as to choose the name Alps S.D. 2681 (Hanna, Alta.) to describe, somewhat loosely, the higher-than-average hills that dotted the terrain.

If a community was located near a junction of something or other, like rivers, roads or railways, the citizens were in the habit of heralding this fact in the name they selected for their district. Union Point S.D. 53 (St. Agathe, Man.), for instance, justified such a title because when it was first formed in 1876 a railway, the Red River and an important prairie trail all passed through the district. The River Junction S.D. (Lethbridge, Alta.) told all and sundry that their community was near the confluence of the St. Mary and Old Man Rivers. The Forks S.D. 3606 (Empress, Alta.) employed a similar plan to indicate its proximity to the junction of the Red Deer and South Saskatchewan Rivers. Delta S.D. 2985 (Bindloss, Alta.) gently suggested that the district was located along the Red Deer River.

The dictionary describes "gore" as a triangular piece of land. The first homesteaders to settle along the fifth meridian some seven miles east of Didsbury, Alta., were quick to notice that this strip of land for some sixty miles resembled a triangle. There was no better way to label this uniqueness than to name it the Gore S.D.

Chinook S.D. 16 (Chinook, Alta.) would understandably derive such an appellation from the warm dry winds that descended the Rocky Mountains and swept across the Alberta plains.

There is no experience quite so exasperating as an attempt to walk on a gumbo soil when it is wet. The tacky soil builds up to such an unusual thickness on the shoes of the promenader that it becomes almost impossible for him to lift his feet due to the added weight. Then just at the point when he is ready to give up the mud suddenly peels off giving him a fresh start. The residents of a rural community near Twining, Alta., considered the gumbo soil to be so characteristic of their area that they designated it the Gumbo S.D.

The shape, or some other singular feature, of a neighboring hill or hills prompted the homesteaders to fabricate such descriptive titles as: Hand Hills, Thigh Hill, Rolling Hill, Golden Hill, Hillsgreen, Rainy Hill, Clover Hill, Hairy Hill, Purple Hill, Teat Hills, Rocky Hill, Horn Hill, Hillsview, Island Hill, Hill End, Sky Hill, Summit Hill, Dawson Hill, Clements Hill, Anthill, Gopher Hill, Hammer Hill, Nose Hill and Mouse Hill.

One district could not think of an appropriate adjective to distinguish their hills so they simply came up with the plain unadulterated name of Hills S.D. 3224. In direct constrast to this lack-lustre method some communities dignified their hills with such imaginative titles as Casa Loma S.D. 3468 (Calgary, Alta.), Onanole S.D. 2262 (Riding Mountain National Park, Man.). The former was named by a Frank Cathre after his father's place in Scotland. It meant "castle on the hill". The latter if sounded phonetically simply states, "on a knoll".

If there were no hills in the surrounding area the pioneers turned their attention to other geographical features to gain an appropriate title, such as Little Gap, Big Gap, Round Prairie, Meadowlands, Silver Valley, Cobblestone, Grassy Slope, Red Willow, and Poplar Dale. Rocky Coulee S.D. 1188 (Granum, Alta.), for instance, derived its descriptive title from the coulee some three miles to the east whose springs provided a watering place on the old North West Mounted Police trail from Lethbridge to Fort MacLeod and Calgary, while the name Springbank S.D. 100 (Calgary, Alta.) originated from the bubbling springs that were discovered on the gentle slope of land that led to the school site. A school district near Snowflake, Man., was so strategically located on the fringe of the beautiful Pembina River Valley that it was aptly called Valley View S.D. 666. The enormous size of a greyish-blue rock, one of the larger glacial erratics in the world at Okotoks, Alta., influenced the early settlers in the immediate vicinity of the town to name their district the Big Rock S.D. 592.

Nature often showed her influence in such school district names as Sunbeam, Sunny Glen, Shady Lane, Golden Grain, Beautyland, Crocus, Flowerdale, Sunnynook, Garden Plain, Sunny Crest, Wildflower, Cherry Valley, Northern Lights, Green Bush and Greenmound.

The majority of the homesteaders were filled with a spirit of optimism as they broke the land and built their shacks. This attitude was manifest in school district names such as Hope Valley, New Bliss, Lucky Strike, Excel, Foremost, Little Gem, Majestic, Superior, New Haven, Linger Longer, Success, Golden Centre, Good Hope. On the other hand the mist of sorrow or disappointment shrouded the hopes of many settlers, so a pessimistic point of view was reflected in such titles as Rearville, Stony Slope, Lonely Trail, Faith, Coffin and Last Chance.

The names of a number of school districts were linked, as were their inhabitants, with places called home many hundreds of miles away.

Buchan S.D. 2330 (Hanna, Alta.) was so called because six of the original settlers of the district had come from the Buchan County in the northeastern portion of Aberdeenshire, Scotland.

A school district in the province of Ontario carried the familiar title of Argyle S.D. 4. The majority of the farmers there had come from Argyle in Scotland so no one was surprised at their ultimate choice of this name for the school.

The selection of the designation of Balmae for a school district near Saskatoon, Sask., resulted in a rather pleasant surprise for the inhabitants. The name had been suggested by a number of farmers who had formerly lived near the Balmae Estate in Scotland. When the owner of this estate heard that he had been honored in Canada by having a school district named after him he contributed a substantial sum of money to get the school under way.

Once in a while a name did not come directly from the Old Country but carried out the transition in two phases. Cambachie S.D. 2264 (Moose

Jaw, Sask.) was a good example of this. The original Cambachie was the name of one of the better known suburbs of Glasgow, Scotland, and when some of the residents migrated to Ontario, Canada, they were not remiss in calling their new home, Cambachie, Ont. Then in 1908 when a few of them decided to go farther west and settle near Moose Jaw, Sask., they retained the old emotionally-charged caption of Cambachie for their third home.

Scapa S.D. 4357 (Hanna, Alta.) derived its name from historic Scapa Flow in the Orkney Islands.

Kirkwall, in the Orkney Islands, was the home of the mother of a Mr. C. M. Coote, the first secretary-treasurer of the newly organized district, so with very little opposition, it became known as Kirkwall S.D. 2463 (Oyen, Alta.)

Peter Lutzak came to Canada with his family in 1900 from a village called Shypenitz in the Ukraine. He bought a homestead and settled near the present village of Hairy Hill, Alta. As a result of corresponding with him, many other natives of Shypenitz became interested and so also migrated to Canada to settle in the same rural community. It was only natural for them to call the new district after their native village of Shypenitz. The district that bordered it was called Berhometh S.D. 1499 after a village in the Ukraine that was located near Shypenitz.

As a good number of the settlers in an area south of Buffalo, Alta., had migrated from the Scandinavian countries the district became known far and wide as "Little Sweden". The school district itself was named Ensleaf S.D., meaning, "one leaf". New Stockholm S.D. 120 (Stockholm, Sask.) had a similar origin. It was first settled in 1888 by immigrants from Sweden and they knew it would make them feel less lonely in a strange land if they could hear the familiar ring of the word "Stockholm" repeated many times a day by both friend and stranger alike.

Bostonia S.D. (Madison, Sask.) was named by the first settlers in the district who hailed from Boston, Wisconsin. They had come in a specially chartered train, which, as it pulled out of Boston station bore on its side the legend, "Saskatoon or Bust"; as they neared their destination the passengers are said to have altered the sign to read, "Saskatoon and Busted."

The title "Eagle" was selected for a district near Airdrie, Alta., in deference to one of its early organizers, an American settler named Mr. Lyse.

When a number of homesteaders moved from Nebraska to Alberta they perpetuated the event by designating their newly-formed community Nebalta S.D. 3670.

Wells School (Lloydminster, Sask.) was named by Mrs. H. H. Cayford, the first woman in the district. She arrived in 1905 and was given the privilege and honor of naming the first school in the Manitou Lake District. She selected "Wells" as that was the name of the school that she and her husband had attended in Skowhegon, Maine.

School district names embodying an English origin abounded everywhere.

Netherby Hull in Cumberland County, England, had been the birthplace of three of the original homesteaders who had settled in an area north of Hanna, Alta. This prompted a Mr. Watson to suggest the name Netherby.

Mr. G. Park, a member of the school board of a newly-organized district was very proud when he first learned that the government had approved his suggestion of Westoe as a name for the school. Westoe was his ancestral home in South Shields, England.

The Lathom S.D. 1538 (Osage, Sask.) had a different English connotation. Mr. John Morris, the incumbent secretary of the district when it was organized in 1906, named it after a Quaker family he admired in England.

The Irish did not forget their homeland either when it came to the matter of selecting names for districts. One such school went by the euphonious title of Bally Hamage S.D. (Midnapore, Alta.) When the school was ready to be opened the trustees called a public meeting to single out a name for it. After several suggestions had been considered someone proposed Bally Hamage, the birthplace of Mr. T. Jamieson, their hardworking secretary. Since everyone liked the melodious lilt of this Irish name it was decided to submit it to the Department of Education for approval. When it came time to write the name down in English no one knew how to spell it. They did their best and came up with "Bally Hamage".

Although there is not even a good-sized hill near Leslie, Sask. the Icelanders who first settled there quickly suggested the name of Mt. Hecla for their school district. Thus they made certain of retaining for generations to come a bond with their native Iceland.

In 1873 the Canadian government advertised an offer throughout many European countries that homestead grants would be allotted to immigrants, on condition that a certain amount of land would be tilled and a number of settlement duties, like building a house, carried out. When these conditions were met the immigrant received the deed to the land on the payment of ten dollars. Several thousand German Mennonites, who lived in Russia, decided to leave their fertile land and come to Canada only because they could not practice their religion there. Many settled near Winkler, Man., and named the district Burwalde S.D. 529 to remind them of the home they had left behind in Russia.

French-Canadian farmers from the eastern provinces contributed generously to the building of the Canadian West. This is evident from the number of school districts whose names were of French origin: Bon Accord, Lac La Biche, Chauvin, Qu'Appelle, Rouleau, Val Marie, Gouverneur, Laporte, Cartier, St. Jean Baptiste, Letellier, Beausejour, St. Lina, Prud-'homme, Lac Vert, Dufresne, Tranquille, Barriere, Marguerite, Lac la Hache, Souris.

Some school boards were able to circumvent the provincial regulation prohibiting two districts from using the same name by employing an equivalent meaning in some other language. Buena Vista S.D. (Camrose, Alta.) and Belvédère S.D. (Dunstable, Alta.) are good examples of this unique practice. Both names mean "beautiful view", the former being in Spanish and the latter in French.

Before the white men came, Indians and wild life shared Canada. Hence the country, from the Atlantic to the Pacific, was strewn with school districts with Indian names. No places could be more Canadian than Blackfoot or Minnehaha.

The Manawan S.D. 382 was located just northeast of Whitford Lake in Alberta. As the lake was bounded by numerous reeds that provided a suitable nesting place for thousands of ducks, the Indians called it "Manawan" meaning "a place where eggs are gathered".

Okotoks S.D. (Okotoks, Alta.) near the Blackfoot ford of Sheep Creek, derived from "sikokotoks", meaning "many stones". Etzikom S.D. in the southeastern part of Alberta is an Indian word signifying "stinking water", while Seebe S.D. west of Calgary, Alta., is the Stony Indian equivalent for "a river". Kananaskis S.D. in the same general area was named after a legendary Indian who was supposed to have survived a severe axe blow. Jumping Pound S.D. (Cochrane, Alta.) was the place where the Indians used to kill buffalo by driving them over a precipice. Arrawanna S.D. (Delia, Alta.) means "rolling prairie" in one of the many prairie Indian dialects.

The Indians also had a part in naming the Big Stick S.D. (Maple Creek, Sask.) According to legend the nearby Big Stick Lake derived its name from the sole tree in the vicinity. It had been struck by lightning and was reduced to a huge charred stick. Since the school district bordered this expanse of alkali mud it soon became known as "Big Stick" as well.

The coming of the railway so elated the early settlers that they fittingly recognized these historical occasions by adopting "railway names" for their district. Hanna S.D. 2912 was named after Mr. D. B. Hanna, the first vice-president of the Canadian National Railways.

While school districts like Federal, Fleet, Loyalist, Coronation, Throne, Veteran and Consort, all located along a fifty-mile stretch of the Canadian

Pacific Railway in eastern Alberta were so named to commemorate the coronation of King George V in 1911.

The Laggan S.D. (Lake Louise, Alta.) fittingly adopted the name of the Subdivision (Laggan) of the Canadian Pacific Railway that passed through this lovely spot in the Canadian Rockies.

Another Canadian Pacific Railway line in Alberta that extended from Bassano to Empress was known as the Royal Line because so many places along it were named after members of the royal family: Empress, Duchess, Princess, Patricia, Rosemary and Countess.

Compounding or combining words was another method used by the early settlers for creating distinctive names for their school districts. The title Lundberg S.D. 2794 (Cereal, Alta.) was composed of the names of two families living at opposite extremities of the district, namely the Lunds and the Bergs.

In another district near Lanfine, Alta. two pioneer families gave their surnames to the district. One was of Scottish origin and the other English, and the names were apparently never completely integrated as each family retained its individuality in the two-word title of Glen Avon.

Mrs. E. Moss was instrumental in organizing the Mossleigh S.D. (Mossleigh, Alta.) in 1905. She was also the secretary-treasurer of the district until her untimely death in 1911. She made up the title by combining her husband's name Moss with her maiden name of Leigh.

Mr. J. E. McPherson, the first chairman of a rural school near Hythe, Alta. was honored in a fitting way at the time of the formation of the district in 1922. The school was named after his two daughters, Ann and Ellen. It became known as Annellen S.D. 4111.

Perhaps the classical example of a compound name is that of Hemaruka S.D. (Veteran, Alta.). It was formed by combining the first two letters of each name of the four daughters of a Mr. A. E. Warren, namely Helen, Mary, Ruth and Kate. He was a general manager of the Canadian National Railways when the railway was being constructed through the area in 1927.

A naming method somewhat similar to compounding was that of transposing the letters in an otherwise familiar proper noun.

The designation of Retlaw S.D. (Taber, Alta.) was contrived by reversing the letters in the name Walter. Walter Baker was the private secretary to the Earl of Dufferin, Governor-General of Canada between 1872 and 1878.

Itipaw may sound like a strange appellation for a school district but because of its proximity to the Wapiti River the local school board came up with the idea of spelling the Indian word backwards.

Red Rows S.D. (Balcarres, Sask.) was so called because the land on which the school was built was donated by a Mr. Sworder. The trustees must have had to deal with a delicate situation in an attempt to honor Mr. Sworder yet not make it too obvious for fear they would hurt the feelings of the other early settlers. The problem was solved by transposing the letters in Mr. Sworder's name and dividing them conveniently into two simple words, Red Rows.

Many school officials saddled with the thankless task of initiating a name for their district followed the procedure that incurred the least amount of strife. This was done impartially by adopting the name of a nearby river, lake, creek, spring, mountain, hill, valley or town. Bull-pound S.D. (Hanna, Alta.) borrowed its name from the Bullpound Creek that meandered through the district. Berry Creek S.D. (Sunnynook, Alta.) adopted the name of a creek originally discovered and named by the explorer, Captain Palliser, in 1887. Blood Indian S.D. (Sunnynook, Alta.) was named after the Blood Indian Creek that flowed through the original Blood Indian country.

A school called John Jo S.D. 2198 was said to have come by this odd title by being named after John Jo Spring near Milk River, Alta. John and Jo were two French trappers who made their home by the spring in the early days. Legend has it that the two men were buried near the spring.

Red Deer Lake School, the 128th school formed in the North West Territories and about the twentieth in future Alberta had several mooted origins as to its name. It could have come from the quantity of deer heads that were strewn along the shores of the lake when the school was first opened in 1887; or from the large numbers of red deer that were found in the area; or even the modification of an Indian name.

The naming of school districts after early or prominent local settlers was a common practice. These names were meaningless to outsiders but to the oldtimers of the district they connotated early history of the area and were cherished and revered. Every section of Canada has honored its pioneers in this manner. Here are a few examples from the Hanna area in Alberta: Watts (the first mail-carrier), Parr (the name of a nephew of the first settler in the district), Elmer (the first child born in the Hand Hills to the Flett family), Scotfield (in honor of John Scott, a South African homesteader). Wiese (the first settler to homestead in the district). Hammond (first woman homesteader near the village of Craigmyle), Peyton (Mr. Peyton organized the school district).

Hillman S.D. 3077 (Dapp, Alta.) was named after Hillman Nutt, the five-year old daughter of the first settler in the district. Belzil S.D. 2979 (St. Paul, Alta.) was selected to memorialize Mr. Joseph Belzil, the founder of the district.

A rural community near Youngstown, Alta., was most eager to avail itself of the name—Niles. In 1919 a homesteader called Niles was killed by lightning while he was unloading his settler's effects in front of his newly-constructed shack. The tragedy so touched the hearts of the people that they felt the least they could do was name their school after him.

There were two good reasons why a Ukrainian district northeast of Edmonton was called Shandro. First it was settled by the Shandro brothers in 1899 and secondly one of the brothers became the first Ukrainian Member of the Legislative Assembly.

A Dr. Potter, his wife and two children with the strange names of Silver and Gold, came from Valley City, North Dakota, in 1901 to take up the first homestead in the Potter Creek district near Rimbey, Alberta. He built his shack beside an unnamed creek which soon became known as Potter Creek. The family stayed for four years but left such a host of friends behind that when it came time to name their school they called it the Potter Creek School.

Various members of the Cravath family had, by either filing or purchase, acquired more than two thousand acres of land near the Red Deer River. Since each family settled on a different corner, the father and mother on the southwest corner, a brother on the southeast corner and so on, the school district when organized in 1911 became known as the Corners S.D. 2579 (Brooks, Alta.).

The generosity of some homesteaders in donating a convenient building site for the school was frequently recognized by naming the school after them. Here are two examples. John Newell presented the school board of his community near Hanna, Alta. with a clear title to three acres of his land. In return for his kindness the trustees called the district, "Newell School District 3005". Priddis S.D. 233 (High River, Alta.) started their school in 1892 in a log shack owned by Charles Priddis. Later he also donated the land on which the new school was built. The community recognized the magnanimity of Mr. Priddis by naming their school the Priddis School.

A complete antithesis to this pattern of naming school districts after open-handed pioneers may be illustrated by the Harts S.D. 4127. The ideal place for locating the school was on Mr. Harts' property but he stubbornly refused to give the school board permission to do so. In spite of his unwillingness to accede to the wishes of the trustees the school district was still named "Harts".

Not all pioneers accepted the prestige of having the district named after them. Take the Lancaster S.D. (Conquerville, Alta.) for example. When the first meeting was held on August 21, 1911, to organize the school district, the people were all in favor of calling the district, Dame S.D. to show deference to a Mr. Dame, one of the early public-minded settlers of the area. He flatly declined the honor on the grounds that the "e" would be left off too often and thus give the school an unsavory nickname.

Jealousy resulting in animosity forced some districts to turn to the names of national or international figures in order to preserve harmony within the community. Others thought that such names were more appropriate than local ones.

Laurier S.D. was named after Sir Wilfrid Laurier, a former Prime Minister of Canada; Earl Gray S.D. after a Prime Minister of England who introduced the famous Reform Bills; Cavendish S.D. (Empress, Alta.) after Lord Cavendish, an outstanding British scientist; Bindloss S.D. (Empress, Alta.) after Harry Bindloss, a celebrated writer of western novels; Atlee S.D. (north of Suffield, Alta.) after Clement Atlee, another British Prime Minister; Ryerson S.D. 3113 (Youngstown, Alta.) after Egerton Ryerson, one of Canada's pioneer educators; Webster S.D. 2592 (Oyen, Alta.) after Noah Webster, America's foremost dictionary writer; Jeanne d'Arc S.D. 2205, after France's national heroine and a beloved saint of the Roman Catholic Church often called the Maid of Orleans.

The origin of the name Herzel S.D. (Lipton, Sask.) had an interesting background. Prior to World War I, a Jewish settlement was established near Lipton, Sask. In time the community expanded and the need for a school was felt. Once the building was erected the question arose as to what they should name it. The late Dr. Theodore Herzel was a beloved leader of the Jewish people throughout the world. Although he died a comparatively young man, his ideas caught fire among the Jewish people in Russia, France, England and indeed throughout the world. He proposed the idea that the only hope for eliminating persecution was to establish a homeland in Israel. He felt sure that such an independent Hebrew state would arise within fifty years of his speech. It was natural, therefore, that the Jewish people at the Lipton colony should call their school "Herzel".

The Aberdeen S.D. 291 (Innisfail, Alta.) was named after Lord Aberdeen, a former Governor-General of Canada. Lord Aberdeen and his wife were making their first tour of the west in 1894, just about the time that a school district six miles east of Innisfail was being organized. When the vice-regal party passed through Innisfail, over the newly completed C & E Railway Line between Calgary and Edmonton, the ratepayers were so overwhelmed by the event that they quickly decided to name their school district—Aberdeen, to commemorate the historical event.

Many school district names recorded events in world history, particularly if such happenings occurred at the time the school was being organized.

During the course of World War I it was fashionable to dub school districts after theatres of war in France where Canadian forces had served gallantly: St. Julien S.D. 3578, Vimy Ridge S.D. 3640, Amiens S.D. 3735 and Jutland. Other rural communities preferred to nomenclate their schools after famous generals, for example: Pershing S.D. 3652, Allenby S.D. 3733, Foch S.D. 3734.

When the Lusitania, a large ocean liner under British registry, was sunk without warning by a German submarine off the coast of Ireland on May 7, 1915, with a loss of over 1200 lives, a school district in Alberta promptly latched on to the renowned name of Lusitania S.D. 3684.

In 1920 when Saarland, the highly industrialized region between France and Germany, was placed under the administration of the League of Nations a group of ratepayers northeast of Hanna settled on Saar S.D. 4399 as an appropriate name for their district.

A few school district names could be traced to incidents involving animals.

Moose Hill was selected as the name for a district near Thorhild, Alta., because a hill just south of the school site used to be crossed by a moose run. It was also the place where a Mr. Parranto, one of the first organizers of the school, had killed a large moose.

A district on the Canadian side of the border between Saskatchewan and North Dakota might have gained as much fame as Capastrano and its swallows if someone had taken the initiative to compose a song about the annual migration of hundreds of humming birds into the area. The best the local citizens could do was to acknowledge this unusual influx of feathered friends by naming their district—Humming Bird S.D.

Bear Flat S.D. in British Columbia derived its name from the numerous black bears that inhabited the forested areas along the north bank of the mighty Peace River. Quite often the children would look up from their lessons to see one ambling across the schoolyard, perhaps accompanied by its cubs, or sniffing curiously at the pony barn.

The trustees of a school district south of Coronation, Alta., had been meeting in their brand-new schoolhouse for more than an hour mulling over the suggested list of names. Since it was getting harder and harder to cogitate on the task at hand they decided to take a break and get a whiff of fresh air. As they gathered on the stoop outside, their clatter woke up a dog that had been sleeping on the platform. One look at the drowsy animal and every man came up with the same idea. "Let's name the school 'Bingo' after the dog!" Sure enough, the Department of Education accepted the suggestion and henceforth the school was officially known as Bingo S.D. 2926.

Some names proved the old adage that things aren't always what they seem.

The fascinating name of Beechwood S.D. for a district in the southern part of Saskatchewan invariably caused most people to imagine a pretty prairie scene set off by clumps of beech trees. Nothing could have been more erroneous. There were no such trees within several hundred miles of this district. In reality Beechwood S.D. was named by a district resident after his former home in Ontario.

It probably took a bit of imagination to saddle a school district on the bald prairies with the homey name of Cosy Nook, but some person must have had a real flight of fancy to come up with the title of Banana Belt S.D. for a district in Saskatchewan given to the many extremes of a continental climate.

A number of people living on the prairies in the early days had an abiding love of music, art and poetry. They in particular selected school district names that were both figurative and melodious, like Westerwind, Nut Grove, Purple Hill, Fairplain, Shallow Waters, Willowgreen. These names had a charm all of their own but certainly did not accurately describe the district.

A person could reason that the name for Peace Valley S.D. must have emanated from the fact that the quarrelsome factions of the district had come to some agreement, or that it described the tranquillity of the forces of nature in the valley, or for some such kindred inference implied in the word "peace". Actually it was nothing like that at all; it was named after a family by the name of Peace who lived in a nearby vale.

Two Fifteen S.D. 2153 (Milk River, Alta.) was a bewildering title unless one realized that the numbers merely gave the township and range of this particular district.

The word "prospect" implies expectation of a particular condition but Prospect S.D. (Portage la Prairie, Man.) belied its original outlook. In 1871 the late S. M. Marlatt came to Portage la Prairie and homesteaded the southwest corner of 30-12-6. Shortly after he moved out on the farm he decided to build a house. There were very few neighbors in those days but he had a building bee and the dwelling was quickly erected. When it was completed they asked Mr. Marlatt what he was going to name the farm. He thought for a while and finally answered, "Prospect". "Why Prospect?" everyone asked. "Because there is a prospect of starving on this farm!" he replied. The old gent was wrong for by 1886 the district became so thickly settled that it was eventually separated into two school districts, namely, East Prospect and West Prospect.

Mica S.D. 2728 (Lomond, Alta.) might lead one to believe that there were deposits of a mineral silicate found somewhere in the region. This was not so. The school was named after "Mike" Sheridan, a jovial and well-liked Irish immigrant, who lived in the district for a time with his brother, during homestead days.

When Mrs. Lucy Sinclair suggested the name Sleepy Hollow (from the legend of Sleepy Hollow) for a school district near Milk River, Alta. little did she realize at the time that she was somewhat sullying the integrity of almost every person living in the district. People from the surrounding districts came to assume, more in jest than anything else, that Sleepy Hollow referred to the lethargic disposition of the natives, rather than the fact that it was only a means of identifying the school area. The women did not brook this effrontery too well and when an institute was first formed in the district, they proudly called themselves "The Wide Awake Women's Institute of Sleepy Hollow".

It is difficult to imagine how handwriting had a part in the naming of a school, but it did happen in the Fosk S.D. (High River, Alta.). The residents decided to call the school district "Forks" as it was situated between the Highwood River and the Pekisko Creek. However, due to the indistinct handwriting of a Mr. Mace, who submitted the name to the Department of Education, it was officially translated as Fosk. And Fosk it remained!

A natural formation of a column of rock often in fantastic form is termed a hoodoo. But there was not the slightest similarity between this idea and the reason for naming a school near Rosthern, Sask., the Hoodoo S.D. Mrs. Olivia, an old French grandmother who homesteaded in that district was responsible for the name. She spoke no English and in greeting people instead of saying, "How do you do," said, "Hoodoo!" This unusual salutation captured the imagination of the residents and before long everyone was using it. Eventually the entire district fell heir to this aberrance. The school, the post office, the church and finally the municipality were all named "Hoodoo".

The name for the Independent S.D. 3101 (New Dayton, Alta.) was also typical. Present among the settlers who had gathered in 1914 to organize a school district in the area was an out-spoken bachelor. He opposed the plan yet when it came time to suggest some names for the district he vouchsafed "Independent". He explained the reason for his choice in this manner. Two of the men present, namely, Henry Bradley and Chris Selk, had enough children of their own to legally start a school. They did not need "to depend" upon any other families to provide the required minimum of twelve children between the ages of five and sixteen. The other settlers not only saw some sound reasoning behind his choice for a name but also an opportunity to pacify him, so in due course the Independent S.D. 3101 came into being.

Another group of settlers had been beset with so many problems in organizing their district that when it was finally accomplished they called it Pandora. No doubt they drew a parallel between all the noises and troubles that inhabited Pandora's Box of fable fame and their own difficulties of establishing a new school.

In many cases an incident or event that took place in a district had a singular way of bestowing an appropriate name on the area. The Mapleine S.D. (Youngstown, Alta.) was one such district. Early in the formative period of the school the trustees were fortunate in hiring an excellent female teacher. In addition to her qualities of a good teacher she was a girl of striking beauty who possessed a charming personality and had a

—J. M. Turnbull

Mapleine S.D. (Youngstown, Alta.,) with its attractive name-plaque donated by the Mapleine Syrup Company.

very fine character. The one word that the residents seemed to favor in describing the model of excellence was "sweet". The school board promptly decided that the name of the district would be Mapleine since the name so aptly described their paragon. Then realizing that the use of the name "Mapleine" might infringe on the copyrights of the Mapleine Syrup Company they wrote to the company. The school board were not only given permission to use the trademark but were advised that if a picture of the school was sent to the Mapleine Syrup Company a name-plate would be provided for the building. The company kept its promise and soon one of the finest plaques to grace a rural school adorned the front of the Mapleine School.

One bleak spring day in 1910 while the wind was whipping clouds of dust around the corners of a newly-constructed schoolhouse near Hanna, Alta., the trustees, Messers Sanders, Portfors and Vowel, decided to name their drought-stricken district Red Rose. They reasoned among themselves that with the unfavorable growing conditions that were prevailing at the time it would be impossible to raise any type of crop let alone any flowers that would remove the drab appearance of the dry prairies so by calling it Red Rose they would beautify their district in name if not in fact.

Ashdown S.D. 4504 (Grande Prairie, Alta.) had a different story to tell. It was so named by Arvid Forsgren because a forest fire had gone

—Mrs. Louis Knauft

In the spring of 1910 when this school (near Hanna, Alta.) was completed the district was experiencing a prolonged drought. The altruistic school board decided to name it "Red Rose" to beautify the locality in name if not in fact.

through the district just prior to the time it was thrown open for homesteading and everything was covered with a fine white ash.

The selection of school site in a district usually precipitated a certain amount of bickering but in a community near Mundare, Alta., it almost ended in physical violence. In time cooler heads came to the rescue and the problem was resolved. However, when time drew near for selecting a name for the school, battle lines again began shaping up. Another community hassle was forestalled by an elderly man who suggested that since an agreement had been reached about choosing a school site why not call it Zhoda, a Ukrainian word meaning "peace". Everyone supported the idea so Zhoda S.D. 1498 came into existence with no further difficulties.

To the general public the word "university" signifies an institution of higher learning but this was evidently not the case for the first settlers in a district near Sibbald, Alta. Mr. T. G. Gray, the sole survivor of the original ratepayers who attended the organizational meeting back in 1911, writes:

> "At the meeting, after several names had been turned down, Mr. Jack MacGower said, 'Why not try University? It is as near as any of our kids will ever get to university and besides you never know what brains may come out of here!' "

A school with an impressive name—University S.D. 2981 (Sibbald, Alta.)

In future years the children of the district realized the true portent of his words. Any time the students from University S.D. 2981 attended a school fair, a sports meet, or any other activity involving a number of school districts they were asked the standard question of, "What school do you attend?" The reply, "University" always brought forth surprised outbursts of, "You are so young to be attending university!" or "You must be brainy to be going to university!" The round of explanations that followed these remarks achieved the original purpose for naming the school "University".

When a frame schoolhouse was finally constructed in 1915 in a district near Alsask, Sask., the homesteaders of the area could only gasp at the splendor of their new edifice. They were impressed with such innovations as smooth plaster, fir floors, hyloplate blackboards, large windows and the high ceiling. One enthusiastic viewer summed up his impressions by repeating over and over again the word, "Superb! Superb! Superb!" An astute member of the school board thoughtfully tacked on an "a" to the adjective "superb" and came up with a better-than-average name for a school, "Superba S.D. 2984".

St. Elmo S.D. 2561 (Youngstown, Alta.) was named after the patron saint of sailors. St. Elmo's light was a flaming phenomenon sometimes seen in stormy weather at prominent points on a ship. A sailor who settled in the district was surprised to see the same and unusual lights show up in and around the farm buildings during rainy weather. His stories of St. Elmo's lights at sea created a good deal of interest in the community so when it came time for selecting a suitable name for the school everyone agreed that St. Elmo was most appropriate.

The homesteaders on the prairie often supplemented their meager rations and ready cash by hunting the so-called moccasin rabbits and selling the pelts. The inhabitants of one such district, near Sunnynook, Alta., became so adept at this activity that they soon earned the title of "moccasin flatters". A few years later when a school district was organized in the area it became known as Moccasin Flats S.D.

Any time the word "new" was prefixed to the title of a school district it implied a previous existence. The New Dunbow S.D. 4383 (De Winton, Alta.), opened in January of 1930, was named for the Dunbow Indian Industrial School founded by Father Lacombe in 1884. This school had continued to operate for over thirty-five years for the purpose of educating and training the young people of the Blackfoot tribe to be self-supporting. The "old" and the "new" Dunbow Schools were situated near the junction of the Highwood and Bow Rivers and it was said the word "Dunbow" described the general muddy appearance of the water in the Bow River.

Hamona S.D. 451 (Spy Hill, Sask.) was first organized to educate the children of one of the first colonies of settlers in the North West Territories. This group took up land in the beautiful Qu'Appelle River Valley near where the Big Cut Arm Creek enters the river. The Colony was managed very much on socialistic lines and principles but as it failed to satisfy all the members it disbanded in 1903. "Hamona" was derived from the name of the Colony (Harmony).

The eccentric activities of an inhabitant or inhabitants often were so noticeable as to give rise to a name for the district. Rush Centre S.D. 2769 (Esther, Alta.) derived its title from the fact that one of its settlers always appeared to be in a hurry. He even persisted in galloping his horse while going for the cows.

The affability of the people in another district was reason enough to label it Social Plains S.D. 2813 (Empress, Alta.).

A story is told of a midwife who braved a severe prairie blizzard to reach the bedside of a woman in labor but who arrived too late to be of much assistance. Since she had shown much fortitude in getting there she was given the honor of naming the baby. The would-be obstetrician selected the name "Olive" after a favorite sister. This incident so stirred the feelings of the members of the school board that they decided to name their school Olive S.D. 3252 (Hanna, Alta.).

A few school district names had religious connotations.

Some school names had a religious connotation like Trinity S.D. (Sibbald, Alta.)

The carpenter who built a rural school near Oakner, Man., in 1889 was asked to name it. His procedure was quite simple. He opened the Bible and saw the name "Eden" and recommended that the district be called Eden S.D. 510. The school retained this title until the town of Eden asked that it be changed. Hence it wasn't long before it became known as the Oakner S.D. after a town that had sprung up nearby.

A school near Steinbech, Man., was also given a name selected from the Bible, namely, Ekron S.D. 2093. The reason for this choice was not too well understood but from the best information available from the oldtimers in the district it had something to do with the Mennonites who were compelled by the Manitoba Government to conduct their schools according to the regulations of the Department of Education rather than by their own religious beliefs.

It goes without saying that the people who selected the name Trinity S.D. 3168 for their district near Sibbald, Alta., must have had a deep interest in theology and philosophy. They were attempting to show that, like the doctrine of the trinity in religion, there was also a similar dogma in education. The home, the school and the church were separate training forces but all three acted as one as to their ultimate purpose in educating a child.

—Mrs. J. M. Heaton

A community feud brought a change in name for this prairie school, from **Fry** to Homestead Coulee (Hanna, Alta.)

The name "Taber" was formed from the first two syllables of the word tabernacle (meaning a place of worship) in deference to the many Mormons who settled in that part of southern Alberta.

There were hundreds of school districts named after saints. The name selected depended upon the religious faith of the settlers in that community and the singular way in which some saint fitted in with the particular aspiration or character of the district. Names like St. Paul, St. John, St. Albert, St. George, Ste. Anne, St. Patrick, St. Andrew, Ste. Mary and St. Peter all have a religious connotation.

Once a school district name had been approved by the Department of Education of a province or state it did not necessarily mean that the designation had to be retained for the lifetime of the community. Occasionally some incident occurred that prompted the passage of a by-law to change the name.

A Mr. Dewar after establishing a home in the Reist S.D. 2568 (Youngstown, Alta.) went to eastern Canada to be married. Upon his return he was instrumental in having the school district's name altered to Marguerite S.D. 2568, his wife's name. The fact that Dr. Dewar was an influential member of the school board and that he wanted to impress his wife facilitated the change.

A school district southwest of Hanna, Alta., was originally known as Fry to honor E. F. Fry, an early settler and the first board chairman. However, after a few years a neighborhood feud developed and the name was changed to Homestead Coulee. Actually the new name was a misnomer for although there was an Olmstead Coulee in the area there was no Homestead Coulee. Perhaps it was an intentional oversight to preclude any future animosity arising from personal envy.

The early Ukrainians who settled near Ridgeville, Man., prior to 1900 haughtily named their district Bukovina S.D. 1218. In 1915 they had a change of heart. They considered that their choice of Bukovina was an outward display of anti-British sentiment particularly so when they were being called New Canadians rather than "those dirty foreigners". The name of the school and district was changed to Lord Roberts.

No matter how a particular school district derived its name it would, over a period of years, develop distinctive characteristics of its own. Is it any wonder then, that it meant so much to the people who resided within its borders? They had become a part of its make-up, its history and its culture. So to hundreds of thousands of men and women in many walks of life and in many places, school district names recall, somewhat nostalgically, the hardships, the privations, the happy days and the friendships of their early lives.

FINANCING THE RURAL SCHOOL

No sooner was the school district organized, the site selected and the board of trustees elected than the problem of financing came to the fore as it always does any time new projects are undertaken. Initial capital had to be secured to contract for: the purchase and preparation of the school grounds; hauling lumber and other supplies; building and equipping the school; construction of outhouses, a coalshed and probably a barn; sinking a well; erecting a fence about the yard; plowing a fireguard about the school; and painting the buildings.

The Dominion Lands Act of 1872 recognized the imperative need for education in a new land and a clause was inserted in the Act whereby certain specified lands were set aside for the express purpose of providing an endowment for educational purposes. It read as follows:

> "And whereas it is expedient to make provision in aid of education in Manitoba and the North-West Territories, therefore sections eleven and twenty-nine in each and every surveyed township throughout the extent of the Dominion Lands, shall be and are hereby set aside as an endowment for the purposes of education."

The operation of the school was a co-operative enterprise and as improvements were made it was realized that the residents had to provide the funds either through taxation or by contributions. Community spirit in most school districts was high. In many instances repairs and even the construction of such buildings as school barns were achieved by community bees. The success of each student was enjoyed by the whole district because everyone had played a part. This spirit of neighborliness and community vigor is an inheritance worth keeping alive today as the more successful rural communities are proving.

The history of rural school financing falls into four well-defined stages: First, when the early settlers provided, without any outside assistance, all the capital required to build and operate the school. Each year the board of trustees made an estimate of the amount needed to run the school and then set a rate of tax commensurate with this. The single land tax system prevailed, the maximum rate being ten cents per acre.

The school board was the sole taxing authority as well as the only collecting agency.

The second stage came into being soon after the various provinces joined confederation in 1867, 1870, 1871 and 1905. Now the cost of maintaining schools was met not only by the taxation method indicated above but by certain legislative grants as well. These were given to schools organized and conducted under the provisions of The School Ordinance of that province or territory.

The third major development in school financing came about as a direct result of the provinces introducing the municipal form of local self-government. When this was effected the provincial authorities improved and extended their legislative grant structure and the school boards now merely requisitioned the municipality, or municipalities, of which they were a part, for the required operating expenses. The municipal officials set the school tax rate at so many mills on every dollar of the assessed value of the property within the school district and once they had collected the taxes, turned them over to the school board.

The advent of the larger unit of school administration was responsible for the fourth and final stage of development. Under this system of centralization the local school boards ceased to exist and the divisional boards took over their powers and responsibilities. This new body prepared the annual budget to meet the needs of the entire division or county and then requisitioned the municipalities for such portion of the revenue that had to come from local taxation. In the meantime the provincial governments in addition to paying out the usual grants made them more generous, as well as introducing the equalization grants to assist the less fortunate school divisions.

The funds for the initial building program in every school district were borrowed on ten-year debentures (15 years, prior to 1910). All the minute books, whether coming from a school district in Nova Scotia or from one in British Columbia, repeated parrot-like the substance of this By-Law Number 1 relating to the issue of debentures. It reads as follows:

A By-Law relating to the issue of Debentures of the Dundee School District No. 4326 of the Province of Aberta

Whereas it is necessary and desirable that the sum of $2500 (Two Thousand Five Hundred Dollars) should be borrowed on the security of the Dundee S.D. No. 4326 of the Province of Alberta for the purpose of building and equipping a school house and necessary out-buildings of frame construction, repayable to the bearer in ten equal consecutive annual instalments with interest at not more than eight per centum per annum.

"Now therefore the Board of Trustees of the said District enacts as follows:

1. That the necessary proceedings be taken under the School Ordinance to obtain the sanction of the Board of Public Utility Commissioners of Alberta to the said loan;
2. That upon the Board of Public Utility Commissioners authorizing in writing the Board of Trustees to borrow the said sum of $2500 (Two Thousand Five Hundred Dollars) or any less sum, pursuant to the said act, debentures of the said District be issued for such amount as is authorized, payable to the bearer in Ten equal consecutive instalments with interest at not more than eight per centum per annum and said debentures shall be executed by the Chairman and Treasurer of this Board.

Done and passed this 30th day of July, 1928.

David Wesley Oke, Secretary-Treasurer   *J. W. Noonan, Chairman*

The amount of money borrowed under the by-law seemed to depend on the year in which it was effected and the extent of the individual district's building program. Money had an uncanny way even in the early years of fluctuating in value. Here are a few examples of what it cost to build the Little White Schoolhouse down through the years. In making any comparisons of these figures it must be noted that, although the schools mentioned were all of frame construction, innovations such as full basements, furnaces and indoor toilets added considerably to the building costs in later years. It is almost a foregone conclusion that these schools differed from each other in architecture as well.

School District	Nearest Town	Cost of Building	Year
Clearwater	Crystal City, Man.	$ 585.00	1881
Forest	Carman, Man.	$ 563.00	1884
Burwalde	Winkler, Man.	$ 700.00	1890
Orangehill	Thornhill, Man.	$ 700.00	1894
Harlington	Swan River, Man.	$ 700.00	1902
Kipp	Davidson, Sask.	$1000.00	1906
Fartown	Marshall, Sask.	$1000.00	1908
Glenbow	Cochrane, Alta.	$1295.00	1910
Hillsgreen	Morrin, Alta.	$1677.50	1912
Westwood	Gadsby, Alta.	$1200.00	1914
Haig	Foremost, Alta.	$2000.00	1918
Bearspaw	Cochrane, Alta.	$2400.00	1919

In general, prior to 1905 it required less than $700.00 to construct and equip a one-room school; between 1905 and 1910 around $1000.00; from 1910 to 1920 about $2000.00; and between 1920 and 1930 the cost had risen to $3000.00. Very few districts considered a building program during the depression years; they merely converted some suitable farm building into a school and operated as best they could. By 1940 building cost had started to skyrocket and it was not uncommon for contractors to quote figures of $5000.00 or higher for erecting one-room schools.

As the original debentures were repaid the secretary-treasurer scrupulously recorded the amount and the date of each repayment in the back of the minute book. Here is one such entry that was duplicated by thousands of districts across Canada.

> "Wildflower School District No. 2560 Debenture Number 1, dated June 1, 1912, for $2000.00 at 6% payable in 10 years at the Union Bank, Alsask, Saskatchewan, with the first payment due 18 months from date of issue."

Coupon Number	Due Date	Amount	Date Paid
1	December 1, 1913	380.00	December 6, 1913
2	December 1, 1914	308.00	November 19, 1914
3	December 1, 1915	296.00	December 4, 1915
4	December 1, 1916	284.00	November 23, 1916
5	December 1, 1917	272.00	November 26, 1917
6	December 1, 1918	260.00	December 1, 1918
7	December 1, 1919	248.00	November 14, 1919
8	December 1, 1920	236.00	November 19, 1920
9	December 1, 1921	224.00	November 28, 1921
10	December 1, 1922	212.00	November 23, 1922

The sale of debentures enabled the school district to make a good start, but what about the operating costs from year to year? There were teachers' salaries to be paid, coal and wood to be bought, maintenance costs to be met, equipment of various types to be purchased and a host of kindred disbursements to be settled. These current expenses were met by a local tax levy and by grants received from the provincial government.

The school taxes brought in a good share of the revenue. The school board estimated their operating expenses for the year, subtracted the amount of government grant and requisitioned the municipality, or municipalities for the remainder. The municipality, as the administrative unit, set the mill rate and collected the taxes.

The school districts retained complete autonomy in the field of taxation for they, and they alone, predetermined the mill rate by the simple expedient of requesting from the municipality a specific sum of money. A high requisition meant a high tax rate while a smaller amount signified a lower mill rate. If some of the school district's land was located outside a municipality the school board assumed all responsibility pertaining to taxation. The School Ordinance of that day stated that the tax on such land should be calculated on the basis of so many cents per acre. Some school boards followed this method of taxation while others, realizing that the land in these unorganized areas was usually poor, thought it only fair to assess both types of property by the same standards and to adopt the same mill rate for every portion of their district. The big question appeared to be whether it was fair to tax poor land at so many cents per acre in order to secure an amount equal in ratio to that raised per acre on better land within the Municipal District, where the land had been assessed in value and was taxed on the basis of so many mills on the dollar. This controversy over a just method for taxing inferior land continued for the entire duration of the rural school.

The municipality fulfilled its function by turning over to the school board the tax money that it had been successful in levying from the ratepayers of the school district. This was done four times a year to enable the board to meet its current expenses. In hard times however the municipality transferred immediately to the school board any amounts that it was fortunate enough to collect. This permitted more than one district to ward off a financial exigency and to continue operating for a few additional months.

The rural tax structure incorporated some interesting features. The distance from the school was one of the determining factors in assessing the value of a particular piece of agricultural land in the days of the one-room school. Prospective farmers when choosing the location of their homestead had an eye on the prospective site for the future school. If it was close by it meant that their children would walk less than a mile as compared to others who might have to walk four or five miles. The school was the only community centre and it was a distinct advantage for any farmer and his family to live nearby no matter whether their interests were social, religious, political or cultural. All these activities were based in the Little White Schoolhouse. Today, this variable factor of distance from school is relatively unimportant from the standpoint of taxation.

The mill rate for a school district was also established at such a figure that those who were able to pay "the shot" bore the brunt of the costs of operating the school. Hence in hard times while very few farmers paid the school tax, the school still functioned by reason of the paid-up taxes of the fortunate ratepayers of the district. Some districts however had assessments so small as to make the operation of an efficient school impossible, so the provincial legislature set aside a special grant to assist in equalizing the educational opportunity for the children in these districts.

The variation in mill rate from school district to school district was quite pronounced. In some districts that did not operate schools, or where circumstances had made necessary the closing of the school, the education tax continued from year to year at the minimum rate of two mills. A neighboring district, on the other hand, that had experienced some difficulty with tax collection over a period of years, or where a large and steady school population had added increased burdens on the school's available resources, may have had a high tax rate of twenty mills. The majority of the schools however operated between these two extremes with an average mill rate of ten mills. It was a measure of local pride to operate

Calvin W. Lowrey

School Tax Notice of 1905, just before Alberta became a province.

the school smoothly and efficiently and to meet all financial obligations along the way.

Although the majority of boards exercised considerable care in financing their schools, practically every district had the experience of facing at least one financial crisis during the course of its existence. Great Bend S.D. (Standard, Alta.) found itself in financial straits inside of a few months. School opened in October, 1904, and was closed in January, 1905, because it ran out of money. The trustees laid down the law to those in arrears, but still had compassion in their bewildered souls. William Lampfert, who had been a faithful ratepayer, had suffered a serious accident. So the board refunded whatever he had paid in.

The rate of taxation in the Great Bend S.D. in 1905 was five cents per acre and once collected went a long way towards paying the bill of R. H. Chapman, who for $151 built the school, including the toilets. Unfortunately there was not enough to pay the teacher as well, so after an operating period of four months school ceased until more tax money came in. This didn't happen until fall.

Educational grants were instituted by the provincial governments to assist the individual school districts in achieving and maintaining a certain standard of education. They also helped newly-organized districts to get established. The administrators of the departments of education across the land were in the habit of modifying the grant structure every few years in an attempt to achieve the best possible distribution of the funds voted by the legislatures. Their objective was to obtain the best education possible for the money available.

Initially, the majority of rural schools operated on the safe premise of "pay as you go" rather than the somewhat servile scheme of "credit financing" that was to follow in later years. Apparently the individual school districts carried on as long as funds were available but once these were spent the trustees promptly closed the school.

The Flowering Valley S.D. (Winnifred, Alta.) continued to operate their school as long as they were able to meet their salary commitment to the teacher. The instant they saw that it was not possible they ended the school term whether the required ten months had been completed or not.

The minute book of the Atlanta S.D. 2909 (Colinton, Alta.) also vividly portrays this grim period of financing in the Thirties:

> ". . . that we petition the government to so amend the School Act to provide for a minimum teacher's salary of $600 per annum for 10 months of school . . ."
>
> ". . . after a lengthy discussion over a request from the teacher for a large dictionary, it was decided to look up prices of some. When this was done the board felt that the ones which would be suitable were too high in price for us to afford at the present time . . ."
>
> "A discussion about the board furnishing funds for the purchase of a bat and softball was not settled."
>
> ". . . that the secretary tell Miss Brooks we feel it our duty to cut down teachers' salary to some extent . . ."

Expressions such as, "Moved . . . that bills be paid when funds are available", or "that we pay salaries due as far as funds will allow" became well-worn in the records of most school boards during the period 1928-40.

The School Grants' Act passed in 1905 in Alberta reads as follows:

> "In aid of schools organized and conducted under the provisions of The School Ordinance there shall be paid out of any legislative appropriation made for that purpose:
>
> 1. To rural districts in an amount to be calculated as follows:
>   (a) To each district containing 6400 acres or less of assessable land as shown by the last revised assessment roll of the district $1.20 per day for each day school is kept open; to each district containing less than 6400 acres as aforementioned one cent more per day for each 160 acres or fractional part thereof less than 6400 acres; and to each district containing more than 6400 acres as aforementioned one cent less per day for each additional 160 acres or fractional part thereof.
>   (b) To each district whose school is kept open more than 160 days in the year 40c per day for each additional day not exceeding 50.
>   (c) To each district engaging a teacher who holds a first class professional certificate under the regulations of the department 10c per day for each day such teacher is actually employed in the school.
>   (d) To each district whose school maintains a percentage of attendance as set forth in the following schedule the sum set opposite thereto for each day school is kept open:

40 - 50 inclusive	5c
51 - 60 "	10c
61 - 70 "	15c
71 - 80 "	20c
81 - 100 "	25c

2. To each district whose school attains a minimum grading on its efficiency in respect to grounds, buildings, equipment, government and progress a sum not exceeding 15 cents per day to be paid in proportion to such grading for each school day school is kept open, and such grading shall be based upon the inspector's report, or reports prescribed by the regulations of the department.

The board of every district receiving a grant under this clause shall expend one-half of the amount of such grant received in each and every year on the purchase of books for a school library and such books shall be selected from a list authorized and furnished by the department.

In 1913 the Act was revised to read as follows:

1. To rural districts in an amount to be calculated as follows:
   (a) To each district the sum of $1.10 per day for each legally authorized teaching day during which the school is kept open.
   (b) An additional sum of 30c per day for each legally authorized teaching day during which the school is kept open in the year of its organization and the three succeeding years.
   (c) A special grant for the encouragement of the teaching of agriculture and school gardening to be fixed and apportioned in accordance with the regulations of the Minister as approved by the Lieutenant-Governor in Council.

2. To each rural district whose school maintains a minimum grading on its efficiency in respect to grounds, buildings, equipment, government and progress a sum not exceeding 15c per day to be paid in proportion to such grading for each day school is kept open; and such grading shall be based upon the inspector's report or reports as prescribed by the regulations of the department.

   Provided, however, that the department may in lieu of such sum or any portion thereof supply to such district for its school library or libraries books of equal value selected from the list authorized by the department for library purposes.

3. To each district having a daily average attendance of at least six pupils in grades above the eighth as classified by the regulations of the department, and not maintaining one or more rooms exclusively for such grades, the sum of $40 per term.

The amount of grant that any particular school district earned was calculated by applying the above grant schedule to the Classification and Attendance Report completed by the teacher at the end of each December and June. Since the school register was the original source of all this pertinent information it became known in the rural areas as the Doomsday Book. In addition to the above report the secretary-treasurer of the district had to submit the Financial Statement, the Auditor's Report, Copy of the Minutes of the Annual Meeting, the names of the Officials of the Board, the

Teacher's Agreement, the School Census and the Vital Statistics. All together these became known as the Term Returns. They took a considerable amount of time to compile and as a result many districts submitted incomplete returns or failed to mail them on time. The Department's instructions in this regard were definite enough, "School Grants will be paid in the order in which the complete returns are received by the Department."

Nevertheless under the best of conditions there was a lag of two or three months from the time that the government received the Term Returns until the school was able to spend its grant. December returns brought payments in March, while June returns were settled in September or October. Hence the school boards were forced to borrow money from the banks in order to meet their indebtedness during these periods of financial destitution. At one stage in the history of the rural school the grants were sent directly by the Department to the teachers as part or full payments on salaries that were badly in arrears. The officials reasoned that school boards faced with economic duress might have the urge to spend money on anything but the teacher's salary if they received the grant directly. At times the Department divided the grant between the teacher and the school board.

Wildflower S.D. 2560, a representative rural school in Alberta, received the following grants from September 1912 to June 1922. The first figure indicates the amount of grant earned up to the end of December of the previous year, while the second figure indicates the sum received for operating during the spring and summer term. It must be realized that a school term included the last four months of one year and the first six months of the next year, but many rural schools varied this by commencing early in July or August and declaring an intermission during the inclement winter months of January, February, and even March:

Year	December Term	June Term	Total Grant
1913	97.75	93.96	$191.71
1914	132.75	93.80	226.55
1915	116.10	44.00	161.10
1916	51.55	90.20	141.75
1917	121.95	62.70	184.65
1918	132.00	107.65	239.65
1919	53.75	114.00	167.75
1920	65.75	71.50	137.25
1921	38.40	117.00	155.40
1922	75.50	123.00	198.50
1923	114.35	140.30	254.65

The Attendance Grant was not the only financial device instituted by the provincial legislature to aid the local boards. There were Grants on Leased Land, Library Grants, High School Grants, and Drought and

Depression Emergency Grants (often referred to as the 2D Grant). These subsidies from public funds forced the districts to provide a certain minimum standard of education before they could qualify for the full grant. This in itself was desirable, and it also had the effect of reducing to some extent the tax burden of the local ratepayer.

School districts had the option of raising money from a few local sources of revenue. A tuition fee of thirty cents per day per child was charged students attending from unorganized districts, or from neighboring districts, whose schools for one reason or another were not operating Some schools were also rented out at a standard fee ($5.00) for functions such as public meetings, dances and for polling booths on election days; while for church services, charity drives and patriotic activities the sponsoring group was given free use of the building, or at most was assessed a nominal charge.

It was the custom of many school boards to organize card parties, auctions, dances and other forms of money-raising projects to provide Christmas treats for the children or to assist the district in the purchase of a piano. This was particularly true during the depression period in the Thirties. The Cherry Valley school board organized a public dance in the schoolhouse on January 11, 1918, in support of the Halifax Relief Fund. This was when two ships, one of them carrying high explosives, collided in the Halifax harbor and the resulting blast almost destroyed the city and killed thousands of people. The income derived from such supplementary sources might appear to be insignificant, but in the "close-to-the vest" financing that most of the boards employed, every penny counted.

Most of the money acquired under the debenture plan went towards paying for the new schoolhouse, the two outbuildings, the coalshed and if required, a barn. The cost of the furnishings and equipment also cut deeply into the fund. The $300.00 required for this probably does not seem large by today's standards but at that time it was considered a sizeable sum of money. A number of business firms came into being as a direct result of the increasing demand for specialized furnishings and supplies by the many one-room schools that mushroomed all over Western Canada soon after 1910. These included the E. M. Moyer Company of Edmonton, the Christie Book Store in Brandon, the Alberta Supply Company of Edmonton and F. E. Osborne of Calgary. E. M. Moyer and F. E. Osborne are still active in the school supply business.

The school board that sparked a bit of business ingenuity requisitioned its requirements by tender and hence effected a better bargain than those that followed the traditional method of ordering directly from the catalogue. The shipment was usually slow in arriving, and when it did finally reach the railway station nearest to the school, the board contracted to have the goods hauled. This was no light task as the supplies had to be freighted long distances in slow horse-drawn lumber wagons over bad roads and mere trails. Sometimes it took several days to make a trip into town and back.

Once the equipment reached its destination the school board was confronted with the additional task of having it unpacked and installed. Desks had to be assembled, blackboards mounted, the stove set up, pipes fitted, shelves built and clothes pegs fastened. A person handy with tools was given the thankless but intriguing task of deciphering and fitting together the jumbled assortment of desk and stove parts, with a few items from the pulley-mounted globe thrown in for good measure. It was a difficult job for there were no plans to follow outside of the illustrations in the catalogue. The board was usually charged $20.00 for this work. When it was finished there was no assurance that the desks would remain upright when supporting their human cargoes or that the grates in the stove would remain level when shaken instead of emptying all the burning coals into the ashtray below.

Here is a representative list of school supplies that were purchased by Cherry Valley S.D. (Oyen, Alberta) on April 20, 1916, from the E. M. Moyer Company, Edmonton, to properly equip the brand-new 25-pupil school.

5 New Empire Single Desks, No. 2 at $4.30	21.50
5 New Empire Single Desks, No. 3 at $4.20	21.00
5 New Empire Single Desks, No. 4 at $4.20	21.00
5 New Empire Single Desks, No. 5 at $4.00	20.00
4 New Empire Single Rear Seats, 1 each of 2-3-4-5	14.70
1 Teacher's Desk, No. 3	18.00
1 Teacher's Chair, No. 2	4.25
1 Visitor's Chair, No. 2	1.65
1 Map—The British Empire (Spring Roller & Back)	8.50
1 Map—Dominion of Canada (Spring Roller & Back)	8.50
1 Map—Alberta (Spring Roller and Back)	5.50
1 Globe No. 222	8.00
1 Broom and Dust Pan	.85
1 Mirror	.75
1 Water Pail	1.00
1 Fire Shovel	.25
1 Waste Paper Basket	.75
1 Coal Hod	.95
1 Wash Basin	.50
1 Holder and 3 Rolls of Sanitary Towels	2.00
100 Square Feet Hydroplate Blackboard	18.00
Necessary Moulding for the Blackboard	4.80
6 Dustless Erasers	1.00
½ Gross Colored Chalk	.75
3 Gross Dustless Chalk	1.95
1 Eight-Day Clock	6.00
1 Thermometer	.75

1 Concise Imperial Dictionary L/2 Morrocco 2.75
1 Hand Numeral Frame .... .75
1 Blackboard Pointer (Steel) .... .25
1 Hand Bell No. 7 .... 1.00
1 Desk Bell No. 720 .... .50
1 Union Jack No. 6 .... 3.25
1 Quart Ink 1.00
1 Moyer Clean Air Furnace No. 18 ....115.00
  Gross Total 317.40
  Trade Discount 18.20
  Net Total $299.20

There were many other expenditures incidental to the opening of a new school. These included: The appointment of a secretary-treasurer at an annual salary of from $25.00 to $50.00; contracting for a three-year fire insurance policy on both the school and its furnishings at a premium of $25.00; the purchase and hauling of a supply of coal and wood for around $50.00; digging and cribbing a well, and equipping it with a pump, or a rope and dip-pail, $75.00; plowing a fireguard around the school yard, $5.00; erecting a suitable fence about the school property, $60.00; bonding of the secretary-treasurer, $5.30; and last but not least, hiring a teacher for an annual salary of between $350.00 and $1200.00.

The secretary-treasurers of many school districts started out with little else for their office equipment than the School Act, a five-cent scribbler and one lead pencil. As these worthy individuals gained experience the board invested in a few essential items. For instance, the Spondon S.D. 3375 (Hanna, Alta.) ordered the following office supplies from the Christie Book Store at Brandon, Man., on September 7, 1916:

1 Rubber Seal $2.00
1 Minute Book .... .75
1 Ledger .... .75
500 Printed Letterheads and Envelopes 5.00
100 Printed 10-inch Envelopes 1.50
2 Shannon Files 2.00
1 Carbon Copy Letter Book 2.00

The school district's seal or stamp was a very significant item. Its imprint on any letter, document or cheque issued on behalf of the trustees lent a dignity and legality which were hard to assess. The mere sight of the school district's name and number in print gave credence to the fact that the district was a reality and no longer a dream. It became the community's crest, trademark, coat of arms and flag all rolled into one. Small wonder it had such an emotional appeal for every resident in the district. Secretary-treasurers were apparently very proud to use the stamp. An examination of any of the first official papers issued by a district shows that the seal or stamp was used with extreme solicitousness, but as the years went by it appeared to be taken for granted and was affixed with more abandonment. Yet today such impresses whether they are found in an old library book or on the faded pages of a minute book are much prized by a generation that has begun to feel the thinning of its ranks. To them it is a tangible part of the past of their Little White Schoolhouse.

It is hard to credit a statement made in the minute book of the Wellington S.D. (Thornhill, Man.) that the total amount spent on supplies for a five-month period from March 14 to August 29 in the year 1899 was $6.45. Yet the school's store account with Kilgour and Jordon verifies the fact that the following purchases were made: crayons 20c, broom 70c, erasers 20c, rake 35c (for Arbor Day, May 9), brushes 90c, sprinkler 60c, matches 15c, colored crayons 40c, 2 brooms 70c, chalk 40c, lock 40c, tubing 15c, brushes 90c.

The school board members were very conservative in money matters. This was not because they lacked generous impulses but because they had very little experience in doing business on a large scale. Their own personal business transactions during a particular year rarely involved amounts in excess of a few hundred dollars. The early settlers formed habits of economy, thrift and self-denial and when they were elected to the school board these characteristics were brought to bear rather heavily when it came to financing their school. The ratepayers were always critical of school expenditures and at every opportunity insisted upon the justification of every expense no matter how small. As a consequence the finances of a school district were handled by the board with as much concern and interest as if their own possessions were involved. Every school business transaction, no matter how big or small, was of common knowledge and concern to every resident in the district. It was like having fifteen auditors checking the same financial statement. The records in the minute books reflect this staid, diminutive and cautious but highly democratic and safe method of financing.

> "Moved by James Parke that the secretary get $1.00 worth of stamps and a broom for the school. Carried."
>
> "Moved by Stephen Heaney that the secretary get a fire guard plowed about the school yard one rod wide to cost no more than $2.50. Carried."
>
> "The secretary was asked to read an account of the receipts and expenses of the district in detail for the year 1922."

The Department of Education, through certain provisions in the School Act, was able to maintain a close tab on the finances of any district. For example, the borrowing and spending powers were limited, the business procedures to be followed and the forms to be used were standardized and the district was required to submit an annual detailed financial statement with an accompanying auditor's report. Instructions from the government like the following made doubly sure that all matters pertaining to school accounting were aboveboard:

> "According to Section 129 of the School Act, the books and accounts of every rural and village school district are required to be audited by AN OFFICIAL AUDITOR. No audit of the books of any rural or village school district will be accepted, nor will the Government Grant to the district be paid unless the name of the auditor employed appears in the list of official auditors. This list will be published in The Provincial Gazette and forwarded to the secretary-treasurer of all school districts towards the close of the year. No audit for the year should be made unless this list has been received."

An entry in the minute book of the Esther S.D. (Esther, Alta.) dated June 20, 1925, indicates that school boards did follow the banking procedures as advocated by the Department of Education:

> "Resolved that Blakely McNeil our chairman, and Olaf O. Olsen our Secretary-Treasurer are hereby authorized for and in the name of the Esther School District No. 4038 to draw, accept, sign, and make all or any Bills of Exchange, Promissory Notes, cheques and orders for payment of money, to pay and receive all monies and to give acquittance for same. To assign and transfer to the Bank all or any Stocks, Bonds, and other Securities from time to time, to borrow money from the Union Bank of Canada either in overdrawing the account of the undersigned or otherwise and generally for and in the name and on behalf of said School District to transact with said Bank any Business they may think fit."
>
> "Also Olaf O. Olsen our Secretary-Treasurer is hereby authorized on behalf of said School District to negotiate with, deposit with, or transfer to said Bank (but for credit of the said School Account only) all or any Bills of Exchange, Promissory notes, cheques or orders for payment of money and other negotiable paper, and for the said purpose to endorse the same or any of them on behalf of said school. Also from time to time to arrange, settle, balance and certify all Books and Accounts between said school and the Bank and to receive all paid cheques and vouchers and to sign the Bank form of Settlement of balance and release."

The Department of Education may have had some measure of authority over each school district's finances but they had no control whatever over the country's economy. The depression era found many school districts in Canada and the United States unable to repay the installments due on their debentures. Many were forced to default. A few like the Forest S.D. (Carman, Man.) continued to make payments for a while through the efforts of some devoted resident, like Mr. J. A. Green, who cashed a note for the required sum. In general the financial picture continued to deteriorate. Many boards announced their district's inability to make settlement on the debenture due that year but they still paid the interest incurred. The next year they requested an extension on time on both the debenture payments and the accrued interest. Finally, seeing no way out of the dilemma, the secretary was instructed to write the

Annual Financial Statement and Auditor's Report

Cherry Valley   School District No. 3087   of the Province of Alberta, for the year 1932.

NOTICE RE OFFICIAL AUDITORS—According to Section 129 of The School Act, the books and accounts of every rural and village school district are required to be audited in each year by AN OFFICIAL AUDITOR. No audit of the books of any rural or village school district will be accepted, nor will the Government Grant to the district be paid unless the name of the auditor employed appears in the list of official auditors. This list will be published in The Alberta Gazette and forwarded to the Secretary-Treasurers of all school districts towards the close of the year, and no audit for the year should be made until this list has been received.
A copy of the Financial Statement and Auditor's Report should be retained by the district, and inserted in the Cash Book; the Cash Books supplied by the Department contain blank pages for this purpose.

STATEMENT OF RECEIPTS AND PAYMENTS

RECEIPTS

Under this heading should be entered all sums of money actually received between January 1st and December 31st. Moneys received after December 31st should not appear in this statement.

Total Balance on Hand January 1st, $ 38.01	Net Balance as at January 1st Dr.	16 24
Outstanding Cheques from last year, $ 54.25	(Deduct outstanding cheques)	
Cash received from debentures sold during the year		
Taxes collected for the current year, $ 7.65 ; Arrears, $ 21.93		29 58
Amount received from Municipal Council, on requisitions		450 00
Government Grants received by Treasurer, $708.25 ; by Teacher, $; in Library Books, $		708 25
Amount the Trustees borrowed by note during the year		
Amount the Trustees borrowed from the Government during the year		
Tuition Fees		
Received from other sources (give particulars) $		
Cash temporarily advanced by Treasurer, $; Bank Overdraft, $		
TOTAL CASH RECEIPTS		$ 1171 59

PAYMENTS

Under this heading should be entered all sums of money actually paid out between January 1st and December 31st. Moneys paid out after December 31st should not appear in this statement.

Paid Teachers' Salaries, $ 892.05 ; By Government Grant, $		$ 892 05
Paid Officials' Salaries, Secretary, Treasurer, Assessor, Auditor, etc.		5 00
Paid on Debentures (this should include only the amount paid during the year)		
Paid on account of Notes, $; Interest, $		
Paid for erecting and repairing school house, stable, outhouses, etc.		121 55
Paid for purchasing and improving school grounds, fence, well, etc.		19 43
Paid for furniture—desks, cupboards and stove, etc.		
Paid for school library and reference books (including library books in lieu of cash grants)		
Paid for apparatus and equipment—globe, maps, charts, reading tablets, etc.		
Paid for supplies, stationery, postage, chalk, brushes, pails, etc.		14 90
Paid for caretaking, $ 46.75 ; Fuel, $ 36.55		83 30
Paid for Insurance, $		
Paid for other purposes (give particulars) School Fair $ 10.00 Treas Bond $ 1.25 Charge a Comm on Collections $ 2.22		13 47

Actual Cash in Hands of Treasurer $				
Total Bank Balance $ 221.89 (Including o/s cheques)	**TOTAL CASH PAYMENTS**		$ 1149	70
Total Balance $ 221.89				
Outstanding Cheques $ 2.00	Net Balance as at December 31st, 1932		$ 21	89
Net Balance $ 21.89 (After deducting o/s cheques)	(N.B.—The Cash Book Balance and Net Balance must agree.)			

I, _____ Felison _____ hereby certify that I have examined all the books, vouchers, minutes of meeting, etc., of the 3087 S.D.
No. _____ of the Province of Alberta for the fiscal year ending December 31, 1932, and I further certify that I have counted the cash and examined the Bank Books, or obtained information from the Bank regarding the Bank Balance, showing that there is a balance on hand represented by

     (a)   Actual cash in hands of Treasurer _____ $

     (b)   Total Bank Balance _____ $ 221.89

     or.   That the overdraft amounts to only _____ $

I have found vouchers and authorization for all the items with the exception of _____

Annual Financial Statement and Auditor's Report of a Rural School.
Cherry Valley S.D. 3087 (Oyen, Alta.)

Outstanding Accounts

AMOUNTS which were due to the District on December 31st, 1932			AMOUNTS which were owed by the District on December 31st, 1932		
Taxes Outstanding			Teachers' salaries unpaid	$	
1. Current $418.84			Officials' salaries unpaid	50	00
2. Arrears $7126.34			Debenture coupons due and unpaid including interest thereon to December 31st.		
3. Reported Arrears.... $340.60	7885	78	Government loan	1086	88
Balance due from the municipality on requisitions .... $	271	45	Other amounts due and unpaid (*Give particulars*)		
Total taxes due, including arrears .. $8157	23		Bank overdrafts .... $		2 31
OTHER AMOUNTS DUE DISTRICT (Give Particulars)			Exchange Amount advanced by Treas. $ .90		
Tuition Fees .... $			stamps Government Advances .... $ 1.41		
Cash on Hand and Actual Bank Balance .... $ (Including outstanding cheques)	221	89			
Total.......... $	221	89	Total amount due and unpaid .... $	1139	19

Assets and Liabilities
December 31st, 1932

ASSETS			LIABILITIES		
Estimated value of property owned by the district:			Total of debenture debt not yet due:— Principal only .... $		
Land and Buildings	$1200		Int. on Principal to Dec. 31 .... $	$	.
Furniture, Apparatus, Maps, Supplies, etc.	315		Other amounts which the district owes on December 31st as follows:—		
Library and Reference Books	84	27	Outstanding Accts. (total amount due and unpaid as shown above) $1139.19	1339	19
Total Taxes due District (as above)	8157	23	Cheques outstanding .... $ 200		
Other Amounts Due District (as above) .. (Including total balance on hand)	221	89	Notes outstanding .... $		
TOTAL ASSETS	$9978	39	TOTAL LIABILITIES .... $	1339	19

Particulars of Assessment, Taxation, etc., for the Year 1932

Total assessable areas .... 7791 acres.	Total amount of arrears	$ 7885.78
Total assessed value $ .... 31,502.	Balance due from the municipality	$ 271.45
	Total number of ratepayers in arrears	
Rate of Taxation.... 13 mills on the dollar	Total number of resident ratepayers in arrears	

Exact cost of operation of the school for the year, $ 1149.70

N.B.—This cost should include all legitimate expenditures in connection with the operation and maintenance of the school for the year, *i.e.*: All salaries (including amounts paid teacher by the Department out of the Government Grants) amount of Debenture Coupons falling due during the above year, general maintenance, interest, etc., but should not include amounts borrowed by note or renewals, nor cost of buildings, grounds, etc., covered by Debenture issues.

Insurance

The property of the district is insured as follows:

Building .... $ 1150.00 ; Furniture and equipment, $ 250.00

The policy expires June 4, 1934

Debenture Indebtedness

The debenture indebtedness of the district remaining unpaid is .... $

I have examined the above Financial Statement, and to the best of my knowledge, believe the same to be true and correct.

J. P. Loratek _____
Treasurer.   Oyen Alta _____ Address.

Remarks or Recommendations

I hereby certify that the above information is in accordance with the books and records of Cherry Valley School District No. 3087 , of the Province of Alberta, and from the information given me I believe the same to be correct. I further certify that I have made a copy of this Report in the back of the School District Cash Book.

C. G. Pierson _____
Official Auditor.

Oyer _____
P.O. Address.

DATE .... Jan 21-1933

Department of Education in regard to the district's unpaid debentures. This turned out to be a mere formality for very little assistance came from that source. All too soon the debenture payments of many districts became badly in arrears and their borrowing powers seemingly lost. By the year 1935 it had become apparent that a financial stalemate had been reached in a large number of school districts. The solution lay in some sort of administrative unit which could deal with the problem over a large area having the power to bring greater resources to bear on the matter. The answer came in each province and state when its legislature amended the School Act and provided for the establishment of School Divisions and Counties. School accounting has become big business now and the days when budgets for $1000.00 and special tax levies for $100.00 were considered, are no longer with us.

4

BUILDING THE SCHOOL

The rural school building program across Western Canada proceeded with caution until 1910, gained momentum between 1911 and 1914 and was curtailed during the war years 1914-18. A wave of immigration after 1918 crowded the existing country schools to such an extent that many new districts had to be organized. This resulted in a new spurt in school construction which continued at a hectic pace until 1925, declined by 1930 and become sporadic thereafter. Nearly as rapidly as the number of settlers had increased from 1910 to 1925, a decided drop took place in rural poulation in the early Thirties. Outside of a few districts formed in the northern portions of the prairie provinces to which many of the inhabitants of the drought-stricken areas had fled there was no need for new schools. With fewer people to tax and the depression at its height many schools went bankrupt. In others, the enrollment dwindled to such small numbers, i.e. two or three students, that it was considered imprudent to continue operating the school. As a result the large unit of administration came into being and many rural children were conveyed to consolidated schools for the first time. Centralization in education had begun.

The building of a school was the first tangible evidence, even to the casual observer, that systematic learning was about to be introduced in the district. The formation of the school district and the borrowing of money by debentures were historical events just as significant as the erection of the school building, but since these preliminaries involved a considerable amount of routine paper work not seen by the general public they went unheralded. It was not until the building supplies began to arrive at the site or the actual construction started that interest and excitement became rampant. Each day's progress was carefully observed and reported. It became the main topic of conversation among the citizens of the district whether it was at home during moments of respite or out in the fields as neighboring farmers rested their horses. The exciting news—"Our school is going up!"—was proudly proclaimed to all and sundry by the settlers involved.

—Mrs. C. Wallator

The Uphill School No. 3541 near Turner Valley, Alta., was erected in 1917 out of rough lumber. Its appearance may lack elegance but the building itself was serviceable.

—Ray MacKay

A stone school erected on the prairies. The Foster School near Abernethy, Sask., was built from the many stones found in the district.

—Mrs. I. Hosie

Swamp Road School near Denbigh, Ontario, built in 1880.

—S. B. Smith

Poplar Dale log schoolhouse was completed in 1927. Poplar Dale School District is near Dapp, Alta.

Prior to 1905 and for many years thereafter there were very few government regulations pertaining to the construction of rural schoolhouses.
Hence it was the custom in those early days for some former carpenter
living in the district to draw up the plans. He supplemented his own
concept of what a school building should be like with the ideas suggested to
him by the various settlers. As a result the finished school resembled those
found in Eastern Canada, the United States or many European countries.

The school supply houses of that period were the first to see the
urgent need for a set of designs for a one-room school. They prepared
some and sold them to districts contemplating building a school.

The Departments of Education of British Columbia, Manitoba, the
Territories and the Midwestern States, did not issue specific drawings but
distributed very general directions for building a school similar to the
following:

> "Every school room shall be built of such dimensions as to allow at least 15
> square feet of floor space and 200 cubic feet of air space for each pupil in
> average attendance. The room should be from two-thirds to five-sixths of
> the length and the ceiling should be at least 11 feet high.
>
> "A roomy porch or inner cloakroom should be provided for the children's
> hats and wraps. The hooks used should be strong and firmly fixed to the
> walls. Shelves for dinner baskets and stands for a washbasin and a water
> pail should also be provided.
>
> "The windows should be placed at the left, and, if necessary behind the
> pupils. Those at the back should be near the left corner. Windows should
> never be placed facing the pupils. The window sills should be from 3½
> to 4 feet high and the top of the window should extend to within 6 inches
> of the ceiling. Storm sashes should be provided when the school is to be
> kept open during the winter months. Light colored curtains should be placed
> on all windows exposed to the direct rays of the sun.
>
> "Due provisions should be made for comfortably heating the schoolroom
> and providing a sufficient supply of fresh air."

When the provinces of Alberta and Saskatchewan came into being in
1905 they adopted many of the regulations and administrative precedents
established by the Territorial Department of Education. Hence the two
new provinces continued the policy of the previous administration in
respect to building new schools. By 1912, however, the various Departments
of Education had made good strides in developing some useful "One Room
District School Plans". Thus the Departments were ready with a good
variety of complete building plans and specifications when the need
became pressing soon after 1918.

The building regulations were there but under pioneering conditions
it was not always possible or even feasible to conform to them. The
settlers built their schools with whatever materials were at hand and in a
way that suited local conditions. There were log schools, stone schools, sod

—Hugh W. Allen

Garnet Truax hauling logs for the Lower Beaver Lodge School 2812
(Grande Prairie, Alta.)

schools, mud schools, brick schools and the common wooden-frame buildings.

The difficulties attending the construction of a new school in those early days were many. The settlers on the prairies particularly found it so. The homesteaders in the forested areas could fell the trees and make their schools out of logs but their unfortunate neighbors living on the vast treeless plains had no such readily available source of building materials. Yet even here the ingenuity and the courage of the early settlers overcame the problem temporarily at least. The historical stories of the organization and the construction of the Grassington Mud School, the Grahamston Stone School and the Aneroid Sod School are worth telling. They typify the undaunted spirit of the early pioneers who attempted to secure an education for their children no matter what the cost.

GRASSINGTON MUD SCHOOL

The pioneers of this prairie district in southwestern Saskatchewan wanted to construct a school but the shortage both of funds and building materials was thwarting their plan. The solution to the problem came from an unexpected source. It was learned that Chris Carsner, who lived in the district and had a number of the school-age children, was skilled at building mud houses. Donald Fraser, the secretary, was instructed by the school committee to contact Mr. Carsner and see if he would superintend the building of a school with mud walls and a timber roof. He readily consented.

Someone brought up the question of securing the consent of the Department of Education of the Territories at Regina for their ambitious undertaking. The answer was, "Oh! That will take too long. We'll build first and notify the Department later. They'll be glad to see any kind of a school out here."

Chris Carsner drew up some working plans and soon the men of the community under his guidance set to work to construct the first and only mud school in that part of the prairie west. Building bees were frequently held and in no time at all the schoolhouse began to take shape. The ladies did their share. They prepared many meals for the volunteer workers.

This was a German-type mud house, of which many were built in the district about that time. The mud was first softened with slough water and then thoroughly impregnated with such binding materials as straw and willow twigs by the workers tramping it in with their bare feet. The scene was almost reminiscent of the old Biblical days when the Egyptians compelled the Hebrews to make bricks without straw.

As soon as the mud reached the right consistency it was poured into a wooden crib to form the wall. It remained there until it hardened. Then the framework was moved to another part of the structure. The process was continued until the wall enclosure was completed. A roof of rough boards but no shingles completed the major part of the construction. The final result was a mud-walled building twenty by twelve feet with one door and three windows but no porch for the children's wraps. These were hung on old-fashioned square pegs driven into the walls. The door and window frames, the floor, and the walls were lined with lumber to give them a more durable finish.

The naming of the school was no problem. A Yorkshireman present suggested "Grassington". This was the name of his native hamlet in the Old Country. The large number of white-walled settlers' huts reminded him of an English village with its buildings of white walls and thatched roofs.

School opened in the fall of 1895 ten years before the province of Saskatchewan was born. The first teacher, or master, as they were known in those days, was Mr. Judson Booth. He taught the three R's sternly and without favor. There was not much choice of subjects in a pioneer school. When the weather became cold a small coal stove was placed in the centre of the room with the pipes leading out through the wooden roof. The fuel bill was not high as this type of insulated building proved to be cozy in the winter and cool in summer. Besides, buffalo chips and the deadfall from a nearby river bank did not cost anything outside of the trouble of collecting and hauling.

This pioneer mud school stood for twenty years. However, with the erection of a modern frame school building, it was used only for public meetings and church services. In 1912 the roof, which was in danger of collapsing, was dismantled. The mud walls stood through the depression years but gradually crumbled away.

Today only a little mound of earth remains to mark the spot where this strange but historic schoolhouse stood.

THE GRAHAMSTON STONE SCHOOL

Samuel Dickson, his two brothers and their families arrived at the village of Innisfail (then called Polar Grove), North West Territories, in May 1892. They homesteaded four and a-half miles southeast of the village. The first school was built and opened in Polar Grove in 1890 and for a time the Dickson children attended this school. In the meantime the parents considered the possibility of building a school closer to home. Neighbors were few and far between and as the majority were bachelors they were not interested in a school and were bitterly opposed to any plan for getting one organized. Mr. Dickson persisted and with the help of the Department of Education of the Territories in Regina mapped out a few quarter sections and opened a school in an old house in 1897.

It was a good school. The first teacher was a Mrs. Flanagan, a ratepayer of the district. Her salary was $30 per month if there was any money in the treasury. If not, the taxpayers contributed a pig, a calf, a colt, or a few chickens in lieu of money. The children had to be educated and the parents were certainly going to do their part. The teacher used the three-month school term to advantage. There were no strikes, no institutes, no teachers' conventions to interrupt her zeal for giving the students the best she knew.

The boundaries of the district were extended when more settlers came into the area. Soon the old house became too small for the number of school children attending. Something had to be done! Again Samuel Dickson took a leading role and organized a school building committee. They surveyed a number of possibilities but each plan was turned down as being beyond the district's ability to pay. The dilemma ended when one of the settlers reported finding a deposit of stone in a nearby coulee. To the majority of settlers this discovery was irrelevant. But to the few Scotsmen it meant much. They were familiar with the many uses to which stone could be put, not the least of these being the construction of buildings. Yes! Why not a stone schoolhouse?

Volunteers quarried the stone from the coulee while three local masons built the schoolhouse. It was completed in the summer of 1898. All the school furniture was homemade with the fathers responsible for building a desk for each of their sons and daughters attending the school. The

—A. H. "Hap" Clarke

The Grahamston "Stone" School near Innisfail, Alta., is still good as new after serving the community for 70 years. It is in use today as a community centre.

teacher's desk was simply a table. This newly-constructed school was appropriately named "Grahamston" to honor the Dickson family who were of the Graham clan.

The Grahamston School, unlike the Grassington School, still stands today, a credit to the craftsmanship of her builders and a landmark of the day when the rural school marked an epoch in the building of the west.

ANEROID'S SOD SCHOOLHOUSE

On the evening of May 10, 1910, a gathering of Aneroid homesteaders was held at the pioneer home of H. C. Douglas. This meeting was an urgent and important one called to organize a local school for the settlers' children. This area some sixty-five miles south of Swift Current had been thrown open for homesteading in 1908 and with a great influx of people it was felt necessary to provide a school for the thirty local children.

The decision of the meeting was unanimous and determined—"We must build a school!" They appointed the following trustees to carry out their plans: H. C. Douglas, M. S. Brooks, J. Stroman and R. B. Lloyd as secretary.

The building of a wooden schoolhouse was out of the question as the lumber would have to be hauled from Swift Current. Some type of temporary building had to be erected until the railway came to Aneroid.

The discussion ranged far and wide until someone suggested the use of prairie sod as building material. The idea seemed preposterous. However when it was pointed out that it had to be a sod schoolhouse or none at all, the idea became more tenable. In fact everyone had seen sod shanties here and there on the prairies so why not a sod schoolhouse? George Corbin, an apprenticed builder from England, swayed the meeting in favor of the plan when he said it could be done.

The newly-appointed secretary, Dick Lloyd, was saddled with the task of convincing the educational authorities at Regina of the feasibility of the scheme. At first the correspondence from the Department of Education gave very little encouragement. "Your proposition is too weird to consider. A building of bricks, logs, stones or boards, yes, but who ever heard of a sod schoolhouse?" Mr. Lloyd persisted. He answered each refusal politely with additional facts, figures and new arguments.

Finally the Department of Education went so far as to arrange a meeting at Swift Current between the Deputy Minister of Education, Mr. H. Calder, and the district's school committee. The afternoon was spent in discussing the bizarre plan and what it would cost. The men from Aneroid became adamant and refused to give up. Eventually the official from the Department acceded to their wishes and gave them permission to proceed with their plans. He added a word of caution, "Remember! yours will be the only sod schoolhouse in the west!"

Such a statement failed to deter the pioneers. In their imagination they could already see the new school made of freshly-cut sods standing majestically with the Union Jack fluttering in the breeze above it. Yes, they even visualized a pretty, white-bloused, dark-skirted teacher presiding over their children.

The homesteaders went to work in earnest under the direction of George Corbin. Bees were held and everyone from miles around came to help. It became a real community undertaking and was the main topic of conversation in every prairie shack. The sods were cut, carefully stacked, and the walls rose rapidly. The window and door frames were homemade while the roof was constructed of rough-hewn lumber. Everything was complete right down to a partition for a cloakroom. True, the walls appeared shaggy but the building was warm in winter and cool in summer. When it rained for one day outside it rained two days on the inside. The children and teacher also discovered they were not the only occupants of the new building when garter snakes kept crawling out of the sidewalls with monotonous regularity.

In searching for a name for the school, Mr. Lloyd suggested that of his home town of Indianola, Iowa. And so, after some further correspondence with the Department of Education, the district became known officially

—Mrs. Margaret Chapman (nee Lloyd)

The Indianola Sod Schoolhouse at Aneroid, Sask., built in 1911.

as Indianola S.D. 2704. School opened with an enrollment of twenty-one pupils on Tuesday, April 4, 1911.

As rural schools go the Indianola Sod School had a very short life. In 1913 a consolidated school was built in the town of Aneroid and the old sod school which had served its original purpose was abandoned. It soon deteriorated. Today only a pile of stones stands in a field two and a-half miles southwest of Aneroid to mark the historic site.

The majority of the rural schools erected after 1914 were of the frame-type construction. Up to this time the Department of Education in consideration for the problems of the early settlers had been quite lenient with the school boards as to their compliance with the various building ordinances. Now they changed their tenor to one of strict observance of all building regulations and procedures. Not only were the instructions modified in keeping with the best knowledge available at the time but by 1919 most Departments had on file over fifteen different "One Room District School" building plans. Each one had been designed to meet a particular set of conditions that could be encountered anywhere in that province. It mattered little whether the school board desired a fifteen-pupil or a forty-pupil school the departmental officials were ready to provide them with the necessary plans. If the trustees expressed a desire for two front entrances rather than one or if they wished the school to parallel a particular road allowance rather than face it, the Department could supply the necessary blueprints.

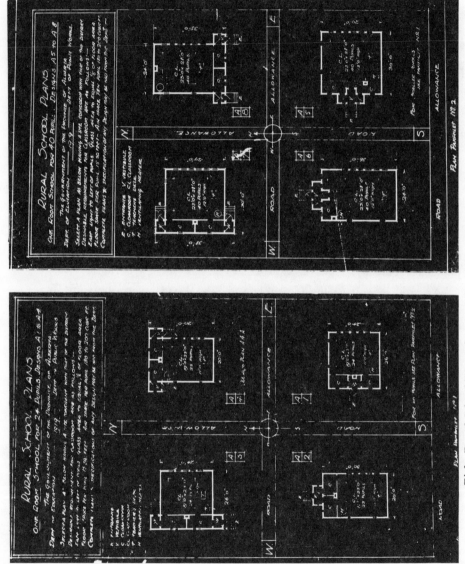

Eight Rural School Plans designed by the Department of Education of Alberta in 1919 for the use of districts planning to build a one-room school.

The school boards were quick to take advantage of this new architectural service. Entries such as the following appear in their minute books:

"Mr. Fleming made a motion that the Government Plan A1 would be a suitable plan for a building for our district. Seconded by C. C. Cameron. Carried." Spondon S.D. 3375 dated March 20, 1918.

"The Departmental School Plan A3 was examined and appeared satisfactory. It was decided to secure an estimate of the cost of constructing such a building." Grassy Slope S.D. 3993 dated October 31, 1921.

"Moved by Mr. Hemstock and seconded by Mr. Rehill that the plan for a school as sent in by the Department of Education, Plan A5, be accepted. Carried." Dundee S.D. 4326 dated April 28, 1928.

A number of school boards made slight modifications in the official plans in order to better meet local conditions. For example, one minute book states:

"The secretary be instructed to write the Department regarding Plan A1, and state that we prefer the cottage roof to the gable one, and where the steps are shown, we would like to build an outside vestibule. Also we want the school building to face west, have a full basement and the entrance changed to the south side."

Another school board had this to recommend:

"The amended plans and two new ones were received from the Department of Education. After reviewing all the drawings the Board concluded that Plan A4 was the best suited for our district, if we were permitted to add a coalhouse to the north end. The secretary was instructed to notify the Department accordingly."

Since official approval had to be secured before any changes could be made the Department of Education made certain that the buildings ultimately erected were functional, compatible and incorporated certain minimum standards. This procedure had a tendency to stifle initiative and resulted in the propagation of hundreds of stereotyped school buildings. The idea of standardization extended even to the colors so is it any wonder that each one blossomed forth in a coat of white paint trimmed with green.

Once the Department of Education approved a particular building plan they sent the local school board a twenty-one page document entitled "Plans and Specifications". This brochure contained all the necessary detailed drawings and work specifications for the precise plan that had been selected whether it was A1 or A16. The following legal documents were also forwarded to the trustees: Conditions of Contract, Form of Advertisement for Tenders, the Form of Tender, the Form of Bond and the Form of Agreement between the contractor and the school board. All the trustees had to do was to follow these instructions diligently and ultimately the contractor turned over the completed school building to them.

—Mrs. O. J. Trudeau

Rouselle S.D. 48 (Big Fork, Montana). The pump and the car in the yard date
the school. This picture shows that rural schools were much alike in Canada
and the United States.

The trustees had the option of advertising the tenders for the schoolhouse in one of two ways. They could request separate tenders for
supplying the building materials and for erecting the building or a
composite tender including both the materials and the construction.

Some school boards felt that if all the materials were purchased locally
they would be able to effect a better saving than would an outside
contractor. Then in addition they had the option of hiring local carpenters
to build the school under this scheme. The trustees reasoned that since
these workers had more than a passing interest in and special devotion to
their own district they were apt to do a better job. In actual practice it
made very little difference financially which type of tender was selected.
Below are the financial statements of two similar country schools built
under different types of tendering.

On June 15, 1918, the Spondon school board opened the tenders for
the supply of materials for building their school and found them as follows:

    Empire Lumber Company—Richdale, Alta. $1500.00
    Crown Lumber Company—Richdale, Alta. 1415.00
    Acorn Lumber Company—Coronation, Alta. 1250.00

They accepted the tender of the Acorn Lumber Company for $1250.00
subject to the approval of the Department of Education. Three months

later, September 5, 1918, the same board opened the tenders for the erection of the building itself.

Messers Williams and Blackmore, Richdale $700.00
Mr. Harry Crego, Whatcheer 650.00
Mr. J. Johanson 595.00

After due consideration the board finally approved the tender of Mr. Harry Crego for $650.00. The total cost of the two tenders amounted to $1900.00.

On the other hand the Grassy Slope school board had asked for tenders covering both the materials and erection of the schoolhouse. When they opened the tenders on June 1, 1922, they decided to accept the bid of B. R. Cramer of Monitor, Alta., for $1915.00.

The ratepayers of the Lothian S.D. 2622 (Veteran, Alta.) must have been thankful to receive Mr. Rube Cross's bid to build their school. This ambitious homesteader of about twenty-three years of age contracted to:

"Haul all the building material required from Veteran, Alta. (22 miles away), supply all the labor necessary to build the school from the bottom of its stone foundation to the top of its brick chimney; varnish and paint it inside and outside; and build two toilets, all for the full sum of $325.00 lawful money of Canada in payment and under conditions aforesaid."

The poetic language of this contract did not detract from its legality for it was duly signed on March 1, 1913 by Mr. A. S. Edwards, secretary-treasurer; R. C. Cross, the contractor; and Mable Edwards, the witness. The district records certify that Mr. Cross fulfilled his commitments nobly but there was some doubt whether he personally made any money on this particular venture.

Sometimes, as was illustrated in the stories of Grassington, Grahamston and Aneroid, the school boards did not call for tenders but undertook to build their schools by day or volunteer labor. This worked very well in the early days but turned out to be a very poor policy in later years. Departments of Education as early as 1912 began to frown on such procedures. The school was usually not built as cheaply or as well as one constructed by a recognized contractor. There were no opportunities for redress and as a result local squabbles were bound to occur.

The expense of hauling building materials to the school site was the responsibility of the local school board and since long distances were usually involved, this outlay added considerably to the cost of erecting the school. In some districts the community spirit was high and the entire task was accomplished by a neighborhood bee at no cost to the school board. In other localities it was simply a business proposition and every farmer in the district was given an equal opportunity to do some hauling.

The Wildflower S.D. kept a careful tabulation of the various loads hauled by each district resident during June 1912 from the end of steel,

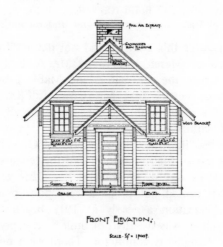

Working drawings for a one-room district school of design "A". These plans
were first issued by the Alberta Department of Education in 1911.

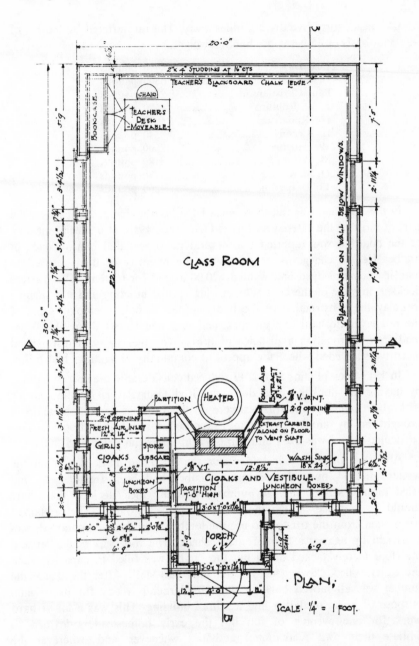

CLASS ROOM

PLAN.

SCALE. ¼" = 1 FOOT.

THE GOVERNMENT OF THE PROVINCE OF ALBERTA.
DEPARTMENT OF EDUCATION.
ONE ROOM DISTRICT SCHOOL – DESIGN A.

DEPARTMENT OF PUBLIC WORK
ARCHITECTURAL BRANCH.
RICHARD P. BLAKEY. A.A.A.
PROVL ARCHITECT.

Alsask, Sask., forty-five driving miles away. The rate offered by the board
was on a basis of 45 cents per hundredweight.

                    Jack Dick .... 4440 pounds
                    D. Garbutt .... 3360 pounds
                    Paul Christianson .... 2720 pounds
                    L. W. Robbins .... 4520 pounds
                    Ira Robertson .... 4030 pounds
                    L. Blegen .... 3340 pounds
                    W. Hughes .... 2900 pounds
                    M. Wilson .... 2180 pounds
                    H. McKee .... 4750 pounds
                    Eli Desjardine .... 4260 pounds

In the Spondon District there must have been a change of heart on the
part of most of the ratepayers for on October 3, 1918, at a special meeting
of the board it was reported that several ratepayers had hauled loads of
lumber free of charge as promised but the majority of them refused to
haul it free as pledged and wanted $20.00 a load for hauling. The trustees
decided, in view of the contractor having started building and not wishing
to delay the construction of the badly-needed school, to employ some of
the ratepayers to haul lumber, rock, and sand and to pay them $14.00 per
load from Coronation a distance of thirty-five miles away. The financial
incentive succeeded where the appeal to community obligations had failed.

In 1913 Social Plains S.D. 2813 reduced considerably the cost of hauling
by having the lumber rafted down the Red Deer River. As the journey
took about ten days the trustees were on the verge of nervous breakdown
brought on by anxiety as to the supposed loss of the supplies. This
particular school was built and furnished at a bargain price of $1200.00.

An interesting story is told about the Highland Park School in the
winter of 1911 once the necessary lumber had been freighted in and
piled on the school site. A number of young men decided that there
should be a dance though there was no place to dance. They obtained
permission from the trustees to use the lumber to build a temporary dance-
hall right up against a homesteader's shack. The roof was made flat and
the floor merely tacked down but the "hall" was filled to capacity when
the caller yelled, "Swing yer Pa and then yer Ma!" After the dance the
lumber was all moved back to the schoolgrounds ready for its original
purpose of being modelled into a school building. This was a lot of hard
work for one evening of fun but the early homesteaders learned to
initiate their own recreational activities whenever and wherever the
opportunity presented itself.

An unusual departure from the normal method of building schools
was exemplified by the Poplar Plain S.D. in 1915. This particular schoolhouse was constructed in a lumberyard and shipped in sections to Sibbald,

Alta., the nearest railroad station. It was reassembled on the selected site in the district to become one of Western Canada's first prefabricated schools.

Contractors experienced many difficulties as they went about their tasks of building schools in the new West. Technical ability was far from what it is today, labor saving devices were few in number, the districts were usually in an isolated part of the country and transportation and communication were very poor.

Max Geldreich, who contracted to build a school in the Fertile Plains District near Foremost, Alta., back in 1910 reminisced about this job fifty-three years later in this manner:

> "The homesteaders were a good class of people. We stored all our building materials and tools in a tent, no lock or a key, and yet not a thing was ever touched. Tom Conquergood helped us shingle the roof. It was the coldest day of the year and we had to heat the nails for the nailing machine. We kept the hot nails in our apron pockets and put our hands in from time to time to warm them."

This contractor also built the Lancaster school in the same general area of Alberta one year later. When he received word to start work on this school in October 1911, he recalls, the weather showed signs of the approaching winter. Claud and Art Page and Fred Nelson who assisted him in building the school decided to erect the barn first. It was here they warmed themselves and ate their lunches while working on the schoolhouse. It was so cold just before Christmas that they had to add seven or eight bags of salt to the cement mixture to provide some assurance against it freezing. The cement was mixed in a trough with a hoe and packed by pails to the forms for the foundation. No ready-mix was available in those days. If a full basement had to be dug it was done by hand using a pick and shovel, while if a speedier job was dictated a scraper and a team of horses were employed.

The majority of the schoolhouses built on the prairies and in the parklands were of frame construction while those in the forested areas were hewn from logs found in the immediate vicinity. The buildings had an average size of twenty feet by thirty feet, a gable roof, a nine-foot wall and an eleven-foot ceiling. The flooring throughout was of two layers with a sub-floor of spruce shiplap nailed diagonally on the joists and a finished floor of one by two and one-half inch edge-grain fir laid over this with a layer of two-ply paper in between. The sidings and roof were also of double thickness for the whole of the studding on the outside was first covered with closely laid spruce shiplap, then two-ply paper and finally for the walls six-inch cedar siding laid four and one-half inch to the weather and cedar shingles for the roof. The entrance at the front was flanked by two windows and prefaced by a four-by-eight-foot stoop. Most

—Mrs. C. A. Bishop

The Farming Valley School near Excel, Alta. under construction in 1911 (left)
and the same school as it looked in 1966 (right).

early school buildings had three windows on each side while those of a
later design accommodated all the windows on one side. Many a youngster
in his imagination pictured the school as a huge four-eyed monster
prowling around the countryside and gulping up little boys and girls.

The influence of church architecture was evident in a number of rural
school buildings for some were surmounted by a belfry that usually, but
not always, contained a bell. The minaret could also double as a cupola
and thus become a vital part of the ventilating system of the school. In
the main these turrets were merely put there for show or to add dignity
to the general appearance of the structure. Old country tradition dictated
that some type of superstructure should grace every public building.

On the inside of the schoolhouse the contractor was directed to lath and
plaster all internal partitions, the inner facings of external walls and the
areas behind the blackboards. The two-coat plastering job had to be half-
an-inch thick on top of laths spaced a quarter-of-an-inch from each other.
The surface was to be well trowelled and polished to an even texture so as
to free it from blisters, cracks or any other defects. This particular work-
specification for plastering is an example of just how detailed the
instructions to the contractor were. The Department of Education was
determined to have only good schoolhouses built.

In some schools only the upper part of each wall was plastered while
the wainscot to the height of three to four feet was finished with four-inch
V-joint fir boards or plain burlap. Then there were the schools whose inner
walls were not plastered at all but left unfinished or covered with narrow
V-joint boards.

The cloakroom in most one-room schools extended right across the
front with a cluster of shelves at both ends for the water pail, the wash
basin and the children's lunch buckets. The part of the vestibule on one

—Isabell Sinclair

A Three-Stage Development of the East Coulee Rural School, Drumheller, Alta. Stage I—A tarpaper shack in a farmer's yard. Chrissie, the teacher, put in the second little window by herself. *Stage II*—A granary on skids. Later this building was used as a teacherage but the skids were never removed. *Stage III*—A well-constructed schoolhouse. The sticks nailed across the casements were to prevent the horses from pushing in the windows. This precaution was necessary as the school was located in a pasture in the Wintering Hills District of Alberta.

side of the front door was the girls' cloakroom while the other section was assigned to the boys. The partition between the cloakroom and the schoolroom proper stopped a few feet from the ceiling in order to permit the circulation of heat and fresh air between the two rooms. In theory this should have worked well but in actual practice it became so cold in winter that the water, the lunches, the clothing and the rubbers had to be brought into the classroom and placed beside the stove to escape the frost.

The architect who positioned this partition must have had a sense of humor. It was placed in such a way as to provide a tantalizing access to the opening in the ceiling that led to the attic. Once it was scaled it was a matter of adventure to crawl along the narrow top to the trapdoor, push it open and then with a daring lunge scramble into the dark, forbidding and mysterious upper room. The spirit of adventure was magnified many times if everyone but the teacher and a few habitual informers knew what feats of climbing and prowling were being performed in the Little White

A VARIETY OF RURAL SCHOOLS OF FRAME CONSTRUCTION

—Mrs. P. Rudick

Hunter's Hill School, Clair, Sask.   Kirkwall School, Oyen, Alta.

Rearville School, Cereal, Alta.   Fordville School, Midnapore, Alta.

—Wesley Dunn

Cappon School, Buffalo, Alta.   Forest S.D. No. 202, Carman, Man.

MORE FRAME SCHOOLS WITH DIFFERENCES IN DESIGN

Burns School, Spondon, Alta.

—Alvin McGill

Huntly School No. 477, Neelin, Man.

Solon School, Hanna, Alta.

Garden Plain School, Garden Plain, Alta.

—Mrs. J. P. Mitchell

Clover Bar S.D. 212, Bremner, Alta.

—Mrs. J. P. Mitchell

Clearwater S.D. 740, Leduc, Alta.

ANOTHER GROUP OF INTERESTING ONE-ROOM SCHOOLS

Egremont School, Egremont, Alta.

Peyton School, Chinook, Alta.

Dundee School, Hanna, Alta.

Merid School, Merid, Sask.

Netherby School, Hanna, Alta.

—Gina Lee

Green Valley School, Wampum, Man.

SOME EXAMPLES OF EARLY SCHOOL ARCHITECTURE

Sanford S.D. 86,
Sanford, Man.,
1912.

—Mrs. George
Ogston

—Mrs. Dorothy W.
Willner

Kipp S.D. 1589,
Davidson, Sask.,
1908.

Tongue Creek
S.D. 128,
High River, Alta.,
1891.

—Mrs. J. E. Blair

Schoolhouse in the teacher's absence. More than one teacher has had to deal with the mysterious paradox of a student "being absent from school" but "being present in the school". Some youngsters were able to negotiate the intricate climb upward but became too frightened to come down. It required emergency measures such as borrowing a ladder from the nearest neighbors to bring the nervous one back to floor level. Needless to say the school board had the trapdoor nailed shut after that to forestall any other such misadventures.

The pioneers who built some of the early rural schools considered the cloakroom as an educational "frill", a luxury, and an unnecessary expense. They excluded them altogether. Such omissions were to create problems later on as experience eventually proved that these anterooms were a necessity. They were not only excellent buffers against the cold every time the outside door was opened but relieved the classroom of many of its less appropriate functions. In the Sunny Crest S.D. 2633 (Lacombe, Alta.) the ratepayers soon realized how valuable a cloakroom could be so they were most anxious to add one to their schoolhouse. The school board although sympathetic to the idea were in no financial position to undertake such a building program. They tabled the proposal. The women of the district were not so easily thwarted. They got together and put on a chicken supper in the Spruceville Community Hall some four miles away. Their project proved to be a financial success so in due course the boys and girls of Sunny Crest School were able to boast of a brand-new cloakroom. The school board members merely smiled, nodded knowingly but said nothing. They knew long before this not to underestimate the power of women.

Log schoolhouses were durable, inexpensive to erect but not as tractable as frame buildings. In the Moose Hill S.D. (Thorhild, Alta.) the logs were chinked with a cement mixture that had the quality of chalk. It was prized by the students for marking out their hopscotch courts and for writing on the logs that had been trimmed flat on the weather side. The inside of the building was lined with plasterboard. The Shining Bank S.D. 4034 (Edson, Alta.) on the other hand was chinked with moss and had no inside finishing. Most of the moss had dried and fallen out so the wind blew between the logs so strongly that it knocked the pictures off the wall. On cold days Kathleen, the schoolmistress, did most of her teaching with the pupils seated around the stove. At times she held the youngest pupil on her knee so the child's feet wouldn't freeze.

The responsibility of the school board did not cease with the awarding of the building contract to a firm or individual. Far from it! The board had the oversight of the entire work program as it progressed from the laying of the foundation to the application of the final coat of paint. Should any variation or discrepancy occur in either drawings, specification

—Jack Hunt

Priddis log schoolhouse, Priddis, Alta., which was built in 1892.

or on the building the contractor was required to refer the matter to the school trustees before proceeding. All the material delivered on the site became the property of the trustees, although the contractor was responsible for its actual care. The trustees or their authorized representative had the right at all times to inspect the works or the workmanship. No completed job could be covered up until it had been inspected and approved.

The board members appeared to be conscientious in their duty of inspecting the schoolhouse during its construction. Unfortunately their combined lack of technical knowledge and any experience pertaining to the overseeing of construction often made these occasional visits a mere mockery. Now and then it was a request by the contractor for a payment on account that sent the board members scurrying on an inspection tour. The minute books recorded these visits in very general terms describing them more as social calls than inspections:

"The trustees inspected the building and found it in a very satisfactory condition. As good progress was shown and a good job was being done the trustees decided that the contractor be paid $300 on account.

"As the school building was finished the trustees visited it, examined it and expressed themselves satisfied with it. A motion to pay the contractor the balance due on his contract was passed unanimously."

At times some appreciation for the efforts of the contractor was voiced.

"The Board of Trustees passed a vote of thanks to the contractor for the manner in which he used the trustees and the good workmanship he effected."

Rarely did the board find things not to their satisfaction but such incidents did occur. The Dundee school board is one example. On October 14, 1928, the first rumblings of discontent were recorded:

"The purpose of the meeting was to inspect the progress of the building of the schoolhouse. Each item in the specifications was read by the secretary and the trustees found a number of things with which the contractor had not complied. It was decided to call the contractor's attention to these things. The completion of the building had been very slow and it was decided to try and get the contractor to speed things up as soon as possible."

By June 17, 1929, the Dundee school board was contemplating some form of legal action against the contractor.

"It was moved and seconded that the chairman and secretary consult a lawyer in regard to taking proceedings to get the contractor to finish the school."

The legal strategy failed to bring any definite results as may be judged by the minutes of the July 22, 1929, meeting.

"The meeting was called in order to inspect the supposed completion of the school as the time limit of 10 days given by the trustees had expired. The list of things found not to be satisfactory to the board were:
(1) The flagpole was not put up in accordance with the specification.
(2) There was no transom hook or pole supplied.
(3) The west windows needed fixing.
(4) More coat hangers were not furnished.
(5) The toilets were not completed.

The Board took things into their own hands at this meeting and passed the following motion:

"That the chairman and the secretary be appointed to try and get someone to finish the list of items named."

By September 9, 1929, the work must have been completed for this was recorded in the minute book:

"That the balance of the contract price, $212.00, together with the deposit of $110.60 be paid the contractor for building the school, deducting therefrom the cost to us of completing the items neglected by the contractor."

The dispute between the contractor and the trustees reached an amiable settlement for eventually each party provided the other with a clearance as to fulfilling the original terms of the contract.

Incidental to the building of the school many events transpired in the district that at times bordered on the tragic and at other times were sources of humor.

The plasterboard that was used to line the inside of the new log schoolhouse in the Moose Hill S.D. 2727 (Thorhild, Alta.) was indirectly responsible for a near tragedy in 1913.

The area of which the Moose Hill district formed a part was not served by a railroad at that time. Consequently the plasterboard was shipped by rail to Westlock and had to be transported the remaining twenty-five miles by team and wagon. The road was crossed by one swamp, a range of sandy hills, several small creeks which had to be forded and at least two lakes. So of necessity this rural thoroughfare meandered a good deal keeping to the high ground as much as possible.

Alonzo Jennison, the youngest son of one of the first pioneer families of the district and a very quiet young man, was assigned the task of going to Westlock to get the plasterboard. Lon, as he was affectionately known in the community, was provided with a spirited team to accomplish his mission. The journey was effected with ease until the last ten miles of the return trip. Lon had received the heavy boarding in good shape and had chained it securely to the wagon gear. He was sitting on top of the load with his legs dangling, reins loosely held, when something startled the horses and they broke into a run. The wagon bounced and jostled over the rutted trail. The load shifted and trapped one of Lon's legs between the boards and the bunkpeg, crushing the bone. It stayed ensnared for a few moments until another good jolt pitched the cargo in the opposite direction and freed him. Lon fell off into the bush unconscious.

The next three days were not clear in his mind. Only in retracing his son's journey could the father and neighbors piece the story together.

It was three days after the accident and some six miles closer home when Opal Ferris, a farmer's wife, heard a weak call for help coming from the trail where it passed their farmstead. They rushed out to find Alonzo Jennison, his leg crudely splinted, crawling along the trail. He had made campfires for the two nights he had spent on the road. The badly injured youth had lain unconscious much of the time and when he was able, dragged himself slowly towards home or some place that was inhabited.

Lon was quickly picked up and taken to his home and the next day moved to a hospital in Edmonton for treatment.

The horses were found safe, free of the wagon, but caught in a clump of spruce trees. They were still firmly hitched together and had devoured all that was edible within their reach. The wagonload of plasterboard was not badly damaged and in due course was used to complete the Moose Hill School.

Alonzo Jennison recovered to the extent that only a slight limp betrayed his accident. He never spoke of it. But others were glad to tell of his courage that was a part of building the Moose Hill School back in 1913.

For the settlers of the Clover Hill S.D. 2584 (Irvine, Alta.) the building of a new school in 1912 came as a complete surprise. In fact most people wondered what it was until they were informed that it was their new school. They could scarcely believe their eyes or ears. The explanation that was noised about was that the idea of a school was the brain-child of a few settlers and was carried out as secretly as possible so that the chosen few were able to share in the work at exorbitant wages. No tenders were let and the wages were very high for those days.

Sometimes it was the trustees of a school district rather than the ratepayers who received the "surprise". The first school board members of the Custer S.D. (Czar, Alta.) requested the Department of Education to send them a number of schoolhouse plans. When they received them they couldn't read the blueprints and after a short meeting to decide what they should do they made up their own drawings.

The good people of Prospy S.D. (Foremost, Alta.) were as frustrated as they could be early in December, 1911. The contractor, Lon Sewell, had promised them that their schoolhouse would be completed in time for Christmas. They took him at his word and had gone to the trouble of preparing their first Christmas concert. But here it was December and the schoolhouse was not finished. What was worse, there was not the slightest chance of having it completed in time for the concert. They were so determined they had their concert anyway. The running gear of a lumber wagon was pulled up to the unfinished building and used as a stage.

The Old Parkside S.D. 1138 (Parkside, Sask.) was built of sturdy tamarac logs that were plentiful in the district at that time. It was frame on the inside and painted a bright blue. There were six windows on each side and two at the back on either side of the door. If the pupils were subject to eyestrain from squinting through all this brilliance no one seemed to be aware of it. For some reason or other the ceiling had not been finished. Possibly they ran out of lumber while building the school and since it had to be hauled by wagon from Prince Albert, fifty miles away, the ceiling remained an eyesore with ugly gaps between the boards. A large ferocious type of woodbug used to tumble through these cracks and drop down the necks of the unsuspecting children below. No one was ever quite fast enough to shake them out of his clothes before being bitten so yelps and screams were taken for granted in Old Parkside.

Not many rural schools could be as unique as the Fossemour S.D. near Swift Current, Sask. It was built in 1917 with an eye to being a community centre as well as a school. The wall between the cloakroom and the classroom was erected in such a manner that it could be easily removed for community dances or any other large public gatherings.

Bells and schools have been very closely associated for as far back as people can remember. So it was not surprising to find early rural communities placing the "bell in the belfry" high on the list of essential school construction.

The Harlington S.D. 1164 (Swan River, Man.) purchased a twenty-eight-inch bell with mountings from the American Bell and Foundry Company at Northville, Michigan, for a price of twenty-five dollars in 1904. The ratepayers put on a concert in the newly-built school to pay for it. As the

The Greenock School near Pinkerton, Ontario, was constructed of brick.
Note the school bell.

bell and mounting together weighed 420 pounds the Harlington school
board attempted, with success, to persuade the company to pay half the
freight bill. The names of members of the first school board, A. E. Smith,
Jas. Jackson, and A. J. Cotton, were inscribed on the bell. The original
bell cracked before the five-year guarantee expired so the company was
forced to replace it. For over sixty years the Harlington School bell has
tolled to call the children to school, the people to church, and the mourners
to the funeral service.

Few teachers have had the experience of teaching in a moving schoolhouse but the series of unique circumstances that developed in the Pelly
S.D. (Pelly, Sask.) forced Hugh Wylie to contend with such a problem. It
all started in 1909 with the arrival of steel on the Thunder Hill branch of
the Canadian Northern Railway. The population of Pelly took such a
sudden jump that the school from the Midhurst S.D., two miles south,
had to be moved into the village to provide education facilities for the
populace. By 1912 even this building was inadequate so during the year
construction on a new two-room brick school was started. In the meantime
classes continued in the old schoolhouse although the building had been
sold to the Anglican Church. The agreement between the school board and
the church vestry stipulated that the old structure was to be moved over

to the church property before a certain date. A contract was a contract in 1912 so in March the task of moving the school began—with the students and teacher inside. The workmen raised it up, placed skids under it and set up a huge windlass nearby preparatory to the actual moving. In the meantime it was pound, pound, pound whether the school was in session or not. Soon all was in readiness for the big moment—a horse hitched to a sweep walked about the mechanical device, the windlass commenced to turn slowly, the ropes began to tighten and after a few uncertain shudders the building started to inch forward. It was a slow and tedious job for the movers but that was the standard method of hauling a building from one location to another in the early days. The contractor was completely indifferent whether lessons were being held inside the school or not for he went on merrily with his job of moving the building. One day Mr. Wylie's expectations were realized—the old stovepipes were jarred loose and came tumbling down in a cloud of soot and dust. No one was hurt and the older pupils acted admirably during the crisis.

The school didn't have to be moved any great distance—just across the road and then swung around to face east rather than south. Even after the building was in place the students and teacher still had to put up with many inconveniences. The blackboards, for instance, were removed from the walls and taken over to the new school. What did Mr. Wylie do to make up for the loss? He put up sheets of tar paper and used them in the manner of flipcharts. The results were so satisfactory that the teacher was ready to dispense with blackboards altogether. However by mid-April when everything was in readiness in the brick school, Mr. Wylie was glad to return to the use of traditional blackboards in a stationary and solid school.

The construction of the girls' and boys' conveniences, also known as: toilets, outhouses, privies, biffies, parliament buildings, commodes, back-houses, closets, water-closets, two-holers and outdoor plumbing, was the contractor's responsibility as well. The Department of Education showed as much concern over the erection of these twin-buildings as they did with the schoolhouse proper. The plans and specifications for these outbuildings were an integral part of the school design.

It was doubtful whether any contractor or school board considered the official blueprints for the toilets very seriously. In actual practice the local design was simpler and produced a more serviceable building. The Department specifications recommended flapdoors for access at the rear for cleaning purposes as well as the installation of galvanized iron soil pails under the seats. The school board soon dispensed with the flapdoors as they provided a handy clandestine method for studying the human anatomy of unsuspecting specimens. In winter the cold icy blasts of wind and snow had an uncanny knack of filtering under the flapdoors causing

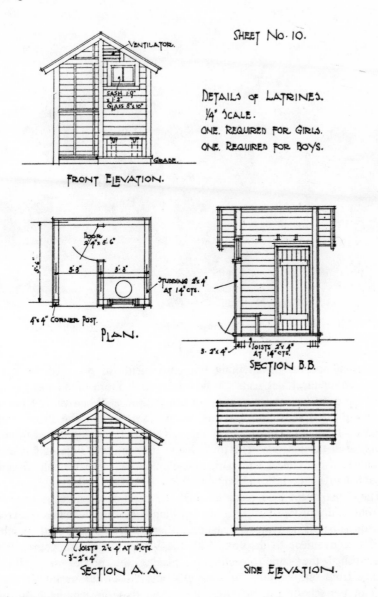

SHEET No. 10.

DETAILS of LATRINES.
¼" SCALE.
ONE. REQUIRED FOR GIRLS.
ONE. REQUIRED FOR BOYS.

VENTILATOR.

SASH 1'-9"
x 1'-2"
GLASS 8"x10"

GRADE.

FRONT ELEVATION.

DOOR
2'4" x 5'-6"

5'-6"

5'-3"   3'-3"

STUDDING 2"x 4"
AT 14" CTS.

4"x 4" CORNER POST.

PLAN.

JOISTS 2"x 4"
AT 14" CTS.

3- 2"x 4"

SECTION B.B.

JOISTS 2"x 4" AT 16" CTS.

3- 2"x 4"

SECTION A.A.

SIDE ELEVATION.

THE GOVERNMENT of THE PROVINCE of ALBERTA.
DEPARTMENT of EDUCATION.
ONE ROOM DISTRICT SCHOOL. DESIGN A.

DEPARTMENT of PUBLIC WORKS
ARCHITECTURAL BRANCH.
RICHARD P. BLAKEY. A.A.A
PROV. ARCHITECT.

The official design for a school privy.

Outdoor plumbing for the Empress View S.D., New Brigden, Alta.

the conveniences to be anything but convenient. In place of the catch-buckets under the toilet seats the board found it more functional to dig a trench beneath the service portion of the outhouse. When the pit became nearly full another excavation was made close by and the privy simply moved over it while the dirt from the newly-dug latrine was used to cover the refuse in the old one. The progression from hole to hole maintained a semblance of cleanliness and sanitation eliminating the extremely disagreeable and unhygienic task of emptying the overflowing pails.

The Department also recommended the erection of a fence to screen the front of the privies but since the resulting enclosures acted as snowtraps or made supervision from a distance rather difficult, the board members found it convenient to dispense with the visual barrier altogether. They accomplished the same objective by placing the privies at a discreet distance from one another. In some districts "discreet" meant the entire width of the schoolyard, in others it implied that the length of the barn should separate them.

The privy was well named for it was an ingenious device for preserving human privacy. The carpenter, by simply shifting the door to one side, was able to use the remainder of the front wall as a blind for the service corner. This, combined with the fact that the door swung inward, screened any "sitting member" from public gaze whether the entrance was open or not. The door usually sagged just enough to scrape the floor so the opening

The two one-holers at Wildflower S.D., Sedalia, Alta.

could be readily adjusted to provide the maximum amount of fresh air, light, and the desired range of view with the minimum chance of self-exposure. Who could ask for more?

This hindrance to the free movement of the door had an added advantage for it stymied the wind from blowing it open when the visitor was otherwise preoccupied. The life expectancy of a latch or inside catch on the door of a school outhouse was extremely short for a "breaking in" or a "breaking out" was always occurring as the students participated in their various shenanigans. The privy was the recognized place of refuge for anyone attempting to escape from pursuing "policemen" or "outlaws". Then if a student had anything of a confidential nature to impart to his friends the "parliament building" was the ideal place in which to do it.

During the summer holidays the vagaries of the weather, the undermining propensities of burrowing animals or the perversity of man would lay prone the silent sentinels of the schoolyard. Prostrate backhouses appeared to be a positive sign that the school was no longer in session. Hence a day or two before school opened in the fall a work-party reactivated the fallen conveniences. A number of school boards became so fed up with the regularity with which these outhouses were overturned that they had them securely anchored with wire braces and stakes. Not even the worst blizzard or dust storm could topple them after that.

Today the rural school outhouse is no more. But it serves to remind the oldtimers of the comfort and even luxury which present-day students

In the Hudson Heights S.D. 3716, (Oyen, Alta.), "discreet" meant that the width of a barn should separate the boys' and girls' "parliament buildings."

enjoy. It's a far cry from the small dilapidated cubical set out beside the horsebarn to the beautifully appointed restrooms, complete with showers, that one finds in the new schools today.

The size of the hole or holes in a school privy did not always complement the size of a student's backside so an occasional rural teacher has had to effect an embarrassing "rescue".

For instance, take the time in the Bryant S.D. (Bindloss, Alta.) that Violet, an unusually small grade one tot, after having secured permission to leave the room dared to become ambitious and decided to roost in a hole much too large for her slender body. Her body jackknifed in the orifice and she was unable to extricate herself. Her stifled cries for help failed to reach the schoolroom. It wasn't until the conscientious teacher missed his entire grade one class and went out into the schoolyard to investigate that he heard her sobs. As he neared the outhouse the whimpering ceased suddenly and he was implored by a seemingly unhurt yet dejected inmate to go back and get her sister. Believing in the old adage that discretion was the better part of valor in such a delicate matter the young man hurried back to the school and summoned the sister. In a matter of minutes both girls were back in the classroom without showing any outward signs of having participated in anything approaching a tragedy. When the teacher questioned the elder sister at recess as to what had happened to Violet he received a shy reply of, "Oh— nothing!" accompanied by healthy blushes. He stopped his interrogation there and then. It wasn't until years after while attending university in Edmonton that the mystery was cleared up for him by the "subject" herself, who by that time was married and had a family of her own attending school in the city.

These two "outdoor conveniences" in the Fairdale S.D. 2611, (Sibbald, Alta.),
were screened from the outside and from each other.

In summer the outhouses seemed quite adequate although stench and flies made them unpleasant, but winter brought a different story. Carelessness made the seats a frozen jungle of filthiness. Sometimes the accumulation built up to a height that made sitting on the bench impossible. Most students will never forget the trip they could not forestall in February or March. after the winds had piled the snow to the very throne of the airy outhouse. The task of climbing over snowbanks and then sweeping or shovelling off the seat to receive only a cold reception wasn't very pleasant. Besides the business of undressing and dressing was not a simple matter. The children wore so many clothes in those days that it was like taking part in an arctic expedition to go to the toilet.

The outdoor biffy of the Green Lake S.D. (Hamlin, Alta.) was located in a hollow of the schoolyard and every spring a lake formed about it. There was only one girl in the school who owned a pair of high rubber boots and she used to transport all the other females piggyback to and from the island outhouse. She accompanied the children even during class time if the need arose. The outhouse could have been moved to higher ground without too much difficulty. It never was. It continued to sit in the middle of the miniature lake for years.

A couple of senior girls in the Otterburn S.D. (Lanigan, Sask.) played a hoax on two little girls. With straight faces they told them that there were snakes in the toilet. Any time that nature called after that the two lassies disappeared behind the barn. Before long a couple of informers told the parents about the strange actions of the pair. A snake bite would have been mild compared to what they received.

Here is a good description of the outdoor plumbing facilities of the Eagle S.D. (Airdrie, Alta.).

"The school barn was flanked on each side, but in the northernmost corners by the outhouses, one for the girls and the other for the boys. Some schools of the era built a sort of L-shaped screen of boards in front of these little buildings to ensure a little privacy but ours stood open to the public and the four winds. They were the "two-holer" variety. The only toilet tissue we ever knew were old issues of Eaton's or Simpson's catalogues, outdated newspapers, a handful of grass, a corn cob, or a piece of stick."

Just as the school privy was the subject and source of ribbald humor as people made light of things that were really trying, it became accepted as an integral part of the history of the Little White Schoolhouse.

Since schools were heated by burning coal, or wood, it was necessary to store these fuels. There was no way of predicting the severity or the length of a particular winter so in the fall the trustees contracted for what they estimated would be enough coal and wood to serve the school for most of the winter. In actual practice the average rural school used nine to fifteen tons of coal and a half a cord of kindling wood per school year. Coal deteriorated when exposed to weather so the trustees were forced to protect their purchase with weather-proof storage.

The schools that boasted a basement or cellar were the most fortunate of all. It required very little investment or skill to construct a bin in one corner. The position of the storage-corner below ground level also facilitated the unloading of the coal from the wagon box or the sleigh. A chute carried the coal from the outside, through the basement window, and then into the coalbin beneath.

If the school had no basement it was necessary to improvise a storage place for fuel. In the Superba S.D. (Oyen, Alta.) an empty piano box was converted into an ideal coalbin. But in most instances a three-by-five foot opening was cut in the floor in the cloakroom and a good-sized pit dug underneath. Then the sides were boarded, a set of steps erected and a trapdoor built. This miniature basement proved to be a ready and convenient place to store the coal and kindling. If the sides of this coalhole were not shored they caved in and the loose dirt mixed with the coal to produce an inferior fuel. It also appeared that every time the trapdoor was left open some unwary youngster plummeted down into the pit and reappeared crying, bruised and blackened with coal dust and covered with an assortment of spider-webs, dead flies and bugs. Such frightening experiences were prevented by stationing a guard over the black void every time someone descended into the coal hole to refill the scuttle.

The idea place for storing fuel was in a specially-constructed coalshed convenient to the school. The average coalshed measured eight by ten feet, had a sloping roof, and was built solidly enough to keep out the rain or snow. It not only safeguarded the several tons of coal and the two or three cords of kindling wood but over the years it turned out to be a

A combination coalshed and storage bin in the Coe S.D. 4381 (Alsask, Sask.).
Notice how convenient it is to the school.

suitable place to store all the useless and broken articles that usually accumulated around a rural school. There would be old maps, broken desks, torn books, cracked water crocks, Christmas concert properties, burned-out grates, a few shattered storm windows, some dilapidated pipes, punctured water pails and the inevitable sawhorses. Teachers always have had the habit of retaining anything that would come into their hands on the assumption that no matter how useless the object might appear at the moment it had the possibility of serving some educational purpose in the future. No school ever built has had enough storage space to house what one teacher and her pupils could collect in one year.

The barn was an integral part of the rural school. Sooner or later the school board was confronted with the problem of building a stable to provide shelter for the many horses that conveyed the children to school. If the exigency occurred at the outset of the school's organization the building of the barn was made a part of the original contract but if not, the construction was delayed until a definite need arose. Then at the appropriate time a tender for the necessary barn was advertised, or alternatively as happened in so many community-minded districts, the school board purchased the materials and the people of the district put on a "building bee" and erected the barn.

The early settlers of the Ridgeview S.D. 489 (Blackie, Alta.) sponsored regular socials in order to obtain sufficient funds with which to build a stable. They celebrated their success most fittingly by holding a Thanksgiving supper in the new barn before turning it over to the school ponies.

SCHOOL BARNS

The roughly-built school barn at Bryant S.D. 2533 (Bindloss, Alta.)

A well-built stable at Carlyle S.D. (Oyen, Alta.)

This large barn in the Bonnie Brier S.D. 3023 (Acadia Valley, Alta.) measured eighteen by twenty-four feet.

Small but comfortable barn at Hills S.D. 3224 near Oyen, Alta.

Most school barns, like this one in the Kirkwall S.D. 2463 (Oyen, Alta.) were always in need of repairs.

Not much of a school barn, only a shelter at Fairacres S.D. 2585 (Excel, Alta.)

The size of the barn, its design, quality, and workmanship were purely a matter of local requirements or preferences. In some districts it was a well-constructed building, in others it was a mere makeshift of two or three buildings that had been neglected and fallen into disrepair. The essential feature was to have it weather-proofed sufficiently to keep the horses comfortable in all weather. A number of boards introduced such additional features as sliding doors, stalls, feed alleys, mangers and a hayloft or a corner of the stable reserved for the storage of feed.

School stables had rather dark, foreboding and smelly interiors. They were drafty, unsanitary and either too hot or too cold. The majority were cleaned irregularly and not too well at that. Although everyone used the stable nobody ever considered it his duty to clean a stall or even to close the door if he were the last to leave. Sometimes the manure accumulated in such high mounds that the horses practically stood on their heads in their stalls. Nature provided the flooring in the stall so it was a matter of conjecture as to where it started and ended.

Smaller children found it convenient to mount their horses inside the barn as there were many supports they could use to scramble up on the backs of their mounts. Yet as the school term progressed this became increasingly difficult to do. The floor rose higher and higher with each day's accumulation of manure and straw until a point was reached where there was insufficient room for the child between the horse's back and the rafters. As a result these little people had to improvise other ways of mounting outside the stable.

John Pearse, a pupil in the Namao S.D. (Namao, Alta.), thought he had the perfect solution to this ever-present problem of cleaning the barn. He brought along a supply of blasting caps to do the job for him. The resulting explosion blew the roof off the barn and gouged out a huge hole in the floor but the manure was still there after the dust had settled. This particular scientific method of cleaning a barn was never repeated although the incident itself was considered worthy of recording in any chronicle ever written about the Namao School District.

At the beginning of the year the school barn was the scene of much bickering regarding stall rights and who was to get the better ones. Later on in the term any activity that was considered of a questionable nature was held in the barn. This secretive routine was followed for fear the teacher would put an end to the entire affair if she ever saw or knew what was taking place. This is why the barn was considered a den of iniquity if left unsupervised. It was the rendezvous for the "stag club" if the weather was inclement. While the girls ate at their desks on such days, the boys repaired to the barn where seated on the mangers they ate their sandwiches while Dobbin munched his hay. The ammoniacal odor that consistently pervaded these barns was of no consequence to a group of

—Wes Plunkett

A school building program never ceases. The Floral S.D. (Saskatoon, Sask.) built its first school in 1902 and constructed a modern building in 1947. This unique picture shows the "old" and the "new" side by side, just before the one was vacated and the other occupied.

hungry farm boys whose appetites were keen after the morning chores and the school games.

Many rural boys learned the routine of visiting the barn rather than the outhouse in times of necessity. The practice was certainly not very hygienic but considering the state of most outdoor school privies during the winter, especially after a spell of blowing snow, one could hardly blame them for their choice. At least the heat generated by the horses made the stable a bit more comfortable than the outhouse. This rural custom of using the barn as a second privy for the males dictated that such places be out-of-bounds to all females. This was not always possible in a rural school as many girls drove or rode horses to school and had to enter the barn on many occasions during the day to take care of their animals. The boys soon learned to use a little discretion under such circumstances. Any time a girl was seen approaching the barn the boys inside were warned by an infallible system of signals from those on the outside.

The majority of fights that started on the school grounds were settled in the safe confines of the barn. Any time an excited youngster yelled, "Fight! Fight!" everyone knew where the match would be. The spy system instituted by the students was so efficient that it was next to impossible for a teacher to approach the barn without the lookouts sounding the alarm if something of a clandestine nature was taking place inside. A number of rural teachers, like Dorothy who taught in the

A radical departure from the standard type of schoolhouse seen at the Red Rows School 3038 (Balcarres, Saskatchewan) which resembled a family residence much more than it did a school building.

Warmley S.D. (Moose Mountain, Sask.) in 1927, solved the problem by making the barn out-of-bounds to the children except for a five-minute period at noon for feeding the horses and ten minutes after school for harnessing.

The final touch to the building program came when the school, the outhouses, and the coalshed, were made resplendent in coats of vivid white paint, with green or black trim. The barn if painted at all was finished in a dull red. Such well-finished school buildings stood out in contrast to the unpainted houses of the settlers. They could be distinguished miles away and appeared to gleam as bright beacons of hope in a dark world of ignorance. The clean, pungent odor of fresh paint and varnish of the new schoolhouse that greeted the children, parents or board members on opening morning still remains to this day in the memory of many a person of the one-room school era.

Just about this time everyone heaved a sigh of relief and said, "We have finished!" Yet this never proved to be the case. Two decades later the school board was hard at work modernizing its old institution or replacing it entirely with a new one. Men may come and men may go but school building programs go on forever.

The Denehurst S.D. 1070 (Brock, Sask.) completed their school in 1913 but in 1925 the building was raised and a full basement constructed under it. Then, after dividing it into several service areas, they proceeded to install a hot-air furnace and two chemical toilets. To complete the renovation they shifted all the windows to one side of the building, put in electric lights and arranged for telephone service. Three years later a small cottage was erected on the schoolgrounds as a dwelling place for the teacher. This ended the progressive building program for in 1944 the Denehurst School was closed for good.

The Floral S.D. (Saskatoon, Sask.) erected their school in 1902 but instead of making any major alterations down through the years they waited until 1947 and then erected a brand-new schoolhouse.

No. 1 Woodyatt S.D. thought they had discovered the perfect solution to the recurring problem of repairs to their school. They covered the entire building with grey metal sheets similar to those once used on grain elevators. The idea didn't work too well. Rain set up such a terrible din against them that any teaching or studying was well-nigh impossible during a shower. The roof leaked in eight places and Beatrice Fines, the teacher, had eight different-sized cans to catch the drops that resounded in different tones — plink, plonk, plunk — as the rain dripped in. The children used to try to arrange the pails in such a way as to play the musical scales or the opening notes of a popular song.

5

THE POT-BELLIED STOVE

The heat for the Little White Schoolhouse was dispensed by a large rotund contraption often referred to as the "station" type or "pot-bellied" stove. One such class of heater was manufactured by the Waterman and Waterbury Company. Anyone who remembers and speaks about the past refers to the Waterman and Waterbury as one of the best heaters that appeared on the market in the early days. The history of the one-room school and that of the Waterman and Waterbury furnace were so intimately bound together that one seldom heard mention of one without the other. They appeared to be inseparable partners of the early era of rural education.

The installation of the furnace followed a set pattern. It was placed in one corner of the schoolroom and then connected to a brick chimney at the opposite end by a string of overhead stovepipes. The longer the system of pipes the more heat radiated from their surface and this assisted in warming the strata of air near the ceiling. The circulation of air in the room was promoted by installing a five-foot high metal jacket, raised six inches off the floor and enveloping all but the front of the stove. A couple of metal troughs were fastened to the upper brackets of the jacket and if kept filled with water or snow a certain degree of humidification of air took place. Some teachers found these buckets to be a convenient way of heating water for washing purposes. For the most part however these waterpans were permitted to run dry and become collectors of dust and garbage rather than humidifiers. To complete the layout a protective sheet of No. 24 gauge galvanized iron was placed on the floor under the heater just about a foot larger than the base of the stove.

There were any number of modifications to this standard method of heating the one-room school. Some school boards installed two small heaters, one at either end of the classroom, assuming that a more even distribution of heat took place. Others believed that they could accomplish the same results by placing the large pot-bellied stove in the centre of the room. In later years a number of schools placed the furnace in the basement and channelled the heat into the classroom through large

The Waterbury stove holding the spotlight in the Bryant School.

conduits and hot-air registers. This arrangement not only provided more floorspace in the school but confined all the untidiness associated with fire-making to the cellar. The furnace was regulated from above by a set of pull-chains attached to the drafts on the stove. It took a little while for the students and teacher to become accustomed to the periodic outbursts of clattering and banging as the large, resonant and tinny furnace-pipes expanded or contracted with the accompanying heating or cooling.

Teachers were quick to make use of the conveniences offered by these hot-air furnaces. One lady in the Cobblestone S.D. (Youngstown, Alta.) found that the warm-air register was an excellent place to put her bread to rise. She was in the habit of taking the dough over to her teacherage at recess and kneading it while watching the children at play through the window. Many teachers used to carry their newly-washed clothes over to the school and spread them over the hot-air outlets to dry.

The ventilation system was relatively simple and depended upon heat from the stove to circulate the air. Warm gases rise so the air above the stove flowed towards the ceiling while the cold air descended and moved along the floor back to the stove. It did not require any complicated mechanical equipment to control these convection currents. A duct installed under the floor connected the air intake on the outside of the

—Edith Mitchell

A typical wood stove doing yeoman service in the Hammond Rural School near Ottawa, Ontario.

building to the heater; if this duct remained closed it promoted recirculation of the air in the school without introducing any cold air from outdoors.

Practically every school board that installed a fresh-air vent as an integral part of their school's heating system found it very unsatisfactory. Their opinion about it was similar to the following view expressed by the Westmoor S.D. 2010 (Punnichy, Sask.):

> "The old stove was taken out in favor of a Waterman-Waterbury with a jacket and a fresh air vent. The vent was just an insult. It turned out to be a cold-air intake, as though we needed more cold air. Finally the vent was closed entirely and we secured our fresh air from under the poorly fitted doors and the sides of the rattling windows."

It didn't take the student very long to discover that the fresh-air intake at the back of the school made an ideal listening post. When someone was kept in after school the other students listened intently to the ensuing dramatic dialogue. If the teacher was forced to administer the strap the auditors could count the number of strokes the victim received on each hand or on his backside. Unfortunately, unless the listeners were extremely quiet the teacher heard them and they too were in trouble.

The outside register was a popular rendezvous when the teacher entertained such visitors as the inspector, trustee, irate parents or even her sweetheart. No present-day radio or television program, outside of Candid Camera, could ever hope to rival in interest and suspense these true-to-life dramas and comedies that unfolded inside the school. The ventilation-shaft communication system was not as one-sided as the children reported it to be. The teachers could also listen to what was going on in the schoolyard as well as hear the various opinions expressed by the students. More than one rural teacher learned only too late about the existence of these spying devices. It is also safe to assume that some never did.

Whether for good or for evil a supply of matches had to be kept in the school to start the fires in the stove. Some settlers found out how embarrassing and inconvenient it could be to travel several miles in below-zero temperatures to get to the school and then discover that they had no matches with which to start the fire. The famous last words that wives always directed to their husbands in those pioneering days were, "Don't forget to take some matches!" The student-janitor did not ordinarily carry matches on his person so a supply was kept in the school. Some precautions had to be observed in storing these wooden matches. It was common practice to place them in a covered metal container in order to prevent any gnawing animals from igniting the matches. Fire insurance companies were adamant in this matter of storing matches in tin receptacles for they realized better than anyone else that a large number of rural schools were lost in fires started by mice chewing on matches.

In order to prevent little children from playing with matches or to discourage any would-be smokers, the box of matches was placed in a metal container and hidden in one of the drawers of the teacher's desk or in a locked cupboard. In such a place the matches were readily available to the authorized persons but not so accessible to illegitimate users.

Many a teacher or student of the Little White Schoolhouse became a master in the art of operating the school stove. They not only understood the scientific principle behind each operation but they also fathomed every idiosyncrasy of the temperamental heating robot. These artists could get a fire going faster than anyone else without filling the school with smoke and they were able to coax heat from the furnace after others had failed. One rural teacher in divulging the secret of his success stated that he treated the stove as gently as if it were a gracious lady and in turn received her many favors.

The boys and girls learned to watch the chimney as they approached the school on a cold morning for the various smoke-signals indicated just what progress the fireman was making in heating the building. No smoke meant no fire. Considerable smoke indicated that the fire had just been started, while if a wisp of smoke curled lazily from the chimney the children could expect to find the school nice and warm.

In winter the stove became the hub of the day's activities. Here the overshoes and outer garments were left to dry or to warm after a session of playing outdoors. Here the lunch pails were dumped on the floor on cold days to thaw out the frozen sandwiches and here the children ate their lunch at noon and enjoyed such social exchange of wit and horseplay as the teacher permitted.

Who will ever forget the picture of a cold winter's morning in the country schoolhouse? The students huddled around the stove, the "janitor" poking the fire and adding coal, while the flames roared up the chimney with the sparkle and crackle of a fireworks display at today's Calgary Stampede. The old Waterbury appeared ready to take off into space. Soon the flaming excitement subsided and the quiet heat just oozed into the bodies of the youngsters who had travelled anywhere up to five miles in buggies or on horseback in twenty-below weather. The odor of burnt leather or cloth permeated the classroom again and again as youngsters extended their shoes or mittens too close to the red-hot stove. The cheeks, noses and ears of the children hugging the stove roasted while at the same time their toes and posteriors were still cold.

With so many children crowded around the pot-bellied stove incidents were bound to occur. In the Rose Lynn S.D. (Sunnynook, Alta.) a pupil stepped on a springy floorboard and a loose leg on the heater fell off. Immediately the stove tipped to a dangerous angle scattering red-hot coals and stovepipes over the oily floor. Quick-thinking youngsters somehow managed to right the stove, gather up the live coals, secure the detached leg, put up the stovepipes and then went on with their studies as though nothing had happened.

In the Bryant S.D. 2533 (Bindloss, Alta.) an overshoe landed on a weak spot at one of the joints in the stovepipes. The two sections parted and, but for the twist of wire supporting them from the ceiling, would have crashed down on the heads of the children below. It was a tense moment for the pupils and teacher watching the flames leap from one pipe to the other over the ever-widening crack and seeing that the pipes in the vicinity of the break were gradually acquiring a reddish tinge. The situation was saved when Alton, the oldest boy in the school, put on his heavy leather mitts, stood on a chair that had been placed on the teacher's desk and gingerly thrust the pipes together again.

The toasting of human bodies continued until the last trace of chilblains had been dissipated and then a progressive migration in the general direction of the desks followed. The boys and girls learned from early experience that in order to avoid getting cold feet it was advisable to sit on the top of school furniture. The region along the floor was always draughty and the last to become impregnated with heat. Many teachers wore felt shoes or moccasins in order to keep their minds on their work and not so much on their frost-nipped toes. Cold mornings found the children perched on desk tops like sparrows in a tree. They were just as restless too for they darted back and forth on the slightest provocation. Ultimately the school bell sounded and this put aside the living subject of cold and brought the children to grips with the abstract subjects of the academic world.

At times it was necessary for the teacher and pupils to remain around the stove for more than an hour before the rest of the school became inhabitable. It was a case of soaking up heat and knowledge simultaneously. The students read, spelled, sang, wrestled with mental arithmetic, acted out scenes from their readers, and did whatever else seemed adaptable to this mode of learning. The normal schools never taught new teachers what to do under such circumstances but the ingenuity of some turned the unfortunate situation into highly productive educational sessions.

The cold mornings in the Eden S.D. 510 (Oakner, Man.) always began with a few minutes of physical exercises and then the children marched around the schoolroom singing "Onward Christian Soldiers" to get warm. However it always took some time before their icy fingers were limbered up enough to enable them to hold their pencils to write properly. More than one youngster sat on his hands for a while, wrote for a few minutes and then went back to warming his fingers. The routine of alternately warming hands and working proceeded for most of the morning. The occasional child, more from mischief than for the purpose of getting warm, would thrust his icy fingers down his neighbor's warm back. Such an unpleasant surprise always prompted the unsuspecting benefactor to shudder and squirm if not to utter a sharp outcry. A sense of humor went a long way towards enabling the rural children to tolerate the many adversities brought on by the extreme cold.

There was no more frustrating experience than for a small boy or girl to reach school on a cold morning expecting to see the welcome sign of a red-hot stove only to find the building still cold or even locked.

One morning the stove in the Eden S.D. 510 (Oakner, Man.) refused to burn and did nothing but smoke. The teacher knew the cause. She gave the primary students a half-day off to play in the yard while she and the older pupils started to clean the pipes. Very few people today can appreciate the enormity of such an undertaking.

First the pipes which were strung some eight feet above the floor and held in place by wire loops suspended from the ceiling had to be disconnected and lowered cautiously to the ground in manageable sections.

Any slight jar of the pipes produced a black cloud of soot. Sometimes a section of pipe broke free, came crashing to the floor and rebounded two or three times with a clatter and a gusto that only hollow tinware could produce. Like a snowfall, the dust and the soot silently blanketed everything below as an aftermath to this noisy outburst. Next the disjointed pipes had to be carried outside to the back of the school and cleaned by thumping them vigorously with a board and the inside swabbed with a mop fashioned from gunny sacking. Anyone who could do this without getting smeared from head to toe with the black soot was a wonder.

Once the pipes had been scraped they were taken back inside, hoisted aloft, fitted snugly together again and the anchor wires tightly drawn. Now the cleansing operation started. This chore was probably the hardest of all. The soot was so light and elusive that dusting only spread it, while the wash-water couldn't dissolve it. By the time the entire task was finished the teacher and students with their innumerable smudges of soot bore a close resemblance to the cast of a minstrel show.

Sometimes the boys undertook to clean the pipes on their own initiative. This happened in the Tongue Creek S.D. (High River, Alta.). The stove in the school didn't work too well and everyone continued to freeze until it decided to burn. On other occasions it gave off plenty of heat but filled the school with so much smoke that it was just as bad as the cold.

After one of these obstinate performances the older boys decided to clean the pipes at noon while the teacher had gone to Mrs. Findlay's for dinner. Of course the long length of pipes fell to the floor spreading soot in every direction. Three of the boys didn't want to miss such a wonderful opportunity so they blackened their faces and clowned around the room for a while. However, when they tried to wash off their make-up with cold water they merely extended the black smudges to their hair, necks and ears. What a sight! The teacher took one look at them and sent them home, despite the bitter cold outside.

A teacher in the Barlay S.D. (Holland, Man.) boarded with a childless couple close to school. They had told her to lock the school and not to permit anyone in if she wasn't there. She followed their suggestion. In summer and the early fall it was all right but when the weather turned chillier the children found it rather discomforting to wait for the teacher.

One cold sleety day the youngsters were forced to stand in the porch soaked and shivering. The situation became so untenable that a grade eight boy forced open a window, crawled in, unlocked the door, let the children in and lit the fire. By the time the teacher arrived the pupils were dry and warm. She was furious with the thoughtful youngster and threatened him with the police and jail for breaking into her school. The school board quickly informed the teacher just who owned the school and instructed her to leave the key in a place where all could use it.

Most of the rural schools were never locked so sometimes the children entered the school long before the tardy firemaker had the school warmed. Then they had to stand around and wait and get colder by the minute. Records indicate that some younger students almost froze to death under such trying circumstances. They were too small or too cold to start a fire by themselves. It was difficult enough for the students to make their way to school for several miles in below-zero weather without being greeted at their destination with more intense cold. They had become progressively colder en route and to find the school just as frigid was almost more than most could stand.

Faith Gibson of the Fertile Plains S.D. (Foremost, Alta.) recalls one such experience that almost ended in tragedy. It was a winter day in 1912 and around thirty-nine degrees below zero with a cold wind. She was walking to school alone and, after becoming drowsy from the cold, lay down to rest. Luckily she was near the school and was seen by the teacher, Mr. Gibbons, who ran out and carried her to school and safety.

A cold Monday morning was the crucial time for building a fire in the Little White Schoolhouse. The coals had been permitted to die out completely over the weekend so the student-janitor or teacher had to start from scratch.

They first cleaned the fire-box of the stove by shaking the grates and tamping with a poker until all the cinders and ashes had been ejected into the ashtray below. Next the bare grates were covered with a few sheets of crumpled paper surmounted by a teepee of kindling wood. Once the lighted match was applied to the paper it in turn set fire to the wood. Just as soon as the flames made sufficient headway in the wood the attendant threw in several small lumps of coal. As far as he was concerned his moment of success was attained when the coal ignited.

Now was the ideal time for emptying the cold and harmless ashes. The moment the caretaker swung open the lower portal of the stove to remove the overflowing pan the powdery ashes flooded the area around the stove and showers of hot sparks from the fire pitted the unprotected floor. The dust and the carbon monoxide of the burning coal permeated the air to such an extent that most of those standing near the stove burst into fits of coughing.

Every schoolyard had a place at the back or at the side designated as the "official ash pile" so the caretaker emptied the refuse there. The final chore was to sweep up the spilled ashes from around the stove. If this wasn't done, a pattern of footsteps appeared fanning out in all directions from the stove just as soon as the rest of the children arrived.

Although the majority of rural schools used the accepted technique in starting a fire in the old Waterman-Waterbury stove a number of districts had their own unique way of doing this. In the Silverton S.D. (Carnduff,

Only the ashes of a former radiance remain in the foreground of the S i l v e r Valley S c h o o l (Watts, Alta.) .

Sask.) for instance, Tim, a seventeen-year-old student used a sheaf of oats to light the fire every morning. It didn't take him very long to produce a roaring fire but there was usually a litter of straw around the stove.

One weekend in the year 1921 the weather turned suddenly cold in the May Hall S.D. 3299 (Schuler, Alta.) and the school was out of fuel. The teacher used a butcher knife to cut splinters off some fence posts in order to get wood. When the nearest neighbor discovered her plight he brought her two sacks of dried cow chips to use until the fuel came on Monday. The trustee, a bachelor, who ordinarily looked after the coal supply had been rebuffed by the teacher in his romantic advances so he employed this plan to redress his grievances. He had purchased a shiny new buggy and a smart dapple-grey horse but the teacher just wasn't interested.

A district like Little Souris S.D. 227 (Brandon, Man.) located near or in a forested area usually installed large box-like iron stoves in their schools. These heating units were built to accommodate cordwood in three-foot lengths but as they cooled off quickly they were refuelled many times during a cold day. The temperature had the habit of fluctuating throughout the day between what one expected to find only in Florida and Alaska. When it became too warm and the pipes turned red hot it was the duty of some youngsters to splash water on the burning wood to try to reduce the blazing inferno in the stove. Smoke and soot billowed out the door with every cupful of water to irritate the eyes and singe the hair of the volunteer fireman but almost immediately the fire began to subside. An hour after school closed the fire was dead. It used to be a common sight around such schools to see groups of men and boys cutting cordwood with crosscut or buck saws. Soon piles and piles of cordwood mushroomed in the vicinity of the school in preparation for the winter ahead.

Instead of relying on volunteer help most districts secured their supply of wood by tender. In 1902 the Harlington S.D. 1164 (Swan River, Man.) let its first tender for ten cords of green white poplar wood cut in four-foot lengths, split (no round wood accepted), delivered and piled on the school grounds at $1.50 a cord. The school children found these stacks of freshly-cut wood an attractive place for playing innumerable games. There was room for imagination, that wonderful world of make-believe which is the greatest joy of childhood.

Many factors militated against the best efforts of the teacher and her pupils to maintain a uniform temperature in the school. First and foremost was the high ceiling. According to the building specifications it had to be "at least eleven feet high". Just as soon as the fire was lit the heat rose to the ceiling and gradually began to inch its way down towards the floor. It was almost possible to trace the slow downward movement of the heat by gauging its warming effects on the various parts of the human anatomy. First the cold cheeks and ears felt comfortable, then the hands and finally if the children were lucky, their toes.

On a cold windy day the distribution of heat was far from adequate. The children sitting on the windward side of the school shivered from the cold while the rest languished in the heat. Some desks, benches or chairs always had to be moved closer to the stove for the pupils who, through the vagaries of the building and the weather, were on the wrong side of the room for that particular day or even hour.

This cold-weather shuttle system enabled the teacher to keep the classes functioning and on schedule. In spite of such makeshift arrangements to keep warm it must be said to the credit of the rural children and teacher that schools were rarely closed because it was too cold inside. Such a luxury was reserved for the present-day schools.

If snow ever blew into the attic of the rural school it became a sorry day for its occupants. As soon as a fire was started in the Waterman-Waterbury stove and enough heat was generated to melt the snow the ceiling would start dripping. Then it became a case of trying to keep warm, dodging drops of water and paying attention to the teacher.

Some of the rural schools were undergoing modernization to overcome a few of these deficiencies in the Mid-Twenties but the idea hadn't struck home as yet in the Wild Rose Valley S.D. (Kindersley, Sask.) in 1925. The farmers in the district were progressive, even well-to-do people with good stock, prepossessing barns and comfortable homes but as one student, Lorne Smith, was to say on a momentous day, "Our parents wouldn't keep their cows in a place like this!" That was the Monday morning following a three-day blizzard, when Miss Vernette Akeley, the teacher, arrived at the

—Mrs V. Mohl

The Spondon School (Hanna, Alta.) after the 1937 blizzard. The Waterbury furnace at the front had to stand idly by until all the fine snow had been swept out and dusted from the interior.

school a little early to start the fire. The desks, ledges, floor and everything else were covered with a three-inch blanket of snow that had seeped in through the cracks around the bleak, frosted window panes. Miss Akeley dared not light the fire until all the powdery, infuriatingly hard-to-handle snow had been shovelled and swept out. Of course the children began to arrive before this was finished and the weekend chill had not been dissipated.

All former rural students will likely recall the coal scuttle that was always empty and the ashtray that was always full. Remember they should, for at one time or another during their scholastic careers, they were saddled with the responsibility of filling the coal pail and emptying the ashes.

The fire had to be tended every hour of the school day. Since there were no thermostats and sometimes not even a thermometer it was the duty of the teacher or an older pupil to judge whether more or less fire was required at any particular time. If the children appeared to be too warm in the opinion of the "human thermostat", he turned the damper off, closed all drafts, left the door slightly ajar and awaited developments. On the other hand if the school was getting chilly the entire routine was reversed and supplemented with such activities as stirring the fire with the poker, shaking the grates and dumping a few more lumps of coal from the scuttle into the heater. It was a strange coincidence but every time the fireman started to stoke the fire, the accompanying clatter always produced a psychologically warming effect on the students long before the real heat had reached them. A sense of satisfaction and well-being was evident the moment the monitor rose to go to the stove.

The routine that accompanied the alternate heating and cooling of a classroom was repeated as many times per day as the temperature inside dictated. In early spring and late fall a small fire of kindling wood was all that was necessary and once the morning chill had been dissipated it was left to burn itself out. During the winter, however, the heater was banked for the night. It was always a real trick to get the fire to persevere all night. Usually one or two large lumps of coal were put in the stove and the drafts set in such a way that the resulting fire took until nine o'clock the next day to consume the coal. In the meantime the schoolroom stayed moderately warm. Next morning by merely opening the drafts, replenishing the coal and removing the ashes the caretaker could have a good fire going in a very few minutes. Unfortunately, sometimes a wind came up during the night and by morning the fireman found only cold ashes instead of glowing coals. Such a discovery was always discouraging for it meant building the fire all over again.

For the most part the school stove was a benevolent friend of the children, devoted to their welfare and, in an unobstrusive way, beaming forth on all with an air of cheerful dignity. In fact its twinkling portals appeared to look a pupil straight in the eyes as he hustled into the school on a cold frosty morning. But once in a while the heater rumbled with anger. This occurred any time its bowels were filled with slack coal and the drafts left closed. All would be peaceful for a while like the calm before a storm, and then without warning a violent muffled explosion would rend the air in the classroom. The doors on the stove flew open, live coals spread over the floor, pipes quivered dangerously and smoke poured profusely from every conceivable opening. Simultaneously the slack coal in the stove burst into a flaming inferno as a pall of smoke settled ominously over the heads of the startled children. After a discreet pause the caretaker or teacher stepped over to the stove and checked it carefully. It seemed such a useless manoeuvre once the damage had been done.

Although heating was the primary function of the pot-bellied stove it also doubled as a drier on numerous occasions. In the spring somebody was willing to try out the rubbery ice on a nearby slough or else go sailing on rafts put together with old fence posts, discarded desks or, failing these materials, to attempt to navigate on a large chunk of ice. The results of such foolhardiness invariably ended with one or two pupils getting soaking wet. For them it meant huddling around the stove for the rest of the day wearing borrowed off-size garments while waiting for their own to dry on the temporary clothesline strung up in the school.

The children of the Eden S.D. 510 (Oakner, Man.) like those of thousands of other rural schools spent most of the pleasant winter days playing out on the snowbanks. The snow invariably clung to their long black hand-knit stockings and formed ice. These youngsters sat through most afternoons with wet stockings and damp long underwear as the icy-snow melted and then slowly evaporated.

The guard-rail about the school stove was a convenient place to dry wet garments such as mitts, scarves, toques, felt boots, moccasins, sweaters and coats. The stove was no respecter of careless boys and girls. If they happened to leave any of their apparel such as shoes or mitts too close to its radiant sides the article was toasted until it shrivelled up into a useless mass of hardened leather. Woollen garments scorched and shrunk in the searing heat. As a consequence the schoolhouse at this time of year reeked of the stifling and unpleasant odor of dank and burnt garments. Not only that, but as spring was the season for numerous minor sicknesses the air became saturated with the aroma of liniment, camphor-ated oil, wintergreen, mustard plasters and goose-grease. The schoolhouse smelled like a hospital. On blustery days with the windows closed and a goodly fire roaring in the stove, more than one teacher grew faint from such a malodorous onslaught. But this wasn't all. There was usually the youngster who brought the unmistakable scent of the stables to the class-room, while children of European parentage often attended exuding the heavy aroma of garlic. To top it off there was the lad who had tended his trap line on the way to school and depending upon whether he had handled weasel, skunk or marten, he added one of several distinctive flavors to the already rich assortment.

What memories and stories these old school stoves could recall! One early fall morning in 1930 the Ribstone Creek S.D. 2861 (Coronation, Alta.) seemed rather chilly so the teacher decided to build a fire. The stove smoked terribly. She told one of the board members about it that evening but he didn't think there was anything wrong. The next day was even colder, so again the teacher started the heater. The smoke was so thick in the school that the children spent most of the morning playing outside. When the board members investigated later in the day they found a partly-consumed rabbit in the chimney. Apparently an owl or a hawk had lost part of its dinner!

It was a standing rule in those days that the first arrivals at school were expected to start the fire in the stove. One very cold morning in 1930 a girl happened to be the first one to get to the Shandro S.D. (Mundare, Alta.). She opened the doors of the stove to perform her duty when from within came the screams of human voices. The frightened girl almost passed out when she saw two grinning boys crawl out. This incident had the effect of discouraging any girls of ever attempting to build a fire in the pot-bellied stove again in that school.

Christine van der Mark Wise will always remember one night in September 1937. That was the time that she nearly set fire to the Meadow-grass School near Hussar, Alta. She was a city girl and completely unacquainted with the secrets of firing a big school stove. This particular evening she stoked it with slack coal. The wind came up and when Christine went back to the school about ten-thirty that night to see how the fire was coming, she found the inside of the school bathed in a brilliant pink glow. The stove was bright red from top to bottom, and the long string of pipes through the centre of the room were just as red. The entire building creaked with the oppressive heat. She spied the pail of drinking water sitting on a shelf near a window, and flinging open the door of the heater she tossed the water on the fire. The next thing she knew, a cloud of steam engulfed her. She was wearing a hip-length sheepskin jacket at the time and it shrivelled right off her in the hot vapor. But under it Christine was unharmed. The stove's color returned to normal once it received its unexpected shower bath and the building started to cool perceptively the instant Christine shovelled snow over the floor.

Since the Green Lake S.D. (Hamlin, Alta.) was heated with wood the children were held responsible for bringing in the firewood and stacking it in the boys' porch. During the school hours the students took turns in keeping the furnace going. Sometimes when the pipes became red-hot the youngsters learned the technique of splashing water on the burning wood to try and reduce the intensity of the flames. Soot and smoke billowed out the door with every cupful of water and stung their eyes. They learned to detest these chores and frequently preferred to tap their feet on the floor to keep warm. Of course the tapping of the frozen boots on the floor used to annoy the teacher. She then had them stand up and march around the school while she looked after the fire herself.

One cold morning the children of the Plain Valley School were doing some warming-up exercises in class when their lively gyrations brought down the pipes just as the student-janitor had succeeded in coaxing the fire into a roaring inferno. Every pupil jumped into action by forming a snow brigade of lunch pails. The heater, bereft of its string of pipes looked like an angry robot spewing bursts of flame and great clouds of smoke in all directions, as bucket after bucket of snow was tossed into its vitals. By the time the combined efforts of the teacher and pupils had extinguished the conflagration, the ceiling was badly blistered and the interior obscured by a mist of pale blue smoke. The hot pipes had also

Bringing in the firewood (Green Lake S.D., Hamlin, Alta.)

scorched the floor and some of the desks. In spite of this minor damage and the fact that everything was a trifle damp from the melting snow, the teacher was able to hold classes in the afternoon.

There were also times in this school when a boy or two livened up a dull afternoon by dropping .22 bullets into the stove. These went off with a loud bang and pleased the children. If the teacher was puzzled by the stove's performance, she no doubt put it down to the sap in the logs.

Charlie Schact did the janitor work in the Braeside S.D. 1748 (Cayley, Alta.) for two dollars a month. He walked two and one-half miles every morning to light the fire. The teacher, Miss Bailey, hung a thermometer on the wall and insisted that Charlie have the temperature up to seventy degrees when she arrived at the school. The lad had his own technique for carrying out this order, whenever for one reason or another the pot-bellied stove failed to give sufficient heat. When he saw Miss Bailey coming down the road he would light a match and hold it near the thermometer until it reached the required temperature. One morning he held it there too long—and shattered the thermometer.

Fate must have smiled sweetly on the rural schools. Why more of them didn't burn down was a mystery. Fire hazards abounded everywhere—the oily floor, the worn and rusty pipes, the unclean chimney, the banked stove, the debris in the coal scuttle, the unlocked school and the ash pile beside the school. Also sad to relate it was the exception rather than the rule to find a school with a fire extinguisher or an adequate and ready supply of water on the premises in case of fire. The excellent record of rural schools in fire losses was due in part to the self-reliance developed by rural students at an early age and the fact that everyone in the community treated school property as their very own and took a personal interest in safeguarding it.

Nevertheless practically every school district can relate incidents of near-fires.

Mrs. Rebecca Peacock, now over ninety-one years of age, recalled one such exigency that arose in the Asplin School at Muskoka, Ontario, in 1884. The youngster who looked after the fires was in a rush one day and instead of emptying the hot ashes in the proper pile he threw them out by the side of the school. A breeze fanned the ashes back to life and sent the flames up against the school until a log caught fire. The teacher fortunately discovered the fire in the log wall later on in the morning and everyone threw snow at the flames until the school was saved. A girl who was late that day made the following pert observation: "It was burning when I came in!"

A new stove had been installed in the Earltown S.D. 2417 (Hanna, Alta.) for the winter of 1922. It was a late model that sat directly on the floor, would not tip, and according to its manufacturers was an excellent heater. It was all that and more. In fact it yielded so much heat one day that the floor caught fire on the underside. The wind blew the smoke out through the air ventilator at the side of the school and it was assumed at first that the fire was ensconced in the wall. It was soon located and a portion of the floor was cut out and the fire extinguished by some of the neighbors who had answered the teacher's emergency call. School had to be closed for a couple of weeks while repairs were made to the fire-damaged floor and the wall.

The old stovepipes contributed more than their share of grief. They smoked, they gathered dust, they filled up with soot, they became red-hot and, on more than one occasion, came tumbling down without the slightest provocation. Yet for all these deficiencies the string of old pipes and the pot-bellied stove provided enough heat to make school possible during the winter months from one end of the country to the other in The Little White Schoolhouse.

6

DESKS AND WRITING MATERIALS

In the early days of the Little White Schoolhouse it was the responsibility of the parents to furnish a sufficient number of desks to accommodate all the members of their family attending school. As a result, the first desks, which were just benches, were built long enough to seat all the children in that family. They were crudely constructed, differed markedly from each other in design and rarely did the four legs touch the floor at the same time. The many protruding nails became such a nuisance that they had to be pounded back into place almost every day. In addition the seats were so rough and full of splinters that it ill-behooved any youngster to attempt to slide off or onto them.

Each child sat at his family's desk and as a result the members of any particular grade were scattered all over the classroom instead of being together. Many students sat on empty nail kegs, wooden crates, or on planks supported by two blocks of wood. They wrote at desks built of two blocks of wood thirty inches high and set about eight feet apart with a plank placed over them and then nailed firmly. Such homemade desks, unless propped up securely against the wall, were never too stable and once in a while they toppled to the floor with a resounding bang and completely disrupted the staid tenor of the classroom. It soon became painfully obvious that it was better for all concerned to hire a skilled carpenter to construct a few standard desks or else buy some of the ready-made models from the furniture factory.

Benches proved unsuitable and were replaced by double desks. The children liked them for they were ideal for playing the many pencil games in which they participated during winter recesses. It was common for a boy and girl, if they happened to be in the same grade, to share one of these double desks. Teachers, however, preferred to have boys sit with boys and girls with girls. One way of punishing a pupil for talking in those days was to have him sit next to a shy, unpopular or silly-mannered member of the opposite sex. This was enough to discourage even the most loquacious individual from attempting to strike up a conversation. In spite of any claims that could be made on behalf of double-

—Mrs M. C. Farwell

The Paddle River School in Northern Alberta was furnished completely with homemade desks. The singular heater shown in the picture was also manufactured locally.

desks most school boards eventually came around to buying the single prototypes.

The factory-made desk, whether single or double, was made of hardwood supported on a couple of iron frames very similar to those still used on treadle sewing machines. It consisted of a large, smooth writing surface, a storage space directly underneath and a hinged seat fastened to the front. There was an unwritten law that when school was dismissed for the day each seat had to be left folded back—or else! The writing surface was complemented with a pencil trough and a two-inch circular opening in the upper right-hand corner to hold the inkwell. When the desks were new they presented a most formidable sight as they stood in the classroom so neatly arranged in rows and just sparkling in their untouched coat of varnish. They looked like a company of well-dressed soldiers on parade. But the desks were not comfortable as they were too hard. Just ask any former student of a rural school who had to sit in them for eight consecutive years!

Since desks came in a variety of sizes most school boards purchased a few of each in the hope that they would meet their needs for a good number of years to come. People have often wondered what the number embellished on the side of the desk meant. It merely indicated the size

—Mrs. R. Christie

A fine view of the interior of a typical rural school showing the children's double desks and the teacher's stand at the front. This is the Shining Bank log school near Edson, Alta.

of the desk. School catalogues of that day were careful to supply the following information to school boards contemplating the purchase of right-sized desks:

Size	Age of Pupil	Class
6	5 to 8 years	Primary
5	8 to 12 years	Second Intermediate
4	10 to 15 years	First Intermediate
3	12 to 18 years	Grammar
2	16 to 20 years	High School
1	Adult	Normal School

Once the desks were set up in rows they formed convenient "learning cells". Each student used the seat of the unit behind him and the desk-proper of the one in front. The distance between the writing surface and the seat was regulated to provide the right space for the slender child or the corpulent one. This didn't always turn out well. For, thanks to the perverted sense of humor of one or two characters, some unfortunate child often found himself either being squeezed vexatiously or separated so far from his work that even if he sat on the edge of the seat he had to stretch embarrassingly to reach it.

Some school boards felt they had been duped in their purchase of desks when they discovered that each row led off with a surplus seat and ended with an unusable desk. Little did they realize that the

—Mrs. N. Charyk

Double desks in the Laggan School 1063 (Lake Louise, Alta.). When picture
was taken in 1928, Kathleen Fraine, daughter of a C.P.R. Vice-President was
teacher.

manufacturer also sold front and back components for this very purpose.
If the trustees failed to buy these specialized units the teachers still made
good use of what they had. They placed ordinary chairs or benches at
the back desks and used the front seats for their recitation classes. It was
astounding the number of schools that never deciphered the mystery of
uncomplementary seats and desks.

In spite of the care exercised initially in purchasing desks of the
right size, succeeding years found a large class of beginners dangling their
dinky legs from seats obviously much too high for them, or, conversely,
big boys attempting like present-day astronauts to squeeze themselves into
diminutive spaces. Several school districts overcame this problem of fluctuating needs by instituting a desk-swapping program with their neighboring
schools every September. It worked very well. A number of furniture
companies came out with adjustable desks but for some reason or other
the mechanical sliding device on them failed to hold so the school boards
were not favorably impressed. A special wrench accompanied these desks
and very often when a husky youth attempted to tighten the bolts on each
side of the desk after adjusting it the cast-iron frame shattered. No one
knew how to weld cast iron so after effecting some temporary repairs

The end of the trail for the desks of a disused and forlorn rural school. These desks were formerly stacked in this manner when they were temporarily removed from the school to make way for a dance, or some other social gathering held in the schoolhouse.

with pieces of baling wire the desk served out the remainder of its days in a shocking state of disrepair.

In most schools the desks were not permanently fastened to the floor. Instead, two or three units were joined together in tandem fashion by securing them to a pair of wooden slats or runners. This made the desks quite stable yet at the same time readily portable. If the floor had to be cleared for a dance the strings of desks could be moved expeditiously and stacked.

The first school day in September brought forth the observance of a custom known as "jockeying for seats". The students rushed to school as early as possible and reserved their seats for the year. At least so they thought! The talkative, the lazy, and the pranksters wanted places at the back. The studious, the inquisitive and the eager beavers selected desks at the front, while the new, the shy and the average chose what was left. Of course when the teacher came round to it a wholesale change in plans resulted. At least the anticipation was nice while it lasted! Some new teachers permitted the youngsters to pick, on a temporary basis, their own seats at the beginning of a new term. In this manner she was able to anticipate the various personality traits of her pupils for they automatically categorized themselves by where they wanted to sit. A strange test, but it frequently worked. The next September saw a similar mad scramble

Double desks in full use in the Bryant School, (Bindloss, Alta.), 1930.

to manoeuvre for certain seats. They never gave up. Who knew? Someday they just could succeed in their stratagem.

There was a right way of arranging the textbooks, the scribblers and the other school paraphernalia inside the desk. It began with the largest book and all the rest were stacked on top in order of diminishing size. If one yielded to temptation and merely shoved the books in to save time, the entire conglomeration had the persistent habit of crashing to the floor with a thunderous bang, with all the odds-and-ends scooting, bouncing or rolling to all corners of the floor. How exasperating! But it taught the youngsters to keep things in order.

True to tradition the students left their marks for posterity on school buildings, fences, barns, pumps, outhouses, coalsheds and huge rocks. But the desks in particular took the brunt of these vain attempts at immortality. Over the years they became well scarred with initials and names of fathers, mothers, uncles and aunts, brothers and sisters. In turn the students felt obligated to add their own names to the family registry. The defacing didn't stop at initials for it included nicknames, hearts encircling pairs of names, phrases of so-and-so loves so-and-so, various types of diagrams, good and bad drawings, many doodles with here and there interspersed among all the rest a few obscene words. Any time former pupils returned to their own Little White Schoolhouse after being away from the district for a number of years they took great delight in pointing out the desk where they used to sit and to the carving they did. Today, the country school is no more, the hieroglyphics are no more and the hundreds of pupils who inscribed these symbols are also gone. Fame is such a fleeting thing!

There was one good way of forestalling any inclination on the part of students to deface desks. Mrs. R. A. Wilson of Lashburn, Sask., recalls participating in one such preventive scheme.

"I remember one teacher saying something about how badly the desks had been cut up and we went about refinishing them by ourselves. Funds were scarce so we borrowed a scraper, bought some sandpaper and each child sanded his own desk. The little ones received help from the older pupils. Then the mothers held a bee one Saturday and varnished everything. Do you know the children took a real pride in their desks for some years after that?"

The notorious inkwell consisted of three components. There was a chrome-plated housing, a half-cylinder glass receptacle that fitted into it and a hinged lid that snapped shut with a resounding "click". The unit was inserted in the circular opening found in the top right-hand corner of every desk. This position had a decided advantage for the right-handed students but it must be remembered that in those early days the practice was for the teacher to change over every left-handed child. What a change! Today we have left-handed desks, left-handed scissors, left-handed electric irons and even left-handed pencil sharpeners!

It is inconceivable but true that such an inconspicuous, mundane object as an inkwell was the bane of so many rural schoolteachers. The ink came ready-mixed in quart or gallon containers, or sometimes in the form of pellets or powder. Since the school boards preferred the latter, it being cheaper, it fell to the lot of the teacher to mix the ink. Teachers were not chemists so the alkali water that they frequently substituted for the hard-to-get distilled water yielded a concoction that at times resembled invisible ink, at other times, India ink. The act of pouring the ink from the quart or gallon container into the small desk inkwells without spilling or topping was an art in itself. Yet the children loved to do it. A student felt highly honored to be given the privilege of filling the inkwells.

Brimming inkwells were potential danger spots. A sudden jar against a desk invariably spattered the ink on the books below. In fact very few children owned books or clothing that had not at one time or another fallen victim to a misadventure with ink. The handkerchief appeared to be the chief casualty in these incidents. Unknown to the mothers, who tried vainly to remove the blue ink spots, the schools used "permanent" rather than the "washable" variety of ink. It was fortunate for the school that the floors were saturated with oil and dirt for hundreds of inkspots were thus hidden from view.

The spatter of ink could come from the least expected source. On one occasion a teacher turned from the blackboard in anger, having been unable to spot the culprit who was filling the air with spit balls. In frustration she flung a piece of chalk on her desk. It split in two and one portion flew down the aisle and landed neatly in a student's inkwell sprinkling her with ink.

Nary a week passed without an ink mishap. Picture the scene. The students thumbing hurriedly through their exercise books searching for blotting paper. The victim, dripping with ink, standing aloof with feet astride and arms spread out, not knowing what to do. The teacher, book in hand, giving instructions on how best to proceed with the clean-up operations, while a few playful souls amused themselves by daming the rivulets of ink or even spreading them. Eventually a number of pieces of blotting-paper made their appearance through donations or borrowings to cover completely the puddles of ink on the desk and the floor, and the boy or girl hurried over to the washbasin to give the stained clothing a token rinse. The final act saw the unfortunate one down on his hands and knees scrubbing the floor around his desk or mopping up generally. Everyone, including the teacher, was most sympathetic and helped in any way he could. And so they should. No one knew who the next ink-casualty would be.

Winter mornings found the ink frozen solid, so subjects that did not require the use of pen-and-ink were scheduled first. It was a common sight to see a number of ink-bottles and inkwells arranged on the floor about the stove where they would thaw out. In one school a youngster thought he could accelerate the process by placing the ink-bottle on top of the stove. The idea was good but the timing was poor. A puff of hissing steam enveloped the top of the stove and sprayed the white ceiling with blue ink. Fortunately for the entire school the boy had taken the precaution of removing the stopper from the bottle before setting it on the stove. In years to come the tattle-tale blue on the ceiling was a mute reminder of the foolhardiness of attempting to melt frozen ink by the direct application of heat to the bottle.

The heat in the classroom had an uncanny way of evaporating some of the liquid in the ink, leaving behind a writing fluid of such a consistency that it clogged the pen-nibs and left them temporarily unserviceable. The students used blotting paper, pencils or even their fingers to remove the residue. It was a messy operation under the best of circumstances and was instrumental in leaving behind a trail of ink stains everywhere.

Stories about ink also had their less serious moments. The boys often could not overcome the temptation of seeing the springy curls of hair dangling so invitingly before them so they dipped the ends in the convenient inkwell. These mischievous youngsters were probably the fore-runners of today's hairdressers. The wise or experienced teacher always made a mental note of this singular weakness on the part of certain boys and planned the seating arrangements accordingly. This problem never would have arisen if the girls of the Little White Schoolhouse days had anticipated the hair-styles of the present generation.

One teacher could not account for the alarming rate at which the ink disappeared from every inkwell in the school, However, by skilful detection, she discovered that a grade one student had cultivated an insatiable taste for ink and was helping herself at every opportunity. The student apparently survived the drinking bout without any harmful effects. It might be said in favor of the little girl that ink does have the bitter-sweet essence that is so characteristic of most soft drinks manufactured today.

No one has come away from a rural school without having at least one sad experience involving ink. They might have worked painstakingly for hours, or even days on some school project, presumably their masterpiece, and then ruined everything by upsetting a bottle of ink over it. The use of an ink eraser, or a sharp knife only increased the damage to the potential work of art.

Teachers knew that three-thirty was at hand without having to look at the clock on the wall, for the steady clicks of inkwell lids as they were closed with a gusto were constant reminders to her that at least one partner of the teacher-pupil fraternity was finished for the day.

Many pioneers like to reminisce about the old-style writing tools and books of the Little White Schoolhouse days.

School slates were well on their way to becoming obsolete by 1915 but some teachers and trustees favored their retention in the lower grades. The equipment consisted of a slate, a slate pencil, a bottle of water and a rag for cleaning the slate. Slate rags yielded a vile stench, particularly after prolonged use. Girls prided themselves on having fancy bottles for holding the cleaning water and frequently swapped them for others that they thought were even fancier. A small vanilla bottle was a favored container because it imparted a pleasant fragrance to the water. No such effeminate practices for the boys! When the teacher wasn't looking they used spit and their shirt or sweater sleeves to clean their slates; otherwise the sissified water-and-rag routine had to be followed. There was one consolation for the boys. The water-bottles were handy for wetting the seat of a neighbor's desk when he was up at the teacher's desk for a recitation or reading class. Imagine the surprise and the embarrassment of the returning classmate as he or she sat down in the usual place.

Slate pencils were very brittle so the rate of breakage was unusually high. However, as they were purchased by the dozen, a family was able to keep pace with the rapid rate of turnover. There were two kinds of slate pencils; hard black with a cover of striped paper like a barber's pole and plain uncovered grey ones. The former were much to be desired. They were soft and wrote quietly with a fine chalk-like line while the latter, the cheaper variety, scratched and soon marred the slates. Everyone knows how nerve-wracking it is to have to listen to the screeching sounds often produced by a novice writing on a blackboard with a long piece of chalk. It makes most people cringe. Yet this experience is mild compared to the hubbub produced by twenty-five pupils all scratching away on their slates. It is no wonder that the slates were superannuated so soon.

The students used pencils for writing in the first three grades. The great year of maturity came in grade four when they changed from pencils to pens. Not the so-called ballpoint pen that everyone uses today, but a "straight pen" with a detachable nib. The nibs came in an assortment of shapes and sizes and were classified according to the width of their writing edge as very fine, fine, medium or coarse. The stores displayed their supply of pen-nibs in an eye-catching counter cabinet that was divided into several compartments each one holding a particular style or grade of nib. The green felt that lined each chamber not only protected the delicate nibs but added glamour and class to the wares. It was a thrilling experience for a student to make his own selection of pen-nibs as the storekeeper invitingly held the glass lid open for him. Some stores kept their supplies in small cardboard containers so it was a simple procedure to satisfy the pupil's requirements as to size and style by taking out the properly-labelled box. The teacher instructed the students to suck each nib before using it in order to remove the protective chemical coating. Otherwise the ink did not adhere to it. The nibs had a variety of extra-curricular uses ranging from a peaceful game of darts to an all-out battle involving lances and ink-sprays. Invariably when the straight pen fell off a desktop it landed on the floor in the manner of a spear with the nib buried deeply in wood. Needless to say the life expectancy of a nib was short.

The straight pens were made out of hardwood with a cylindrical metal nib-insert at the end. They came in a variety of bright colors and shapes to appeal to the individual preferences of students. The more expensive pens were shaped to fit the hand and had a rubber or cork holder surrounding the base. This was ideal for soaking up the ink and the dirt that the youngsters collected on their fingers. The manufacturers of straight pens never came up with a model that was bite-proof so by mid-term the majority of pens were chewed down to the point where writing became extremely difficult, or even impossible. No research work ever explained the reason for these beaver-like propensities on the part of students. Some attribute it to the nervous tension generated by all learning situations, others to the fact that the manufacturer made the wood as nourishing and tasteful as possible to increase his sales.

Items such as loose-leaf sheets were not popular and zipper-binders were still to be invented. The students made their notes and did their

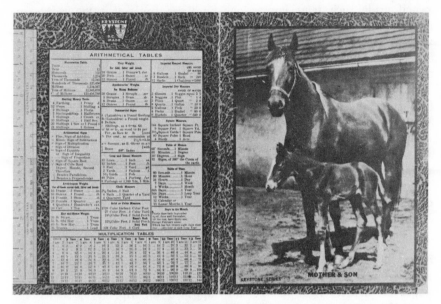

The front and back of a five-cent scribbler that was very popular during the days of the one-room school.

exercises in "scribblers". These could be bought for either pen or pencil use. They contained an attractive picture on the front while the back was covered with mathematical tables of all sorts featuring the multiplication tables up to twelve times twelve. The larger scribblers of fifty pages or more had plain covers with blanks for the student's name, grade, and school on the front. The most pretentious of all pen-and-ink books was one enclosed in flexible or hard glossy black covers. It was the ambition of every youngster to own one of these black notebooks for it carried a status symbol signifying scholarship and wealth. The run-of-the-mill scribblers could be purchased at the rate of six for twenty-five cents, or five, ten, or twenty-five cents each for the better ones, but this special hard-covered one required an outlay of at least fifty cents!

Pictures on the covers of the scribblers came in a full range of colors and subjects. There were pictures of birds, animals, children at play and breathtaking scenes of all parts of Canada. A youngster could not be blamed for buying a particular scribbler exclusively for the illustration on the cover. Needless to say the students had a scribbler for each subject and since there were so few pages in each book it required several of them to contain the year's work. The children were often heard to boast about the number of scribblers they had filled since school started.

Arithmetic was done in pencil scribblers comprised of pages of unglazed paper similar to newsprint. Some were lined, others left plain. A hard lead pencil made such faint impressions on these pages that the words or numbers were barely perceptible. Since these mathematics exercise books were a couple of inches longer than the standard scribblers they created a storage problem, and as a consequence the pages ended up being dog-eared. The fragile paper easily disintegrated under the pressure of an eraser and since the eraser was and still is an indispensable tool in doing arithmetic, these exercise books contained numerous tattered and torn pages. The use of a moistened index finger as a substitute for the ever-elusive eraser wrought even more devastation. It was utterly hopeless to write with ink on paper specifically designed for pencil. The ink diffused through the porous paper as if it were a blotter and the words became obliterated in a chaos of blots. Yet almost daily there were children attempting the impossible! Is it any wonder the pencil scribblers were the bane of so many students and teachers.

Pen-and-ink days were also the days of the blotting paper. It would have been foolhardy in those days to attempt to write with ink without having a blotter handy. If the pen-nib flooded, a dab or two with the blotting paper set matters right. If the ink happened to drip on the notebook or on the desk it could be easily removed the same way. If a bottle of ink tipped over, the blotter was indispensable. Students did not have to wait for the ink to dry at the bottom of a completed page before turning it. All they had to do was to smooth their blotter over the moist writing and all was dry, otherwise the writing smudged and inverted inscriptions appeared on the opposite page. Blotting-paper spitballs were the most succulent missiles ever devised by young minds. Thus it may be seen that there were many uses for blotting paper whether for school work or recreation. In those days if a scribbler was opened at the last place where any entries had been made a blotter could always be found there. Yes it was torn and covered with hundreds of ink blots, but like an old soldier, it was ready to step into the breach at any moment.

The blotting paper came in an assortment of colors: pink, blue, green, grey and plain white. The majority of retail firms used the blotter as a convenient method for advertising their business. They distributed blotters that were beautifully lithographed to capture the attention of the public. Everyone could use a blotter so it was a delightful and profitable way to reach the potential customer. Many such blotters come to light today after having outlived the firm that they advertised thirty or forty years ago.

A teacher could spot the student who was the best scrounger by his collection of blotters. Every blotter represented an achievement whether from the standpoint of business connections or having a host of friends. The blotters were as much a status symbol in The Little White Schoolhouse as record collections are today. The words, "Would you like a nice blotter, teacher?" were enough to melt the coldest professorial heart.

When students of the Little White Schoolhouse era think of pencils they remember the pencil-box. It was merely a narrow wooden container with a sliding lid that enabled one to safely store his pencils, pens, pen-nibs, erasers, and other odds and ends. Manufacturers must have been involved in a competition to see who could produce the most grandiose one, for the market was flooded with a never-ending stream of newly-designed pencil-boxes. Every student aspired to the ownership of a "double-decker" type that contained two sliding drawers. When the top lid was slid back it revealed a grooved floor compartment wherein one could deposit several pencils and pens, while the lower drawer was fashioned to hold erasers, pen-nibs, a small pencil sharpener and a variety of other school trinkets. The box was varnished and had a floral design burned in the top or an appropriate picture pasted on the lid. The secretive nature of the pencil-box and the fact that it offered a lawful way to tinker in school, made it a popular item. Just imagine how one youngster could arouse the curiosity of the entire school by simply saying, "Wait till you see what I have in my pencil-box?"

The children who for one reason or another were unable to own a "store-bought" pencil-box substituted boxes of their own. Cedar cigar-boxes and cardboard chocolate-boxes were the favorites. These make-shift pencil-boxes had one advantage—they could hold more. Adding to the contents of the box, especially to the ones owned by girls, was a prank of the boys. The addendum included grasshoppers, spiders, gopher tails, baby mice, birds' eggs or anything else that would startle the unsuspecting owner when she opened the box. The more consternation a particular female exhibited while making the discovery the more likely were the perpetrators to repeat their performance with her box. In spite of these misdirected uses for a pencil-box a child's school equipment was judged incomplete unless he possessed one. This went for both girls and boys, no matter whether they were in grade one or nine.

The mail-order catalogue was a popular source from which to order supplies. It featured bargains! The catalogue illustrated all the writing equipment that could be purchased for the one low all-inclusive price. The list was amazing in its scope. There would be a schoolbag, a pencil-box, a ruler, a box of crayons, a pencil sharpener, a dozen ink scribblers, six giant-sized unruled books, a packet of blotting paper, a dozen pencils, three pen holders, ink and pencil erasers, plus an assortment of pen-nibs. Who could ask for more? Everybody bought them. Teachers were forced to accede to this trend in standardization of school supplies instead of dictating their personal preferences.

7

OTHER SCHOOL FACILITIES

No schoolroom could ever be worthy of the name unless it contained blackboards. They stretched right across the front of the room and frequently down one side as well. In the early days they were made of compressed paper, wallboard or strips of wood. Whatever their composition, they were surfaced with a veneer, or a paint, that was considered best by the local authorities. Instances have been recorded where blackboards were furbished with black enamel. Result? Beautiful to behold but useless as a writing surface. The chalk skimmed freely over the smooth surface but did not leave as much as a single mark on it.

The first teacher in the Riversvale S.D. 4775 in the Peace River country in 1937 writes an interesting account of her experience in putting up blackboards.

> "The superintendent informed me a few days before school opened that the building was nearly ready and that two pieces of plasterboard for the blackboards had been sent. He instructed me to take some sizing and a paint brush along. His suggested sizing was a light brown sugar syrup. So armed with three pounds of brown sugar, a paint brush, a trunkful of equipment and all the fresh ideas of a Normalite, I was on my way.
>
> The second night at Riversdale a school board member and his wife came to help me put up the blackboards. By nailing rough scantling to rougher log walls we eventually got the boards in place. It was the teacher's duty to put on two coats of sizing and two of paint. It took me two weeks before the blackboards were fully operational."

Brown-sugar syrup may have proved to be a satisfactory sizing for the blackboards in the Riversdale School but not so for the Orangehill S.D. (Thornhill, Man.). The financial statement for the year 1895 recorded an expenditure of $1.30 to a Mr. H. B. Brown for two gallons of beer for the blackboards.

There was an art in installing blackboards. Some had to be fastened to the wall no more than two feet off the floor so the little people could use them, with others secured at a much higher level to accommodate the senior students. Unfortunately in the early days the persons usually hired to set up the furnishings in a new school never realized this and put them up at a height to suit themselves. Teachers overcame this problem by reserving the lower portions for the primary grades, the middle sections for the elementary students and the top areas for the tall students. In most cases the blackboards were finished with a strip of wooden moulding along the top and sides, and a chalk ledge at the bottom.

The blackboard that contained a paper base served equally well as bulletin boards. Tacks could be pushed easily into them. Modern classrooms boast of magnetic blackboards for holding instructional materials in place but the oldtime paperbacked ones could be adapted for this function just as readily. Unfortunately, after being punctured by hundreds of tacks over a period of twenty or thirty years the surface attained the appearance of a smallpox victim. They defied anyone to write legibly on them. Commas and periods appeared in places where they had no right to be. The letters and words resembled chopped-up alphabet soup. Students had to resort to guessing the meaning of some of the sentences that appeared on the pitted blackboard.

The blackboards were always a source of perplexity and vexation to early school officials. This is how a teacher of the amalgamated districts of Wilfred and Dorothy (Sunnynook, Alta.) described the inside of her unusual fourteen-by-twenty-foot school.

> "The aisles were so narrow that the children turned sideways to get out. The blackboards were so high I could only use the lower two feet unless I stood on a chair. I am 5 feet 4 inches tall."

The installation of blackboards in the Cameron S.D. 406 (Minnedosa, Man.) in 1885 just missed being an absurdity.

In many districts there were always some eager souls who sought the honor of being identified with any praiseworthy project in-the-making. Thus, in the Cameron District, it fell to one of these self-appointed benefactors to measure the length of the potential blackboard. But as he had neither tape measure nor ruler he used a piece of straw. What happened when he converted the straw-lengths into feet and inches no one ever knew. Anyway, on arrival, the blackboard was far too short. To remedy the botched job the local carpenter divided the error equally between the two ends. Any person who ever visited the Cameron School was always amazed to find such an abbreviated blackboard. In answer to the questions that were bound to be asked the local resident, with injured pride, invariably mumbled uncomplimentary remarks about certain Cameron people, who, even if they were doing it gratis, took on jobs they were incapable of handling.

A rather unique feature of the Rocky Coulee S.D. 1188 (Granum, Alta.) classroom was its blackboard. It was fashioned in 1906 out of the ordinary narrow flooring strips and then painted black. The cracks between the boards provided guide-lines for anyone writing on it. Novel as was the idea it did not prove entirely satisfactory so in 1909 it was replaced, or rather covered, with a hyloplate blackboard.

It wasn't long before the Department of Education took the matter of blackboards under advisement and from then on the problem was somewhat lessened. The Alberta Department of Education for instance, issued the following directive in 1906:

> "Every room shall be provided with at least sixty square feet of blackboard space. The blackboard should be at least four feet wide and not more than 2 and a half feet from the floor and should extend across the room behind the teacher's desk. Additional blackboard space should be provided on the side of the room that has no windows. At the lower edge of each blackboard there should be a concave shelf or trough three inches wide for holding chalk and brushes. Blackboards may be of slate, hyloplate, cloth, plaster or wood. Owing to the difficulty experienced in making durable and service-able plaster blackboards they do not meet with favour. Blackboards of wood or cloth are not recommended except for temporary use. Considering the cost, durability and serviceableness of the various blackboards in use, hyloplate gives very general satisfaction."

Hyloplate was the sheet of slate that was glued by a special heat treatment to the face of the blackboard to furnish a superior writing surface.

One difficulty with blackboards was that any time frost formed it was impossible to write on them with chalk. Since most country schools remained unheated over the weekends this was a usual problem every Monday morning throughout the winter months.

Perfectly-executed letters of the alphabet, both lower case and capitals, graced the space along the top of the blackboard. The students were expected to imitate these models in their own writing. Did the ruse succeed? Probably not as much as some educators would have one believe. The real value lay in the fact that the students were challenged to improve their writing. The daily writing periods provided the opportunity for practice. The digits and letters directly before the students supplied the accepted form. Thus eight years of looking and doing were instrumental in developing good penmanship among the majority of the students in the Little White Schoolhouse.

During World War I years colored chalk and blackboard stencils came on the scene. The teacher tapped a chalk-filled eraser on a paper stencil held snugly against the blackboard and presto—borders or scenes appeared as if by magic. There were witches and pumpkins for Hallowe'en, a chimney and Santa Claus for Christmas, doves and hearts for St. Valentine's Day, baby chicks and lilies for Easter, and flags for Victoria Day. No one ever considered it a chore to fill in the dotted outlines with colored chalk. One felt proud to be a part of this ever-changing panorama of festivities and scenes. Students courted the favor of the teacher for the privilege of doing next month's stencil. It was for this reason that the seasons or holidays did not sneak-up-on-a-person as they do today. Nor did they suddenly burst with all their glory leaving everyone wilted, unprepared, and exasperated. Instead, each event became a feeling, an anticipation and finally something to be shared and enjoyed.

"Up-at-the-blackboard" was a favorite spot during winter recesses and noon hours. The children could play such intelligent competitive games as hang-the-man, tic-tac-toe, x's and o's, or if they were in no mood to engage in thinking games they could "just doodle." The custom of everyone using the blackboard any time they desired made life uncertain for blackboard exercises. They could be erased in a split second. Teachers were forced to protect them by writing the terse command. "Do not erase!" by the required transcription. Grade ones could not read. Which exercise or work did the teacher mean? There was no embarrassment to a child quite equal to that of discovering that he had erased some of the work that the teacher still required.

Teachers wrote questions for an examination on the blackboard the evening before or early in the morning before the students arrived at school. These were kept screened from prying eyes until the time set for the test by hanging a map over them. However, a word or two always peered enticingly from just beyond the boundaries of the map. Consternation reigned supreme among the students. Guessing was the order of the day but the teacher met each conjecture with the same knowing smile.

The examination hour arrives. The map goes up. Once again the futility of second-guessing the examiner is proved.

Students with the best penmanship or artistic ability were recognized. They transcribed material or drew pictures on the blackboard for the teacher. The procedure not only saved the busy teacher precious time but also provided some students with a psychological boost. They were being recognized publicly for their ability to write or draw well. The rural schools studied each learning situation intensively in order to provide opportunities for their students to succeed and then made certain that the achievement received some form of public recognition.

The duty of cleaning blackboards and brushes was assigned by the teacher early in September. Who wanted to clean the blackboards? Up went the hands of youngsters eager to please. Who would like to clean the brushes? A few more waving hands were raised. What if there was a dead silence and no arms were elevated? Only a sign that the volunteer system of doing chores had been momentarily suspended or that the teacher was not liked. Nevertheless the teacher drew up a schedule of chores and held the students responsible for doing them, voluntarily or under duress.

At times the spotless blackboards were a delight to behold, while at other times it was questionable whether they had been cleaned at all. There was a knack to this business of cleaning blackboards and brushes. Some students acquired the skill very early in their school careers. Others never did, or never wanted to. A few who were pressed into service complained, at least to each other, that since the teacher had dirtied the blackboards and brushes, it was only right that she should clean them herself. No one could clean the blackboards better than the senior girls. Even an inexperienced observer could tell that masters had been at work. The blackboards, really black for the first time, sparkled like a mirror. The last vestige of chalk had been flicked from the chalk ledge while the brushes, glowing with a new-found cleanliness, were arranged neatly thereon with their red, white and blue felts facing out. It was almost a sacrilege for anyone to dirty the blackboard and erasers again.

No teacher will ever forget the ghastly appearance of some grade one child after his initial attempt at cleaning brushes. In his wild enthusiasm he tapped the brushes so vigorously that a cloud of chalk dust enveloped him. Eventually it settled on every part of his clothing and on his hands and face. School could be fun! Besides, he was helping the teacher. He was important. If his movements had not been so vigorous an onlooker could have imagined that a marble statue of "The Little Worker" had been erected beside the school. It would have been far easier to have cleaned the brushes in the first instance than to remove the chalk dust now deeply entrenched in the fibres of his clothing. The schoolhouses withstood the banging of the brushes against their sides very well. If they had been painted any other color but white the telltale brush marks would have certainly detracted from their aesthetic appearance.

Blackboard equipment consisted of a yardstick and a pointer. These not only served their intended purpose but when the occasion arose could be used as instruments of correction as well. Many a rap across the knuckles or the shoulders brought students in line smartly. Sometimes this was harder on the equipment than on the child. The wooden stick often shattered dramatically at time of impact, the pieces sailing through the air to all parts of the room. The teachers were not altogether responsible for all the broken linear objects. The students contributed their share by engaging in clandestine duels using rulers or pointers as weapons. Now and then a student made a rational observation. An abbreviated rule or pointer in the hands of a teacher only inflicted a mediocre blow. What to do? Accidents happened sometimes. Expectant characters participated in activities that contributed to the shortening process.

Every rural school boasted a few wall-maps and a globe. The countries and the capitals of the world remained on a more-or-less permanent basis in those days so a map purchased in 1920 was still as good as new in 1932. The Neilson Chocolate Company found a novel way of advertising their products to the children. They issued, free of charge, lithographed wall-maps to all schools that were willing to use them. Schools by the hundreds availed themselves of the opportunity. In many places they were the only maps owned by the school. What effect did this advertising have on the sale of Neilson Chocolates? Not many know. But it is certain that thousands of school children learned their first geography from the Neilson maps. Thirty years have gone by since these free maps were distributed. Yet it is not uncommon to find them in some classrooms today.

Trustees knew a bargain when they purchased a complete set of wall-maps. The compact case with the maps mounted on roller-springs on the inside was installed just above the front blackboard. The teacher was fortunate indeed! The world was at her finger tips. All she had to do was to pull down the required map. The rolling down was the simple operation. The rolling back necessitated some technical skill. Sometimes the map snapped back into position with such a thunderous crash that it startled everyone in the room, not to mention the barrage of dust it let loose or the fact that the map and roller had parted company. At other times it produced a provocative bulge and refused to roll. The experts said it was all a matter of spring tension in the rollers. Many a teacher gave up the task of outwitting a fickle spring that operated normally one moment and rebelled the next. Years passed. The maps found new resting places. Corners, blackboard ledges, tops of cupboards and cloakrooms were the favorite spots. A few reposed in the coalshed or the cellar. The map-case in the meantime remained in its original place yawning forth its emptiness to an unresponsive classroom. Why was it never taken down? No one wanted to acknowledge defeat.

Some good sprang from the map rollers. Many female teachers felt that it was beyond their technical knowledge and skill to bother with mechanical things. They asked for help. If she was young and pretty assistance came from many quarters. Eventually the map roller was running smoothly and the teacher was going steady with some local swain. It is a matter of conjecture whether any of these "roller-spring romances" culminated in a marriage. But the exploits associated with the map-rollers will prompt more than one person to reminisce about the days of The Little White Schoolhouse.

Globes in the rural school seemed to be accident prone. The inquisitive fingers of students inevitably made inroads in the earth's crust. They just had to discover what was on the inside. The mice relished the glue that the manufacturer employed in fabricating the globe. Whether the revolving globe was mounted or not made no difference to them. They still managed to crawl to the extremities of the North Pole. A new sparkling globe could exhibit a number of neatly chewed fissures in its surface overnight. If left in the same place for a few more days the teacher was bound to discover a family of pink baby mice taking up residence on the inside. The globe also assumed the role of a piece of sports equipment in the interval between the arrival of the first pupil and the eventual appearance of the teacher. No globe could withstand the combined onslaught of mice, children and athletes, and hope to survive. It didn't. School boards complained bitterly. They believed that one globe should serve the school for the duration.

A practical solution to the problem became apparent when the suspended globe was introduced. A system of ropes and pulleys enabled the teacher to hoist the earth aloft almost up to the ceiling. Now it was safe from all destructive forces. Not quite! The pupils occasionally launched missiles that scarred the lower part of the globe while the flies completed the job of stippling it from above. Notwithstanding all this the globe served its purpose admirably.

People looking into an empty rural schoolhouse today often wonder about the presence of a rusty pulley and a few pieces of cord dangling from the ceiling but these are mute reminders of geography lessons of another era.

Drinking facilities in the early rural schools were inadequate or even non-existent. A galvanized tin-pail and a dipper served adequately for many years until the demand for more sanitation produced a covered porcelain crock with a push-button tap at the bottom. This in turn was superseded by a fountain-type of drinking container. A catch-bucket placed beside the pail or under the latter types of dispensers took care of any waste water. A few schools never went beyond the pail-and-dipper stage but generally the majority adopted the earthenware crock with the tap outlet dispenser. Not many rural schools ever invested in the fountain as it was expensive and wasted too much precious water.

The school board of Stewartfield S.D. 4164 (Stewartfield, Alta.) ordered one of these costly drinking fountains but it never arrived. All the freight had to be hauled from the C.N.R. siding at Cherhill and as there was no agent there the trustees received very little satisfaction from their complaints about not receiving the modern water dispenser. Years later the remains of the fountain were discovered quite by accident in a farmer's yard near Cherhill. He had been using it as a still.

At the beginning of the year each student was required to bring an individual drinking cup from home. These could be filled from the dipper or tap under sanitary conditions whenever the youngster wanted a drink. But as the year wore on the children found it more convenient to use any drinking container that was handy rather than walk a few steps to get their own. The tin or porcelain cup was stored in the desk of the individual student and frequently tumbled to the floor with such a clatter that it often disrupted the class that was reciting at the time. As these cups were never washed with hot water and soap the original sanitary purpose was defeated. For the most part they remained in the desks and gathered dust, a commodity of which the rural school was never short. The interior of the pail or crock, nevertheless, received its weekly swish of the wash-cloth. In addition the drinking water left in the dispenser at the end of the day was emptied into another container to become the wash water for the morrow and as a result it was regularly rinsed in the process.

Winter increased the vigilance that had to be exercised in safeguarding the drinking facilities. If the water remaining in the crock at the end of the day was not emptied it froze during the night and cracked the earthen-ware. Many a teacher or school caretaker would wake up with a start some cold night and wonder if they had emptied the fragile container. It was with a sense of relief that they viewed the object of their concern the next morning if it was still intact. Sometimes the worst did happen! Then the reliable water-pail was reinstated. It never cracked under the most adverse of weather conditions.

There was one thing about taking a drink from a dipper—it offered many moments of amusement and relaxation. The dipper could be floated on the surface of the water in the pail with the finesse of a sailboat. Nothing was so exasperating as to watch the dipper take on water and with a final gurgle, sink gently to the bottom of the pail. It required skilful fishing to recover the ladle without wetting the hands.

Then there was no sound quite like that produced by the dipper as it clanked along the corrugated bottom of the pail to recoup the last few drops of water. The teacher also heard it and this was her signal to appoint some youngster to get a fresh supply.

Opportunities for fun at the drinking fountain were many. The water remaining in the dipper after a drink could be swished suddenly into the face of an inquisitive bystander or thrown with a flourish over many innocent victims. The long handle made it easy to thump an unsuspecting classmate over the head or across the seat with the bowl of the dipper. The blow didn't hurt but the accompanying hollow sound was enough to lower anybody's dignity.

One of the most serious problems confronting rural school boards was that of obtaining a satisfactory water-supply. Most districts could not afford to drill a well, the only type that was sanitary, so they did the second best thing and dug or bored one. Such wells contained too much water and became receptacles for sticks, filthy surface water and a multi-tude of small animals and insects. When the board decided on a particular spot in the schoolyard there was no assurance that they would find an ample supply of suitable water. It was always a hit-and-miss proposition.

The trustees of the Cameron S.D. 406 (Minnedosa, Man.) put their faith in a divining rod in 1886 when they tried to locate a likely place in the schoolyard where water could be found. The divining rod was a forked willow twig and when the ends were grasped in each hand by a gifted person who walked slowly about in the schoolgrounds the butt end turned downward against the human grasp to where the water was located. The school board appeared to be in luck for the favorable spot lay quite near the northwest corner of the school building. So with shovels, a bucket and a windlass, the men began to dig. At first up came a mixture of loam and black soil which gradually changed to a greyish material. The signs were not encouraging. Had the divining rod lied? This became more apparent when, after more digging, blue clay, which is impervious to water, began to show. Dry holes were not uncommon in the district and this was another. It had to be filled in.

Where should they try next? Near the east side of the school rose a knob-like elevation. One trustee liked the location and reasoned that since failure had resulted from what was judged a likely spot why not try this one without the benefit of the divining rod. He won his point. So moving their gear to the new spot they commenced work again and were down scarcely ten feet when they struck gravel. That was a good sign. Within another ten feet water began to show and a few minutes later the man below was sloshing around in his gumboots. It was good water too! When it had finally settled it came up clear and ice-cold. To many in the Cameron District who in dry months had to resort to seepage water from a well dug near the edge of a slough it was indeed a blessing. From that day no one at Cameron ever spoke about divining rods except by way of a joke. The well it didn't divine is still there and to thirsty students and any travellers who might pass that way the creaking, discordant pump never fails.

Many school districts were most unfortunate in their attempts to bore suitable wells. After trying two or three times they still ended up with dry holes or, if they reached water, it proved to be too alkaline or unsuitable for some other reason. A dozen wells were drilled in the Notre Dame S.D. (Aneroid, Sask.) and the only usable one was located a mile from the school. One well in particular must have contained water with very unusual properties. When the pigs drank it they all became extremely sick and when it was given to chickens their combs turned black. No further experiments were attempted and the school board, fearful that some of the children might drink it, had the well filled in immediately.

Under such dire circumstances a number of school boards, the Cambachie S.D. 2264 (Moose Jaw, Sask.) among them, constructed a cistern just inside the front of the school. It ordinarily had a capacity of fourteen barrels and was kept replenished with good drinking water by having it hauled by tank from any reliable source within or outside of the district. These cisterns were covered with a trapdoor and surmounted by a pump to bring the water to the surface. Storing the water in such an enclosed reservoir was no assurance that it remained pure. It became stagnant and since trapdoors aroused the curiosity of the young fry, it was not surprising to find the odd grasshopper or mouse floating in the water in the hitherto impervious cistern.

Once a successful well was dug or bored the sides were cribbed with heavy lumber and a protective cover built over the top. There were two ways of bringing up the water. The cheapest and most expedient method was to lower a pail on the end of a rope into the well, tilt the bucket to fill it with water and then haul up the load by pulling on the rope hand-over-hand like a sailor. Other trustees, more mechanically-minded, suspended a pulley from a single rigging constructed over the head of the shaft or they built a windlass. These devices enabled even the youngest child to raise a pail of water from the bottom of the well.

The rope-bucket method of drawing water created no difficulties during the summer but in winter the well was a nightmare. Ice gradually built up about the well until by the end of December a virtual mound of it resulted. The rope became so stiff with ice that it could hardly be handled and would not run through the pulley. The boy whose duty it was to get the bucket of water morning and noon would let the pail down hand over hand. To bring it up he had to lean perilously over the open well, balance on the icy knoll, and then quickly flip the dripping pail over the well mouth to safety. Under such circumstances accidents were bound to happen and two districts at least reported cases where young boys lost their lives while attempting to get drinking water for the school.

The well had an attraction all of its own that very few youngsters could resist. Every recess and noon hour inevitably found the children having an exciting but damp time about the pump. Usually there was a tin-cup chained to it and the boys and girls took delight in filling the battered mug to overflowing every time they had a drink, which was often. As a result most of the water that gushed from the spout drained back into the well along with a generous supply of surface impurities. The children in the Moose Hill School even found another use for the well rope. They used it for skipping. When they saw the teacher getting ready to call school they quickly tied the rope to the pail again so all could get a drink of nice cold refreshing water before going back to their classes.

In time each district that had an open well boarded it over and installed a pump. The wooden pump which was first introduced in most of the sylvan areas at the turn of the century rapidly gave way to its steel counterpart. School pumps were never noted for their efficiency so priming them almost became a daily chore. In fact some wit made the observation

Pupils of School Section No. 15,
Clarence Township, Hammond, Ontario, gather around the school pump
at recess.

that, "It always took water to beget water". This operation wasn't too
demanding during the summer season for the small amount of water
needed could be obtained from a nearby slough, the slop bucket or a
mud puddle. Stories have been told about some schools on the prairies
where the shortage of water was so acute that urine was used to prime
the pump. Such an act may appear to border on the ridiculous but it
certainly proved to be practical. The advent of cold weather added
considerably to the difficulties of using the pump. It now had to be
primed with boiling water for, if not, the water froze before reaching far
enough down to be effective. To obtain the priming water, snow was
melted. The students also had to remember to drain the pump after each
use otherwise it froze solid. When such a calamity occurred the pump
remained useless for the rest of the winter unless some benefactor undertook the unpleasant task of thawing it out.

The cribbing and the plank covering did not get the attention they
should have received from the school board. Once neglected, the rotting
wood imparted an unpleasant taste to the water. The occasional mouse
or gopher that tumbled into the well through the breaks in the siding did
even less for the water. As the cover became loose and worn the children
took advantage of the opportunity to drop things down the well. The
delayed-action splashes were so mystifying that the smaller children were

encouraged to try again. There was always the danger that one of these tots might remove a rotten plank or two and tumble into the well. More than one rural teacher has had nightmares after realizing the potential dangers that prevailed while the children were playing so happily about the old school pump.

In September the first job was to pump out the well and remove all foreign objects that had accumulated. This in some mysterious fashion made the water fit for human consumption for another year. It was only when copious quantities of water were pumped from a well that fresh water flowed in. The rural school was not a large user so in the main the water became stagnant and tainted with an organic flavor. In addition the majority of the wells yielded hard water. This not only stained every container in which it was poured but acted as a purgative for those who drank too much.

Pleasant Plains S.D. 1533 (High River, Alta.) was one rural school that did not have to face up to the problems that attended the scarcity of water. If anything they had too much. In 1906 the school board hired the Snyder-Bricker outfit to drill a well in the schoolyard. The results could best be described as stupendous. After going down 150 feet the drill struck such an excellent flow of water that it gushed out like a geyser at 300 gallons per minute. The land surrounding the school was soon inundated and the children wore rubbers to get in and out of the building and the schoolyard. For some reason or other no casing was used to shore the inside of the well and the resulting cave-ins formed a huge abyss around the head of the well. The farmers of the district hauled some thirty loads of stone to fill this almost bottomless pit.

At first a wooden trough was built to carry away the water from the schoolyard and then a pipe was inserted into the gusher to permit the children to get their drinking water without too much difficulty. In due course a small building was erected over the spot to protect the students and any wandering livestock. The youngsters enjoyed the sparkling ice-cold water that the well supplied during the hot summer days but also the large skating surface that it provided during the winter when it spread over the pasture areas and froze solid.

It is said that this well in the Pleasant Plain District is still flowing today just as energetically as it did the first day it was brought in over half a century ago.

In the Round Plain S.D. 30 (Wishart, Sask.) drinking water was most scarce and sometimes sheer desperation forced the children to dip a tin cup into a nearby slough. Then they strained the contents through a corner of an apron, a handkerchief or a sun-bonnet tail before quenching their thirst.

Drinking water for the teacherage and the Aurora S.D. 1050 (Winnipeg, Man.) was secured from a well some fifty feet from the school. The supply was cold, pure and received regular government inspection to keep it that way. There was one period when it may have fallen below the standard. The Thirties were not only known for dirt and drought, they also had grasshoppers. Somehow, despite all attempts to get rid of them, the pesky insects kept getting into the school well. The pioneer blood which settled the land couldn't have all disappeared by that time for someone decided that a few "hoppers" in the drinking water wasn't an insurmountable problem. Consequently the children found the pump equipped one day with a small white cotton bag. The purpose of the bag was to strain out the extraneous items in the water. In this regard it was successful and the water which came from the spout and percolated through the cotton bag filled the drinking pail with cool and clear water. When the bag became a bit bulky it was removed and the sodden mass of drowned grasshoppers was dumped to one side. Strangely enough, it didn't bother the youngsters at all.

Gertrude, who first attended the Elnora S.D. (Elnora, Alta.) in 1911, still remembers the somewhat peculiar taste of the school's drinking water.

> "The drinking water was from a rusty pump in the schoolyard. The old granite mug was chipped and needed washing. The water itself tasted of rust, iron, dead gophers and mice."

Every youngster in the Floral S.D. 344 (Saskatoon, Sask.) enjoyed the cold sparkling water from the school well until one day the partly decomposed body of a gopher was brought to the surface. It must have been in the well for several months. The discovery was so repulsive that everyone refused to take another drink. The students preferred to take turns carrying water half a mile from the closest farm than to have anything further to do with the clear but supposedly contaminated school well.

According to Dorothy, the students of Old Parkside S.D. 1138 (Parkside Sask.) were fortunate to escape typhoid fever.

> "Our drinking water was taken from an open well down which a pail was lowered in summer. During the winters we mostly ate snow or icicles off the porch. There was no set pattern for carrying water. Any boy not lucky enough to escape in time was delegated to take another with him and get a pail of water. This no doubt was insurance against his falling in and having no one to report the matter. On his return to school with the water, any thirsty child could take his turn with the one cup that served the forty-eight children. Later another well was dug and a pump installed."

The students may not have been squeamish about the type of water they drank, but the teachers were. When Lennie Lewis, the teacher in the Hall's Prairie S.D. (Langley, B.C.) heard that a dead cow had been found in the Campbell River a couple of miles upstream she refused to drink any of the school water as it was taken from this particular stream. Every morning she used to bring a small keg of spring water from her home in Langley five miles away. Miss Lewis kept up the practice for the entire eight years that she taught in the Hall's Prairie School.

The apparent abhorrence with which most teachers viewed polluted water prompted some of the pupils to try to press this weakness to their advantage. One year in the Jura S.D. (Princeton, B.C.) some mice actually did drown in the well, which was a cistern sunk in a spring across the road from the school. Thereafter the boys tried out each new teacher by complaining that a mouse had drowned in the well. They vehemently protested that the water was unfit for drinking and asked how the students could continue attending school without suitable water. Of course the more shocked and unnerved the teacher became at this terrifying revelation the better the boys liked it. However, most of the teachers took it rather calmly much to the boys' disappointment.

School children in those days did not stand for any ceremony from their own classmates. A child that exhibited any signs of queasiness while using a common dipper or refusing to drink water from a particular source was generally ostracized in one way or other. A girl who attended the Union Point S.D. 53 (south of Winnipeg on Number 75 Highway) in 1900 received just such treatment. She was in the habit of drinking from the common cup by placing her mouth in the region above the handle and thus earned the nickname of "Snooty". The name stuck for years even after she was married and had children of her own attending school.

Many schools did not possess a well of any description. As this was particularly true during homestead days each child was required to bring sufficient water in a bottle or can to meet his individual requirements. Throughout the winter they quenched their thirst by eating snow or icicles off the school roof or barn. Later it became the common practice for school boards to hire some responsible youngster to haul a fresh supply of drinking water daily. So the designated juvenile filled a cream can or a large honey pail with water from his father's well or spring and brought it in a buckboard when he came to school. Girls often undertook the job. They were probably even more conscientious than the boys in carrying out their duties. These water haulers became experts in estimating the amount of water the children would drink on any particular day.

In the winter the job of chopping the ice that formed over the springs or thawing out pumps added to the difficulties of supplying drinking water. A delicate crust of ice often started to form over the surface of the water by the time it was delivered to the school. There was one consolation. Regardless of thirst it never took much of the cold water to satisfy the boys and girls.

If a good spring, well or stream existed near the school the students assumed the task of carrying water. There was no lack of volunteers when the weather was fine for it meant an escape from the humdrum routine of the classroom. But in winter only the intrepid were equal to the task.

"Going for water" was an experience. A pail was the method and two pupils were the means. The trip always took more time than those waiting for the water thought it should. There were rabbits and gophers to chase, sunshine to enjoy, stones to throw, birds to hear and yes—water to get. On the return journey the two students grasped the curved handle of the water-pail from either side and carried it between them. Teamwork was essential. Jostling spilled the precious liquid. It not only splashed on the ground but all over the porters as well, trickling down their legs and into their shoes, or between their toes if they were barefooted. Changing sides enabled the youngsters to rest their tired arms and to hasten the drying of the wet clothes on that part of the body.

But in spite of all these difficulties the much-abused pail and what was left of the water finally was delivered to the school and placed in its rightful spot on the shelf in the corner. The rest of the students were quick to criticize. The water was too warm. There was dust on it. How did the blades of grass get in the water? The best part had been spilled. But they drank the water just the same. It was cool and fresh. They drank eagerly and noisily from their tin cups or the dipper. One could hear the short punctuated intakes of air as each child impatiently quenched his thirst. All too soon the water became warm and torpid. The children still drank it, although now they could not refrain from referring to its sole redeeming quality: "At least it's still wet!"

Sometimes on a hot summer's day the youngsters became so thirsty that even the insides of their mouths felt dry-as-dust. While they impatiently watched for the full water-bucket to appear they played games in keeping with their mood. A favorite stunt was to see who could spit under such arid conditions. Very few ever succeeded but they never gave up trying.

Washing facilities were simple. An enamel or tin basin was provided along with a roller towel. The students assumed the responsibility for taking the towel home for laundering. A few families were not as co-operative as they might have been or else confusion arose as to whose turn it was for at times the common towel remained unchanged for days. This often stretched into weeks. Many children dried their hands on handkerchiefs. This was possible. The so-called bandanna was large and its red or blue color did not show the dirt. Failing a handkerchief, the youngster rubbed wet hands back and forth over the sides of shirt, pinafore, or dress. It was a common sight to see a boy entering the

Relics of the past — well, pump and outhouse — still remain in the yard of the Silver Valley School (Watts, Alta.) as mute evidence of school days that are no more.

classroom giving his wet hands one last brush against the clothing on the small of his back.

The soap was not the soft, perfumed and tinted variety of today. A yellow bar of stalwart laundry soap by the trade name of Fels Naphtha or Sunlight served the purpose instead. The child's face and hands glowed with a healthy rosy tint after washing with it. He also felt a hot prickling sensation where the soap had touched his skin. The irritation was produced by the chemicals that formed the ingredients of the soap, notably lye. A pleasant, clean smell of naphtha permeated the corner where the wash basin was located. It reminded one of wash day at home. More than one pail of drinking water had to be thrown out as a result of the community bar of soap accidentally or otherwise slipping into it.

The combination of hard water and hard soap yielded very little lather. Ordinarily a curdy precipitate, not unlike grease, was the net result. As a consequence the inside of every school washbasin was etched by myriads of darkly colored whorls of sediment. Very few urban visitors to a rural school will ever forget the feeling of revulsion that overwhelmed them as they merely contemplated the possibility of washing their hands in such a grubby basin. A scientific explanation for the unkempt appearance of the bowl never once entered their minds.

A mirror occupied a place on the wall beside the towel. Not many girls and still fewer boys used it. In most cases it was soo small—eight-by-twelve inches—that it became necessary to advance to within a nose-length for a person to see himself. At that only the subject's face was visible. It required many contortions on his part to obtain a mosaic pattern of his complete head. This action before the mirror was a certain sign that one had become egotistical. The surface often became so bespattered with soapy water that it even failed to reflect a partial image. A few were so badly marred by cracks that they resembled jig-saw puzzles. The children of small stature found it difficult to reach the mirror. It was of no use to them without a stool or chair.

In spite of all these deficiencies the mirror was popular during dances and other social affairs held in the schoolhouse. It also glittered bright and clear during the Christmas concert and when the inspector made his annual visit to the school. Useful or not, the mirror was a part of the anteroom setting.

The unsanitary arrangements of a common washbasin, a common towel and a common drinking cup should have spread infectious diseases like wildfire throughout the school. Such was not the case. A siege of measles or colds might develop but no serious epidemic. The explanations that rural children immunized themselves or that they were tougher than the germs are mere conjectures.

The following accounts by Hilda, who used to teach at Georges S.D. 1386 (Qu'Appelle Valley, Sask.); Miss Mary Dickie, a former teacher at No. 7 Greenock (Pinkerton, Ont.); and Kay, who attended the Alpha S.D. (Hanna, Alta.) in the Twenties, give a good indication that communicable diseases could become quite severe in a rural school.

"In this school some of the children had had cases of impetigo. The health officer came out to the school and said that seeing the parents were not trying to effect a cure the only way was for the teacher to doctor them at school. This I did by putting on sweet oil to soften the scabs and then applying antiseptic ointment. I secured good results for the first half-year but after the summer holidays they came back as bad as ever. The parents of the children who had not contracted the disease put in a complaint saying that they did not consider the teacher should have to do this type of work. But in the meantime I got the disease myself and lost two weeks school over it."

"One time I noticed that my pupils had many sores on their hands. I secured some phenol and had each child wash his hands, his desk, his slate and anything else he used regularly in a solution of this disinfectant. The boys said I had made them wash in "sheep dip" but their lesions soon disappeared."

"Epidemics were common and caused our school to close on two occasions that I remember. Once during the spring break-up the Bull Pound flat was flooded and resulted in spreading typhoid fever throughout the district, and secondly, when cholera-infantum swept through the Russian-German homes south of the school and wiped out many families. This was the first introduction to death for many of my pupils, as they never saw their classmates again."

There may have been a time when the only use made of the cream can was the original and intended one—that of conveying cream from the farm to the creamery. But the rural schools changed all that. Many had no wells on the premises while others although they had wells could not use them because the water for one reason or another was unfit for human consumption, so at varying intervals the cream can came to school in the guise of a water container. The first few years it arrived in a school buggy, democrat, wagon or Bennett buggy, and in later years in the back of a car or a pick-up truck.

The strange feature about cream cans was that once they assumed their new role they remained in the custody of the school officials. No one ever seemed to miss them. They rusted away for years in their accustomed spot in the school anteroom. It wasn't until the rural school closed that some farmer went back to pick up his cream can from the school porch for the last time. He probably returned it to its original use if it had not been damaged or worn too much for the purpose.

If the school had a teacherage a second cream can eventually made its appearance. It just took time. The quickest way for a teacher to assure herself of a cream can was to sponsor a community party in the school and someone always left one behind.

Most country teachers have labored under the tyranny of the cream can at one time or another in their careers. In cold weather she had to lug the can into the teacherage near the stove, or to a shady side of her shack if the day was hot. Some of the cream cans were of gigantic proportions and had been designed to be handled by two men, not by one little female teacher.

Then there was always the fun, if you could call it that, of removing the lid. No doubt a creamery was equipped with a tool for this express purpose but no school board ever thought of providing one for their teacher. Any attempt to wrestle or pull the lid off by brute strength always ended in victory for the cream can. Heavy blows with a large stick of firewood helped to loosen the stubborn lid a trifle. While prying with a poker or stove lifter completed the job.

Another difficulty was that the amount of water required by the school or the teacher seldom corresponded with that provided. Some mornings the teacher's dipper struck the bottom of the can with an ominous hollow sound that portended little coffee that day. Of course she could go over to the school and fill her kettle from cream can number one if she had no qualms about depriving the students of their drinking water or didn't mind using water that had been lashed about by a variety of cups and many human hands. Some school-ma'ams soon discovered that the only way to lick the recurring problem of an inadequate or unsuitable water supply was to acquire a local boy friend who owned a truck or car—and an extra cream can.

Irksome as the rule of the cream can was, without it conditions were even worse. Janet once rashly declared that she hoped never to see a cream can again. The next year she taught at a rural school which boasted a well so she thought her servitude to a cream can was at an end. The water that came from this particular well resembled spoiled tomato juice in appearance and made tea and coffee that tasted the same—both like vitriol. However the young lady was assured by the local authorities that the water had been tested as pure. She ultimately began to wish for the return of the cream can she had once despised.

Friday night a surprise appeared in the form of a cream can full of imported water to make coffee for a community gathering that evidently didn't care for "nice pure water". Janet didn't rest until a cream can was permanently placed in her teacherage. She took back every disparaging remark she had made about cream cans.

Catherine, another teacher of the cream-can schooldays, eulogized it in these words, "Dear old cream can, you frayed our fingernails and our tempers; but we could never do without you."

A singular feature of the early rural school was the small platform that monopolized about one-third of the space at the front of the classroom. It was possibly no more than four feet by nine feet and about eight inches high yet it served a definite educational purpose.

Classes in the rural schools were brought to the front of the room for their recitation periods and the platforms provided a convenient place for holding these lessons. When the pupils recited, read or engaged in other educational activities from these miniature stages they had a feeling that they were performing in public before a real audience—the rest of the students and teacher. A reading given at the side of a desk was an artificial situation and did not capture the imagination of the children as much.

The position of the teacher on the platform had a favorable psychological effect on the learning situation. She was now both physically and mentally on a higher level than the boys and girls she was teaching. Instead of saying, "Step into my office!" to a student as is done today it was "Come up to the front!" More than one rural teacher was glad of the presence of the dais when it became necessary to admonish or strap a big pupil. The few inches that were added to the teacher's stature were of inestimable value. Offices, cloakrooms, staff rooms and special washrooms insure some privacy for the modern teacher but in the days of the Little White Schoolhouse the "platform" was her only private domain. Rural students were primarily honest, so if a teacher left anything of value or importance in or about her desk it was left untouched. In fact it would have been very strange indeed in those homestead days to find a lock and key anywhere. Property was respected and there were few cases of pilfering.

Public gatherings of any sort always made good use of the platform in the school. The chairman and the secretary-treasurer took their rightful places up on the stage and this arrangement provided the necessary physical separation and evidence of leadership so essential to the proper conduct of a meeting. Entertainers of all sorts found the platform a good vantage point from which to amuse their audiences. This was especially true with dance orchestras, quadrille callers, public speakers, singers and actors. The rural school platform proved to be a useful innovation.

Today infinite care is taken to insure that every student is provided with a certain minimum standard of illumination at his desk or the blackboard. If the windows permit too much sunlight to enter, blinds are installed to reduce the glare. Then when the blinds are drawn it is necessary to switch on the electric lights to restore the intensity of the light on the reading or writing surface. A coninuous battle is being waged to maintain a certain degree of luminescence. Paradoxically there was very little concern about the lighting in the Little White Schoolhouse as long as the official regulation, "the total area of window glass must be equal to at least one-fifth of the floor space" was observed superficially. Originally schools were constructed with windows on both sides and it took physiologists and educators many years to convince the rural school boards of the harmful effects of cross-lighting on the eyes of the children. It was considered more important for each settler, no matter in what direction he lived from the school, to see the lights "go on" in the school when a meeting or a social gathering was being held than to consider ophthalmological conditions. There were no surveyed road-allowances, fences or other landmarks by which night travellers might steer their course. The school light blinking in the windows was a most welcome sight to the settlers who were out travelling after dark. No doubt other homesteaders, lonely and isolated, were cheered by merely seeing the lights of the school in the distance.

During the winter school started at nine-thirty in the morning rather than the usual nine o'clock. This later opening gave the caretaker an extra half-hour in which to warm the school in the coldest months of the year and saved the school board the extra fuss and expense of providing some form of artificial lighting. Thus it was indeed difficult to find a rural school that could boast of any kind of lamp as part of its regular equipment. If the school had to be used for a public gathering after nightfall farmers living near the school brought their own lamps or used the ordinary barn lantern to provide the necessary illumination.

At the dawn of the Little White Schoolhouse era the coal-oil lamps were in common use. They did not provide a very bright light but they were reliable and quite simple to operate. As long as the wick holder was kept clean, the glass chimney polished, the bowl filled with kerosene and the wick trimmed and adjusted they rendered good service. These lamps had the habit of smoking when placed in drafts so their use was rather limited in a public place such as a school. Some school boards put up metal brackets along the walls to support the kerosene lamps to their best advantage as well as keep them out of harm's way. It was so easy to accidentally upset a lamp or topple the glass chimney if it was left unattended on a table or desk.

More than one rural teacher had the habit of returning to school in the evening to finish putting her work on the blackboard by lamplight. Eventually it became a common sight in most rural schools to see a coal-oil lamp holding down a place of honor on top of the piano or organ. Of course some were safely put away in the cupboard and remained there until required. By that time the kerosene had mysteriously disappeared, the chimney broken and the lamp itself sprinkled with dead flies and covered with a thick layer of dust. No wonder people preferred to bring their own lamps rather than put their trust in the one kept at the school.

Although the common coal-oil lamp with its reflector attachment remained as the standard method of lighting rural schools on ordinary occasions the hurricane (Aladdin) or gasoline lamps took over on special evenings such as Christmas concerts or social gatherings. The source of illumination of the hurricane lamp was the chemically-treated cotton-mantles. These lamps were similar in structure to the present Coleman camp-lamp and burned a mixture of air and alcohol. Although this particular type projected a very bright light it had to be pumped up at least once an hour to replenish the air otherwise it spluttered and went out.

The gasoline mantle-lamp was the most efficient of all but very difficult and dangerous to operate. It burned a fuel composed of high-test gasoline and air under a pressure of some ten pounds per square inch. The lamp was lit and then suspended from a suitable place on the ceiling by means of a hook. Here it hissed and sputtered all evening out of harm's way, although sometimes a very tall person or someone carrying an object overhead forgot about its presence and knocked the blazing inferno to the floor. It took quick action and presence of mind to avert a fire if such an accident ever came to pass. Not infrequently the temperamental gasoline lamp died out completely midway through the Christmas concert or some such important event. So, while the lamp was being serviced, the program ground to a halt.

The greatest drawback to keeping a hurricane or gasoline lamp in the school was the mantles. The gleaming white protuberances attracted the curiosity of the children and unless the lamp was placed in an inaccessible spot the youngsters damaged the mantles by poking holes through them with their fingers or pencils. A sudden jar or a flying object also wrecked the lacy sheaths. It required time and care to replace the all-important Welsbach mantles not to mention the smoke-filled room that accompanied such activity.

It might seem strange but no sooner had the school been built and put into operation than the district made a concerted effort to procure an organ or a piano for it. The initiative for such an undertaking frequently stemmed from three sources. First, as the school began to assume more and more its function as a community centre, it was felt that a musical instrument of some sort should be placed there. An organ or piano increased the number and variety of activities that could be sponsored at the school. The building was often used for church and Sunday school so the people involved were very keen to secure a piano or organ to complement their religious services and make them more interesting. Then someone always suggested to the school board that the children should be getting a musical education now that they had a school.

Once the community set its mind on a piano or organ there was no turning back. No matter what group or what individuals engaged in a money-raising scheme for its purchase, everyone supported the idea. On September 20, 1912, a box social was sponsored in the Kirkwall S.D. 2463 (Oyen, Alta.) by the Sunday school for the purpose of getting funds to purchase an organ. They realized a sum of $40.50 and by October of that year a new Dougherty organ was in use at the school. Not all districts were as fortunate as Kirkwall and many had to settle for second-hand instruments while others were forced to borrow a piano or organ from someone in the area to meet their needs for special occasions.

It was one thing to have a piano or organ in the school and still another thing to use it. School boards always advertised for a teacher with some knowledge of music but not very often were they successful in securing one who actually played the instrument. If they did, everyone in the community awaited with keen anticipation the annual Christmas concert or some such event to hear the musically-trained boys and girls perform. In most cases rural schools lacked a teacher who could play the piano so unless a qualified member of the community assisted in training the students the piano or organ stood in the corner of the schoolroom, draped and silent. Mice took more than a passing interest in the unused organ for they gnawed holes in the bellows and built comfortable nests inside. The pianos were not as convenient hiding places as the organs but even here nests of shredded paper mysteriously appeared snuggled around the bases of the strings.

There was no scene more pathetic than to see someone who knew how to play a musical instrument come to the school to show off his ability. It required so much energy to pedal the organ to maintain any air pressure in the leaky reservoir that the musician became exhausted in a matter of minutes. The school piano usually had two or three keys that produced either the most heart-rending notes imaginable or remained so silent that even the least musical person noticed the disparity .

A teacher who was able to carry a note or who could read music well enough to play some standard selection like O Canada or the Maple Leaf Forever was considered a find. Music stirred a full gamut of emotions in the hearts of the isolated homesteaders as they thought of other places, other people, and the faded dreams of another day. Farmers travelled miles on horseback or by buggy, in all types of weather, to attend a program that included a musical number or two. Music certainly had charm for the early inhabitants of the West.

The children were no different. Everyone aspired to be a Beethoven or a Paderewski when the piano or organ was first placed in the school. Some of the boys or girls had never seen or heard a musical instrument in their lives before so they were enthralled by a performance. Many former rural students are still able to recall those exciting days although they occurred over fifty years ago.

Caroline Barnes of Moose Hill S.D. 2727 (Thorhild, Alta.) remembers her first school organ with affection.

"Eventually an old organ was bought and placed in the school. Such a joy it brought to us youngsters! On cold winter days during recess and noon hours that organ was never quiet. "Twenty Froggies" was learned by heart by anyone who cared to extend his or her knowledge that much. I'm sure the poor teachers were driven frantic.

"The up-keep of the organ fell to my father who had a superficial knowledge of the principle of it, and loved to tinker. Mother played for the services of course. But it was two or three years before a teacher came who could play for us.

"That year we learned several songs to our great joy. Also a class of us girls learned the Irish Washer Woman Jig to perform at our Christmas concert. The grade three class that year did a drill to organ music. Well do I remember the centre girl in the line, two inches taller than anyone else, with a shining face, manfully marking time and swinging her Christmas bell utterly opposite to everyone else. Poor Miss Menzies! She couldn't stop playing to direct Olga and yet I can still feel her chagrin. The applause was tremendous anyway."

The teacher in the Rough Meadow S.D. 2180 (Coronation, Alta.) reminisces in a different vein.

"We had a little old organ and although it was out of key and a few reeds broken, it served very well for our Christmas concerts and our daily singing."

Alongside the organ, and there years before it, was the school library housed in a large sectional bookcase or in a homemade cupboard. Not infrequently it took only a shelf or two to hold the twenty-five books that the school had. Some libraries were quite adequate and contained volumes that covered as completely as possible all the fields required, while others were very poor and contained only a few useful books. The district's attitude toward books in particular and education in general was reflected in the quality and extent of the school library. Perhaps it was the manner in which the books were used rather than the number of volumes that should have been the criterion in judging a rural school library.

There wasn't anything more plebian than a rural-school cloakroom. It turned out to be just the bare anteroom fitted with a couple of boards running parallel to each other about eighteen inches apart and nailed to the walls. These strips supported the three or four dozen bronzed coat hooks. Such a set-up provided a ready place for the students to hang their outdoor clothes. A similar array of hangers on the partition near the stove inside the classroom was reserved for cold-weather use. It must be remembered that in those days every boy and girl wore a hat and coat. The students also travelled such long distances to school that they came dressed to meet every eventuality in weather, so it was imperative that ample cloakroom space be provided for them. The standard procedure was to reserve the hooks on one side of the entrance for the girls and the other side for the boys. Wise teachers tagged each peg with the name of the student for whom it was intended and this prevented any selfish youngster from monopolizing several coat-hooks. The original bronzed clothes hooks did not last very long as they were snapped off one by one under the duress of gymnastic displays. Their places were taken by spikes driven deep into the wall. They were less aesthetic looking but certainly more serviceable.

No description of the interior of a rural school would be complete without some reference to the huge wall clock, the fire extinguisher, the pictures of the reigning monarchs, the flag and the Confederation plaque.

A large pendulum clock, in either an octagonal or hexagonal frame of varnished oak, occupied a prominent place on the front wall. Its strong and steady beat could be heard distinctly above all classroom noises. The tick-tock, tick-tock became particularly noticeable during examination or detention periods when the classroom was unusually quiet. At times like this it became a friendly sound. The grade one and two pupils learned to tell time from it, as for some reason or other their parents never bothered teaching them.

In later years these same pupils tended to become clock-watchers on some beautiful spring day when all nature called to them to come out and gather wild flowers, trap gophers or just run around in an ecstacy of being young and vibrant. The teacher wisèly draped a cloth over the face of the clock during such heady seasons.

Fire extinguishers were considered more of a novelty than an out-and-out protective device therefore very few school boards considered them essential. Three models found their way to the Little White Schoolhouse where they were fastened to the door frame nearest the stove. One type was an unusually long red tinny cylinder containing a brown powder, another was an eye-catching glass-sphere filled with a mysterious red, blue or green fluid, while the third was a bronzed tubular-container eight inches long and four inches in diameter with a plunger on one end and a nozzle on the other. Once the excitement of putting them up had subsided they remained in their allotted places for years getting very little attention but gathering a thick coat of dust. If a fire had occurred it is doubtful whether the aging chemicals would have retained enough of their potency to activate the extinguisher. R. G. Spokes, who attended the Aurora S.D. 1050 (Winnipeg, Man.) between 1932 and 1940, describes with some reservation the value of the fire extinguisher that protected his school.

> "Beside both the entry doors and the rear exit and fastened securely to the door-frame was our only fire-fighting equipment. It was a red metal tube about two feet long and two inches in diameter. I never saw one of these in use but the printed instructions exhorted the user to tear open the top of the tube and swing it vigorously at the base of the fire. I am sure that we were fortunate in never having to call on these fire-preventives of such dubious value."

In most schools the picture of the reigning British monarchs occupied a place of honor in the classroom. It could have been Queen Victoria, King Edward VII and Queen Alexandra, or King George V and Queen Mary. They appeared to gaze down on the pupils with dignified solemnity. Many a beginner's first impression of school had to do with these portraits. Helen, a grade one miss from Manitoba, described it in this way:

> "I used to wonder about the big picture of the old gentleman with whiskers who stared down at us. Later, I learned it was King George V in a naval uniform. To me, somehow, he stood for law and order. I was frightened

of him and remained so until about grade four. His picture could be also found in the front of our readers."

A flag was always prominently displayed on the wall inside and another one on the flagpole outside. They were Canadian flags—or so they were called. Every homesteader with children dreamed of the day when he would be able to look out from his farm and see nearby the completed Little White Schoolhouse with a Union Jack flying majestically above it. A flag was important. Patriotism was taught with a fervor unknown today. Every morning the students were required to stand and salute the flag as well as sing a national song or two.

Soon after 1927 each school began to display still another symbol of Canada's growth and development. It was the Confederation plaque issued to every classroom that year to commemorate the sixtieth anniversary of Canadian Confederation. This rectangular bronze plate, eight inches by sixteen inches, mounted in a wooden frame and bearing the imprint of the Canadian coat-of-arms and an appropriate epigraph, was not attractive. It was too dark and sombre in appearance to portray anything as joyful as the sixtieth anniversary of a country. It even had a tinny sound when dropped. Soon the plaque lost its rightful place at the top of the front blackboard and joined the broken desks and torn maps in the coalshed or basement.

An interesting corner of the Bryant S.D. 2533 (Bindloss, Alta.) showing a
draped organ, a lamp, Confederation Plaque, chimney cupboard, blackboard
stencils, ink-bottles, pupils ranging from grade one to grade ten and an eight-
grade timetable. There was a water "cooler" in the corner formed by the blackboard and the chimney cupboard right behind the serious lad with the striped
necktie and overalls.

8

THE RURAL STUDENTS

What can we do? Where can we go? We're bored to death with nothing to do. These are the common plaintive cries of today's children. Youngsters of the Little White Schoolhouse were never bored with life and no one ever complained of having nothing to do. They worked before going to school in the morning and again upon returning home in the late afternoon. It took more time to train a child to be useful on a farm than to train him to work. Farming took special skills and more judgment than were required for most other jobs. Plowing, milking, taking care of livestock, harvesting, harnessing and driving horses were not things that the father could tell a son or daughter how to do. They demanded the same type of attention, ability and practice as were required to succeed at any skill, whether it was playing hockey or extracting a tooth. The farm raised boys and girls who were self-reliant and capable. The children were partners in the farming enterprise and contributed a good deal to the farm effort. Such a life established a sense of values and responsibilities which made for success in any field of endeavor. School was no exception.

The hundred-and-one tasks that had to be done about the farm, although not always pleasant or easy, provided the boys and girls with numerous opportunities for discovery and the cultivation of new depths of feeling. There were time and solitude for meditation and self-evaluation. Many of the farm chores forced the youngsters to spend long periods of time by themselves. It might be a lonely wagon journey into town to deliver a load of wheat to the elevator or a short trip out to the pasture to water the stock or bring in the milk cows. The child would be alone the entire day if he was stooking, fencing, plowing, mowing or raking. No transistor radio could be turned on to drown out the need for reflection. The rural student had to live with himself.

The children learned to enjoy sounds. the cluck of wagon wheels and the jingle of trace-chains provided a musical accompaniment for an otherwise dull trip. The characteristically sharp rattle of the buggy wheels or the rhythmic beat of horse hoofs made travelling to and from school a daily adventure. The binder or the mowing machine produced a crisp whirr as the cutter knife shuttled back and forth in time with the clack-clack of the pitmen. The whistle of the steam engine used to break the quietness of the countryside and entice imaginary glimpses of the bigger and more interesting world of cities just beyond the horizon.

Not all farm melodies were supplied by machinery. The watering of livestock was always attended by the bawling of cattle, the staccato pounding of the pump, the intermittent splurge of water and the sipping, sucking sounds of animals quenching their thirst. There was something sinister during a cold winter's evening when the entire family gathered in the kitchen around a crackling fire in hearing the north wind shriek and wail about the corners of the farmhouse. The howl of the coyotes with their eerie choral responses gave rural children a feeling of uneasiness and loneliness as they snuggled a little deeper into their comfortable beds. No pupil will ever forget the exciting cries of the wild geese mingled sharply with the whirr of their wings as they passed overhead in the spring or the fall of the year. Not only were the birds many times more numerous than now but they flew lower. There may be songs more beautiful than those of the meadowlark but not to the prairie youngster. A single rhapsody always portrayed to him the majesty, the expanse as well as the friendliness of the prairies.

Emotional experiences attach themselves to sense experiences so not only sounds but even smells added zest to everyday living for the rural child. There wasn't anything associated with farm life which had not the distinctive aroma of a newly-cut or curing grain or hay crop. An indescribable sweetness and freshness seemed to permeate the entire atmosphere. The youngsters could not inhale enough of this heaven-sent ambrosia. Even in the depth of winter when the hay was thrown down from the loft to the appreciative cows and horses below the fragrance of harvest was still there. Any boy or girl who found it necessary to return to the stable on a winter's evening to make one final check of the livestock probably sensed the spirit of peace and contentment among the animals. The air in the barn would be permeated with a healthy warm aroma of livestock well cared for. The leather and the oil of the harness and the saddles always gave the barn a characteristically shoe-repair-shop smell both summer and winter. The dank penetrating smell of newly-plowed fields combined with the suffocating smoke of burning stubble fields and straw stacks used to delineate a typical evening on the farm during spring. The first rains of the season always brought forth a fragrance that was both refreshing and rejuvenating as if to bring back to life a world that had lost touch with summer. Thunderstorms and chinook winds also had a singular way of imparting a piquant odor to the atmosphere. Rural children learned to appreciate these multifarious scents of nature. The schoolhouse had its own distinctive odors. No teacher or child would likely forget the smell of varnish especially on hot summer days. Everything in the classroom seemed to be varnished, the floor, the walls of V-joint, the desks and the cupboards. This aroma coupled with chalk dust, floor dust and oil made what is often described as the typical "school smell", not unpleasant but impossible to resolve.

Just going to and from school was a fascinating experience for the young. If they walked rather than rode so much the better for then there was more to do, more to see, and more to hear. Generally those who rode to school dismounted upon catching up with their comrades and joined them in walking the rest of the way. The horse or horses also enjoyed the stroll for they wandered all over nibbling at tuffs of grass along the roadside. In the spring the sloughs filled and streams became swollen. Students waded, caught frogs, screened out tadpoles, rode a raft, or merely sailed paper boats. Occasionally they fished out the masses of green scum or jelly-like frog eggs and threw them at each other. There was always the duck's or snipe's nest to be investigated near the water's edge. Young gophers appeared for the first time and they made perfect targets for stone-throwing. There were moments of excitement when the children startled a wild animal like a badger, a porcupine, a chipmunk, a skunk, a weasel or a coyote from its hiding place. Feeding the birds was a pleasurable pastime of which the boys and girls never tired. Any time a cock pheasant challenged the right of the youngsters to be in his territory they counteracted by a closer inspection. It was a thrill to come across an antelope or a deer grazing in some vale with a fawn or two nearby. Flowers of every description dotted the landscape and it was up to the children to discover them. They did. It was not unusual for them to also find a wild strawberry patch, a raspberry or a gooseberry bush or even shrubs bearing saskatoons, wild cherries or cranberries. These wild berries were always welcome as any type of fresh fruit was considered a luxury in those days. In years when the rabbits were plentiful the children counted the number they were able to spot while going to or from school. The students had more fun out of leisurely strolling home after school watching a garter snake slither along and trace an interesting and intricate pattern in the dust of the road than students do now riding home on a Honda. There was pleasure even in walking in the rain. Perhaps the words of the Bible, "He that has eyes to see, let him see" had a special significance for rural children as they travelled to and from school.

A common practice in most schools was to record the names of students who were the first to notice the signs that portended the coming of spring. It could be the sighting of the first flock of geese, the first crow, the first gopher, the first blade of grass, the first crocus, the first meadow-lark, the first robin, or even the first grasshopper. A careful entry was made of the event on the blackboard or in a special book kept for the purpose, listing the time and place of the observation, what was seen and finally the name of the student making the discovery. The grade one tots soon learned to be as keen observers of nature as their more experienced and older classmates. It satisfied their ego to have their accomplishments recorded for all to see. Such incentives encouraged the rural child to become an interested and sagacious observer of nature. This practice gained for the youngster an ever-broadening appreciation of his environment. He soon learned to enjoy nature to the full. A meadowlark's song sprinkling the air with joy, a hawk overhead swinging at anchor, the flaming beauty of a prairie sunset, the sky wearing a necklace of wild geese, the winter mornings whiskered with hoar frost, the water chuckling out of a hillside, the summer rusting into autumn, these are simple things in themselves but to an appreciative individual they touch his soul and give life a new meaning. The rural child was rich in such a legacy.

Mrs. Sofia Porayko Kyforuk, a 1907 pioneer of the Vienna S.D. 831 (St. Michael, Alta.), laments the passive attitude of most present-day school children toward nature. She likes to turn back the pages of time to the days of the rural school when children hearkened to William Wordworth's plea of:

> "Come forth into the light of things,
> Let Nature be your teacher."

She recalls:

> "There is something enchanting about peeking into a bird's nest and then excitedly awaiting the day when the young would hatch. But how ugly they would appear in their flimsy covering of feather down, not to mention their gigantic mouths, their closed eyes, their wobbly heads that appeared to be mounted on strings like puppets and then tied to bulging bodies that looked to be all stomachs. Yet the parent birds would show unflinching devotion to their broods. If anyone dared to venture near the nest they would remonstrate with a barrage of alarming screeches, much faking of injury and finally, if these actions failed to repulse the adventurer, to make a physical attack—no matter what the odds."

It must not be assumed that going to school was always pleasant. Sometimes it was attended by discomfort, difficulties and dangers.

In the Superba S.D. (Alsask, Sask.) in 1915 (the year of a bumper crop), Harvey Johnstone, a seven-year-old lad, became lost taking a shortcut through a tall stand of wheat. It was probably a minor incident but to a small boy it was as frightening an experience as being lost in a dense forest.

When the homesteaders first came to settle on the prairies or the parklands, the entire countryside was covered with grass so thick and deep that it was difficult even to walk through it. Hence it was not uncommon for the children to become wet to the waist every time they waded through this sea of dew-laden grass on their way to school. Special precautions had to be taken to prevent this daily drenching.

Mr. G. H. McCracken remembers attending school in Action S.D. (Neepawa, Man.) in 1892 along with a brother and two sisters. The four walked about three miles in single file with the leader carrying a stick to beat the dew from the grass. J. P. Parsons of the Forest S.D. (Carman, Man.) overcame the same problem in a different way. When school first opened in 1884 he plowed a furrow with his oxen two and a-half miles long from his home to the school. Thus neither the children nor the teacher who boarded with his family had to walk through wet grass.

In the Glendale S.D. (Cochrane, Alta.) when Edith and Lena, the twin daughters of Mr. Willis, first started to school in January 1911, they had to walk across an open section of land to reach it. The father drove in stakes and tied pieces of rag to them to show the girls the right cow trail to follow to bring them within sight of the school. The four members of the Williams family of Ames S.D. 1411 (Tugaske, Sask.) were not so fortunate in having such a well-marked trail to their school. For a mile they followed a well-worn buffalo trail that went by their sodhouse and for the remaining mile and a-half steered a course of their own. The scheme worked well on clear days but whenever a snowstorm, dust storm or mist obliterated the landscape the father went out to guide the children home.

On cold winter days some students came to school in a vehicle called a caboose. It was a box-like structure mounted on runners and pulled by a horse, with a small stove inside to keep the children warm. Most teachers looked askance at these contraptions for they always looked as if an accident could easily happen. Mrs. Everatt of Banff, Alta., relates a sad experience she had because of one such contingency.

"One day one of the older boys came to school with his hands badly blistered from burns. He had tried to right a stove in the caboose as it tipped when he drove over a snowbank. I could see that the youngster was in agony but there wasn't much I could do. The school didn't have a first-aid kit. He sat suffering for a while and then asked if he could spread the butter from his sandwiches on his hands. Cold shivers still run up and down my spine when I think of how that poor boy must have suffered."

The majority of the old one-room schools were drafty and cold in winter. The floors were continually swept by chilly breezes. The following nostalgic verses penned by a pioneer poet about days spent in a rural school aptly describe the airy interior:

"Our dear old school was cold and dark,
And winds came whistling through
A hundred cracks in walls and doors
And down the chimney too.

An old pot-bellied stove was used
To heat the ancient shack.
One's face got hot as mustard pie
While chills crept up one's back."

This seasonal discomfort combined with the ill-effects of being exposed to the extreme cold while walking or riding to and from school resulted in many youngsters getting chilblains. The accompanying inflammatory swelling and the severe itching of the toes and heels were almost unbearable. Since the suffering parts were encased in some type of foot-gear, scratching was out of question, so the unfortunate child sought relief the only way he knew how. He tapped his foot against the desk or floor, or engaged in some other such footplay. Sympathetic teachers accepted the commotion with good grace but there were many who attempted to stop it by resorting to such sarcastic remarks as: "Margaret! stop trying to imitate a dancing puppet." "If you have a kidney disorder please leave the room before you have an accident." "Jack, you must have a nervous disorder to be banging your feet like that." After such uncalled-for statements the youngster suffered from both mental anguish and physical pain. Chilblains? We never hear of such distresses today.

The students of the Bar-Vee S.D. (Foremost, Alta.) always looked forward to spring except when the chinook winds rapidly melted the snow and made the coulees run to overflowing and washed away the bridges that most of them had to use. When this happened they walked the fence to get across to the other side. It took them more than an hour to traverse the swirling waters with six or more youngsters filing across one at a time. This was a risky way of crossing flash floods but at other times they were more fortunate in having someone's saddle horse to do the ferrying.

In the Bruan S.D. 888 (Rossburn, Man.) the students placed their trust in Winna, their teacher, rather than in any fence to get them across the swollen Bruan Creek in spring. The teacher was the only one who had a pair of long rubber wading boots so she carried five students over the creek twice a day. One boy, Alex Sinclair, was almost as tall as Winna, but she ferried him across in turn just as she did the smaller and more helpless youngsters.

Mosquitoes were particularly bothersome in the early days. School children used to wear nets on their hats for protection against the pests. Before passing a slough they took a deep breath and then ran by as fast as they could. Even so, mosquitoes rose like a big black cloud and swarmed after them. At times the air became so thick with them that in breathing the children drew them into their nostrils. It was a favorite pastime in the Rush Centre S.D. (Esther, Alta.) to permit a mosquito to settle on an arm or leg and watch it gorge itself on blood. Then when it was well-bloated the child crushed it. The blood was permitted to dry on the skin until recess or the noon hour when a competition was held to see who had succeeded in getting the largest splotch of blood. The reason the pupils enjoyed this game was that they had become immune to mosquito bites—to the extent that there was no swelling or itching.

The Netherby School (Hanna, Alta.) in common with most rural schools of those days did not have screen doors so the mosquito season was anything but welcome. It was said that when a student suddenly closed his reader there were enough of the pests crushed on the two pages to make them unreadable. Very often the situation became so critical that the teacher had to bring a smudge bucket into the classroom and set it up in the middle of the floor to clear the air of pests.

In the Granville S.D. (Boyle, Alta.) mosquitoes were assisted by large black bull flies in tormenting the children. The Department of Education building regulations ordered that all schools have windows on only one side. At Granville it turned out to be on the sunny side of the classroom. The weather became very hot in summer and it was necessary to keep the doors and windows open most of the time. The bull flies entered by the thousands. The school district did not have much money to buy such frills as screens so the teacher and students secured an old pan and kept it on top of the stove with a smudge in it. As long as there was smoke the humans enjoyed peace. One day Inspector Le Blanc arrived. He stood in the doorway and surveyed the smoky scene and then wanted to know what it was all about. He was furious after hearing the explanation. Within a couple of days of his visit a screen door and screens for the windows appeared secretly at the school.

Houseflies were another obnoxious insect that tormented rural students. Although they did not bite like the mosquitoes they were more of a pesky nuisance, especially in the fall of the year. With no screens on the school's door or windows these more than amiable creatures wandered in and out just as they pleased, but mostly in. At first their visits provided the children with an excuse for a diversion from their studies so the flies were tolerated, but it didn't take the youngsters long to discern how badly they had been duped. The flies danced the tango in the scholars' hair, they drowned in the drinking water, they walked defiantly over the written work before it was even dry and frequently caressed and tickled the faces of the girls and boys with their tufted feet during times they did not want to be disturbed.

It was total warfare at lunch time. The insects became so persistent at the sight of food that the children had to fend them off with one hand while feeding themselves with the other. Not infrequently some of the most obstinate foes came to an untimely end when they darted recklessly towards a morsel of food the instant the child thrust it into his mouth.

The spitting, sputtering and regurgitating that followed were enough to condemn every fly in the school.

On chilly mornings the students were thankful to be freed from pests. Yet no sooner did the heat revive the torpid insects than they returned to their favorite pastime of harassment. Their sluggishness caused them to be doubly unpleasant at this time of day.

Fly fighting was all but a lost cause in the Little White Schoolhouse for an endless supply came from the barn, the outhouses and the ashpile. It wasn't until later years when astute inventors came up with devices such as Tanglefoot, coiled fly-paper and poison fly-pads, that there was even a glimmer of hope of controlling the fly menace. The double sheets of sticky paper had to be warmed by a fire, carefully pulled apart and then spread out on any surface where the insects had the habit of assembling. To catch flies that preferred the ceiling, stores sold viscid paper packaged in small cardboard cylinders. These also had to be heated until it was easy to pull out the long spiral of gummy paper from the inside. The coil was then suspended from the ceiling. Users of the poison exterminator were directed to place the circular brown pads in shallow containers such as old pie plates, add water and then position them near a darkened window. The aroma quickly attracted flies and when they came to feast they died almost instantly.

These devices may have worked well in most places but not so in the schoolhouse. The children or their pets stuck to the gluey pads, the girls' hair and ribbons became caught in the dangling serpentines while the liquid poisons were often spilled and the trays knocked to the floor. Such misadventures with flies were so common that people of that day made up songs about their experiences such as, "Shoo Fly! Don't Bother Me", "The Cat In the Flypaper", "The Blue Tail Fly", "I Know An Old Lady Who Swallowed a Fly", and "There's No Flies on Grandpa."

Flies may have annoyed the rural students but lice persecuted them. Country schools were good places from which to spread or catch lice. Some of the children came from families that either through ignorance or carelessness failed to run clean households. These places soon became sources of lice infestations. It was a simple thing for one child to pass on the parasite to another as they sat close together in their double desks, draped their clothes over pegs that were only a few inches apart, or handled each others' books and played games that brought them in contact with everyone in the school.

A teacher in the Lahaieville S.D. 2637 (Athabasca, Alta.) in a brave attempt to prevent lice from spreading separated the pupils "with lice" from those "without lice". She drew a heavy white line down the centre of the room and after each morning head-inspection assigned the pupils to their proper enclave. The method didn't work!

The treatment for lice started with a good bath and a thorough scrubbing. Then the shock of hair was saturated with coal oil and combed meticulously with a fine-toothed comb. This therapy proved to be an arduous task for mothers as most girls wore their hair long and done up in curls or braids. The cure was repeated day after day until a close examination revealed that all the eggs had hatched and the nits finally routed. While the remedy was in progress every sheet, blanket, quilt, pillow and article of clothing in the house was boiled to make sure that they didn't shelter nests or lice.

A child infected with lice suffered from a form of skin irritation but not as severe as that caused by the prairie itch. If one student saw another clawing at himself it was a good sign that before long everybody in the school, including the teacher, would be frantically engaging in this type of activity. The itch was caused by a tiny mite that was very catching and presto! the entire school population contracted it. Fortunately the pest, unlike the louse, was easily expunged. An ointment of sulfur and lard destroyed it and stopped the itching at the same time. Children allergic to sulfur frequently found themselves suffering more from the effects of the balm than the vermin.

So much for pests. There were others but these few related illustrations will suffice to recall some of the less enjoyable aspects of The Little White Schoolhouse. But the usually dynamic rural student was up to much more than catching and killing bugs on his way to and from school, and while there.

Two sisters in the Namaka S.D. came across a poor old horse lying near a pond while on their way to school. The animal was nearly dead from shoulder sores, thirst and starvation. The girls emptied their lunch into a hat and used the bucket to carry water. For the first few days they had to scoop the water into the horse's mouth with their hands before he had the strength to hold up his head. The girls took feed from his master's field and granary to nourish him and used powder and salve from their father's supply for treating the sore shoulders. All that summer the two left early every morning for school to have time to nurse their patient. Finally they had him on his feet and healed. Imagine their chagrin when the owner reclaimed the horse and put him back to work.

Namaka S.D., organized in 1904, was situated on the western border of the largest Blackfoot Indian Reservation in Western Canada so the children had experiences with real Indians. Mrs. Clarence Garriott (Irene Peterson) of High River describes one such personal encounter.

"After a few years father bought a little sorrel mare which was hitched to a large two-seat democrat. It carried six of us and others that we often picked up along the way to school. There were two very steep hills over which we had to travel one at each end of the school route. The small horse could not pull the load up or hold back going down. So we would all pile out and push the vehicle all the way up and on the way down we would dig our heels in the ground to serve as brakes.

"The little mare turned out to have been stolen from the Indians and sold a few times thereafter. So whenever these Indians encountered us along the road we would be stopped, the horse unhitched, unharnessed, and then led away. Twice she was taken from the school barn. No policemen were nearby so she was reported missing to the storekeeper. He threatened not to sell the Indians anything until they had returned the horse. They always brought the sorrel mare back to the place where they got her.

"Three years ago as I sat on the parade route during the Calgary Stampede one of the old Indians looked my way. I recognized him as the horse snatcher of my school days. It gave me a queer feeling."

Mischief in one form or another was often instigated on the road to or from school.

One of the highlights of the Wheatbelt S.D. 2059 best remembered by its former students was the race which took place each day shortly after dismissal. All the conveyances, no matter what their size or form, were drawn up at the starting line and at a given signal the race began. Dowler's donkey and cart had the unique distinction of always bringing up the rear in this daily school derby.

The pupils of University S.D. 2981 (Sibbald, Alta.) had similar races but instead of keeping to the road allowance they planned their course over the roughest terrain and through a deep slough. They were not held as frequently either. The race track with its many obstacles was dangerous in itself but the dash through the slough was foolhardy. The horses were forced to swim to the other side and after the race the slough had all the appearance of a shipwreck at sea with lunch pails, books, blankets, coats, hats, and even a board or two floating on the surface. These races were such well-kept secrets that neither the teacher nor the parents had any inkling of the perilous events.

Not many people would care to quench their thirst by the method once used by the Peterson sisters of the Grand View Farm. On their way home from the Namaka School, some five miles away, they fed a few docile cows through the fence and then milked them directly into their mouths. This went on for a couple of summers until the owner discovered the real reason for his cows drying up so quickly.

The history of the Little White Schoolhouse abounds in acts of heroism but no awards were ever given. Perhaps lending a helping hand to someone in distress was ample reward in itself. Children are truly happy only when they are giving. They are "big" or "small" according to the size of their helping hand. The rural youngsters were unusually generous in this regard.

This type of courage was exhibited by an eleven-year-old girl in the Alexandra S.D. The four Holden children were on their way to school riding double on their two horses. The two younger ones were up on Bob, a reliable old pony, and the other two were mounted on a half-bred hunter. In teaching the latter to carry double a stock saddle was being used instead of the usual military variety. Unfortunately the colt put her foot through a hole in a broken culvert, rolled over, and broke the young girl's wrist and thigh. The brother, who was her riding partner, scrambled up the fence, mounted the unhurt colt and rode home calmly to tell his parents what had happened. The father and the hired man left immediately to rescue the girl. They found her lying in the mud on the edge of the road all alone. She had been there the better part of an hour. When asked where the two younger children were she quietly replied, "I sent them on to school. It was no use for them to be late." The fractures turned out to be of a serious nature so the intrepid youngster was forced to spend several weeks in hospital. She did not miss much schooling either for she kept up with all the lessons and assignment, thanks to a friendly and understanding teacher.

Georgina Thomson, a thirteen-year-old girl in the Porcupine S.D., also displayed a dauntless spirit in warding off an attack of range cattle while her younger sister, Chaddy, dashed to the area beyond the nearest fence for safety. Wild cattle were not accustomed to seeing people on foot and hence, were suspicious of any biped that showed up. The two sisters had been warned by their father never to walk through a pasture containing range cattle as they were always dangerous. On this particular spring morning in 1906 they decided to cut across the open range to save time and not be late for school. There were a few cattle grazing quietly and they appeared very much unconcerned. All went well until the two intruders were perhaps three-quarters of the way across when some of the animals began to raise their heads, stare at them, and then take a few steps in their direction. Soon the entire herd was moving towards them. It was uncanny how their mood could be interpreted in the manner in which they tossed their horned heads and lustily swung their long tails. Georgina began waving her schoolbag high in the air by its long shoulder strap as she ran and yelled at the oncoming cattle. The beasts stopped an instant and stared but still they pressed forward. In the meantime Chaddy had reached the fence and quickly rolled under the lower strand of barbed wire to safety. The wild cattle kept edging towards Georgina as she backed up cautiously towards the fence, until, with one final lunge and a loud yell, she also joined her sister on the other side. The girls were safe but the barbed wire had left its trademark on their clothes and skin.

A prairie fire raced towards the Denehurst S.D. (Brock, Sask.) one fall day in 1917, and before the students became aware of its presence the stable caught fire. The children exhibited more than average courage as they entered the blazing interior, untied the ponies and led them to safety. The grass around the school was worn off and this prevented the fire from destroying that building as well. The children were also instrumental in saving a granary full of flax for a farmer who owned the land just across from the school. In due time he rewarded them with a box of chocolates for their benevolent act. Such sweets were considered a rich man's luxury and for the majority of the boys and girls they were the first chocolates they had ever tasted in their lives.

When the Rae S.D. 1253 (Holland, Man.) was closed by the Department of Education on account of the low enrollment, the Smith children, a boy of ten years and a girl of six, drove an old horse and cart to another school four miles away. As this school was located across the river from the Rae District, the two youngsters had to ride the ferry twice a day. The Smith family became concerned when the river rose and a car ran off the end of the ferry resulting in three drownings. The school board immediately notified the Department of Education and described their plight. When the inspector and his wife came out to investigate the situation she almost suffered a heart failure brought on by the fear of crossing the river on the dilapidated old ferry. The Rae trustees were given special permission immediately to re-open school with only seven pupils.

One time before the re-opening a high wind from the wrong direction rendered the ferry inoperative so the old ferryman tied it up and went off to town. The two Smith children came to the ferry on their way home from school and finding it deserted, drove on with the horse and brought the ferry across alone. When the ten-year-old lad saw a neighbor arrive on the other side, he tied his horse to a nearby tree, took the ferry back for him and transported him across as well. One strong gust of wind could have drowned the two youngsters. It was remarkable how a boy so young could have manipulated the ropes and cable properly to cross safely in such a strong flurry. Unless a person has ridden on a river ferry he would never appreciate the skill required to operate one during periods of high winds and water.

Transportation was a problem in the Kennell S.D. 1616 (Craven, Sask.) in 1923, so the school trustees made an arrangement whereby a number of the children and their teacher, Sylvia, were all driven in one sleigh during the winter. Everyone enjoyed these daily trips as they were all together and could sing songs, play sitting games or just talk in raised voices. All went well until the spring breakup. The ravines filled with rushing water while the snow still clung to the sides.

One afternoon a young and inexperienced driver was sent to pick up the students and the teacher. While travelling through the gully he chose to keep to the old sleigh road which had built up with ice. The sleigh tipped and everyone was dumped into the rushing water. The older students and the teacher had a few anxious moments as they quickly pulled several of the smaller children to safety by their mufflers. It didn't seem to bother them in the least for no sooner were they safely rescued than they raced for home to tell their parents about the adventure. The sleigh box in the meantime had floated quite a distance downstream. A thirteen-year-old boy went back into the swirling waters to retrieve the teacher's books and her precious timetable which he had seen her labor over for several days. The driver, the thoughtful thirteen-year-old and the teacher rode home on the sleigh runners.

Such misadventures which taxed the ingenuity and courage of rural youngsters occurred infrequently and for the most part the students led a commonplace existence characterized by long hours of hard work and very little time for relaxation. The majority of the children, however, were sufficiently independent and imaginative to devise their own fun. Here are a few illustrations.

As the Winter family boarded the teacher of the Wolf Willow S.D. 3370 (Alsask, Sask.) Ken, his younger brother and sister, didn't have the same fun going to and from the school. The presence of the teacher had a dampening effect. But by and large the Wolf Willow teachers were good sports and most of them were young ladies between seventeen and twenty years of age. Usually the Winter children told long continued off-the-cuff adventures or fairy tales to while away the miles or played such games as "I packed my trunk" and "Animal, vegetable or mineral". The teacher also joined in with the three youngsters in these activities.

Wolf Willow had one teacher who liked to do all her homework directly after three-thirty so Ken and his brother used to hitch up the horse, tie it to the flagpole and catch a ride with the Francis family to an abandoned farm half a mile down the road from the school. There they fooled around until their sister and the teacher came by with the rig. The Francis youngsters then continued in a southeast direction while the two Winter boys climbed aboard their buggy and went southward.

The children had a lot of fun exploring the deserted farm buildings and playing with a variety of discarded junk. They discovered an old phonograph and records in the attic and set up a dance-hall in the kitchen. The group pretended they were a gang of robbers with their gun molls, the Francis girls. Once William Francis said, "Old man Huston made a batch of homebrew before he left here. Mrs. Huston made him smash all the bottles but it was rumored he hid a few in the barn and used to have a few drinks at odd times". No sooner did the adventurers hear about the cache than they set to work to discover it. Sure enough they found it inside the straw wall of the barn. Now they boasted of a saloon as well as a dance-hall. They sampled the homebrew but it was so unpalatable that they only managed a sip or two. Every day they participated for an hour or so in their wild-west show with a dance-hall, a saloon and mock fights. They even managed to locate two old rusty bread knives for fighting the duels. In spite of so many intriguing things to do, the gang kept a wary eye out for the Smith buggy and were careful to be out on the road when it came by so the teacher never had to search the house for them. The youngsters kept the secret so well that neither the Smith nor Francis parents ever found out about their unusual rendezvous.

The attitude of the home was often reflected in the manner in which the children conducted themselves at school. This maxim could well be illustrated by an incident that occurred in the Nevis S.D. (Stettler, Alta.). It was in the spring during the last year of World War I, and from listening to the adults at home discuss the war news the youngsters had begun to regard any reference to the "Kaiser" as something very mysterious and terrifying. On this particular day the sun had been shining in the morning but by noon a strong wind and dust had obliterated it. The children spent a gloomy hour huddled together in the schoolhouse listening to the moaning wind and the creaking building. To make matters worse they heard several loud but muffled explosions caused by blasting at a coal mine a couple of miles west of the school. The students had been accustomed to hearing the sounds separately but when they occurred simultaneously and when someone at this psychological moment shouted hysterically, "The Kaiser is coming!" all the children became panic-stricken. It wasn't until after the teacher had returned from her lunch that the alarmed students were able to relax and resume their ordinary classroom activities.

School clothing in those days caused very little concern providing it fitted to within one or two sizes and was warm in winter. The extra large size was to allow for growing. The boys wore bib overalls, cotton shirts, felt hats, stockings and heavy boots. They discarded their underwear and started to go barefooted after each May twenty-fourth. Their winter attire consisted of long underwear, black stockings that came up above the knees and held up by garters made from pieces of inch-wide black elastic, overalls, a flannel shirt, leather or felt boots, two-buckle over-shoes, a toque or a peaked cap with ear flaps, a huge scarf to wrap about the face and collar, either a smock and sweater or a Mackinaw coat and sweater, woollen mitts, and a pair of leather pullovers. Sometimes the boys donned several pairs of socks and wore moccasins rather than boots. A boy's dress suit until he was sixteen years had short bloomer-like pants. In fact up until 1923 it was still possible to see a boy or two starting normal school wearing short pants. There was a great deal of merit

A study in school clothes of year 1913 with the children of Peyton S.D.
(Chinook, Alta.) as the subjects.

in those days in making things do or in wearing things out completely.
Planned obsolescence was unknown.

Girls wore pinafores made from dark prints over their everyday
dresses or else middy blouses and skirts or calico or cotton dresses. The
hidden articles of clothing, the petticoats and bloomer pants were either
white or tattletale grey and made of flannel. The maturer girls also
wore corsets. Other articles of wearing apparel included long black or
white stockings, high buttoned-shoes, a large ribbon bow in the hair, and
a sunbonnet. The high shoes soon changed to slippers or sandals. With the
coming of winter the girls put on long underwear, changed to heavier
petticoats, wore sweaters over their dresses, and substituted red and black
felt boots or moccasins for leather shoes. Outdoor wear also included
woollen toques, mittens, scarves, warm coats, and overshoes.

The combined effect of wearing the long underwear and the woollen
stockings made it appear as if girls had severe cases of varicose veins on
their pipestem legs. More than one pioneer woman after looking at the
skimpily-dressed girls of today has had a good laugh after remembering
what she herself must have looked like in several layers of thick clothing
on a cold winter's morning. Each such heavily-attired girl harbored a
secret resentment in her heart for she thought that her mother was the
only one subjecting her to such indignities. But the other girls were going
through the same torture. The schools were so cold that at times it was
not uncommon to wear nearly as many clothes inside the classroom as
outdoors.

Boys and girls were very sensitive as to what others thought of their
clothing. At Mount Hecla S.D. (Leslie, Sask.) a youngster by the name

—Mrs. I. Hosie

The pupils of the Potter Creek School (Rimbey, Alta.) in 1909 wearing the
style of school clothing that was fashionable in those early days.

of Edmund Blake, after being outfitted with a brand new coat complete
with a warm sheepskin collar, cut it off. He was afraid of being called a
"farmer" by the village children. What his poor widowed mother thought
of his indiscriminate tailoring can only be imagined!

It is said that some mothers sewed their offsprings into the long and
heavy winter underwear with the first sign of cold weather and did
not unshackle them until late spring. The sanitary implications must
have been many but at least the parent was assured of the child being
warm day or night.

Every teacher unfamiliar with rural living can well remember her
feeling of disdain and revulsion when she first noticed the manure-
spattered shoes and rubbers of her students. Resentment soon disappeared
once she realized just how much time farm children spent in and around
barns doing the many chores. The teacher accepted the soiled footwear
as a mark of rural living. As long as the pupils cleaned their shoes
reasonably well before coming into the school and the smell was not too
strong she did very little about it. Even the pronounced horse-and-stable
odors that permeated the clothes of her pupils at the beginning of the
school term seemed to grow less noticeable with each passing day. Little
did the teacher realize that she was becoming acclimatized to the rural
environment.

A former teacher of the Clydebank S.D. (Eriksdale, Man.) likes to recall the Polish family of four who attended school in 1927. Two of the girls presented a delightful picture as they came to school in long flowing skirts and very dainty gold rings in their pierced ears. Their little brother who had just started school had the habit of coming into the school every few minutes during the recess and asking the teacher, "How many more minutes?" These repeated excursions into the classroom made up his only recreational activity. He liked his teacher.

During the depression, makeshift clothing was worn by everyone, Instead of wearing shoes the children came to school with their feet wrapped in gunny sacks secured with binder twine. Some sprinkled cayenne pepper in their stockings and others wore their big brother's or sister's moccasins stuffed with rags of every description. It was not unusual for girls to own just one cotton dress apiece. Monday and Tuesday it would be worn front side, Wednesday and Thursday back to front, and Friday inside out. Slips were often absent in summer. All the undergarments were made of flour or sugar sacking. These articles of clothing eventually earned the name of the "Bennett Underwear". Throughout the winter one or two of the children of a large family stayed home from school in order to enable those who had been selected to go, to have enough clothing to keep them warm.

It was rare for people to buy new clothes during those hard times but if they did they made sure that they received the most material for the price paid. Dresses, trousers and overalls were bought as long as possible. The extra lengths were cut off and used as patching material or else fashioned into wearing apparel for the small children. It was the accepted practice for school children in those days to wear clothes that were mended or patched.

Margaret (Cravath) Bell, a former teacher in the Cravath Corners School, wrote to the Red Cross Society in Calgary and informed them how the clothing of her pupils had become inadequate for the cold winter.

She received an encouraging reply and was asked to supply a list of the children with their ages. Almost immediately a complete outfit of clothing for each child arrived as well as a few follow-up donations months later. It was gratifying to both parents and pupils alike to be presented with never-to-be-forgotten hand-outs at the time of their destitution.

Many relief organizations, church and Sunday school groups, welfare societies and women's institutes of all types from the cities and towns across Canada, worked through the rural teacher to provide assistance to the students in the form of clothing, books and small Christmas gifts during the hard times in the Thirties.

In the majority of rural schools janitor work was done by students. A number of school boards spelled out the specific duties for these caretakers and in most cases it consisted of sweeping the floor, lighting and attending to the fire, supplying the drinking water and doing the dusting. The quality of work varied with the degree of competence and interest of the youngster undertaking the job. The rural children were given responsibilities at an early age so it was not surprising to find boys or girls of only eleven or twelve years assuming janitorial duties. Their impressions of doing this work indicate some of the miseries to which they were subjected.

"My cousin and I took over the janitor work in the Ridgeway School when we were ten or eleven years of age. We continued doing it until we left at grade eight when we were thirteen. We did it week about as we couldn't agree to work together. Our duties consisted of sweeping the floor, splitting wood for kindling, bringing in coal from the outside coal bin, carrying out ashes and clinkers, getting a pail of water every day, and dusting occasionally. My dad frequently split some wood for me but the temperature had to be considerably below zero before he would put the fire on for me. Otherwise he always called me before eight o'clock in the morning. I would go to school, get the fire going, and then return home for breakfast. My cousin had to walk one and a-half miles and then build the fire. We were paid $50 a year, $25 each for about twenty weeks of work."

Keeping the floor clean was a big problem. Right or wrong the majority of school boards decided that the floor should be oiled to keep down the dust. This practice resulted in the floors getting darker and darker until after a few years they became almost as black as pitch. The lighting in the school suffered accordingly while the murkiness provided a protective environment for the dirt. Every time the floor was oiled the children's clothing suffered. The oil seemed to creep up on top of their shoes, which they sometimes placed quite high on the seat ahead. Very few early schools used sweeping compounds and most didn't even have a dustpan. The usual procedure was to sweep the refuse right out the door, and no doubt most of it found its way back into the school on the feet of the youngsters. In hot weather the teacher often instructed the student caretaker to sprinkle the floor with water to cool the building a bit. The aroma produced by an oily floor particularly on such days became so characteristic of most rural schools that in time it also became known as the "school smell". The same could be said of the odor of the green sweeping compound known as Dustbane. Most oldtimers say that when they come across any of these smells today it brings back nostalgic memories of their school days.

Children raised on a farm were not afraid of work so when an opportunity to earn a little spending money presented itself they invariably took advantage of it. In the Mooreland S.D. (Kedleston, Sask.) the boys and girls were in the habit of stooking during recesses and the noon hours for the farmer whose land adjoined the school. Many students in the Petersburg S.D. (Balgonie, Sask.) used to set traps for muskrats and weasels while on their way to school during the winter and empty them on their return. Practically every district had students who, at one time or another, hauled drinking water, cleaned the barn, cultivated the fire guard, dug pits for the outhouses, made all types of repairs and collected bounties on such things as gopher tails and crows' eggs.

Rural children provided with only the education that they received within the walls of the lowly Little White Schoolhouse have gone forth to succeed in every walk of life. There was much the children learned besides the factual information that they gleaned from the printed page. The older children assumed the responsibility of looking after the younger ones on the playground. In many cases they kept the games from getting too rough or unfair, and were democratic enough to see that the smaller children were given an equal opportunity to participate in all sports and other diversions.

The enrollment in the Stoney Trail S.D. fifty miles south of Shaunavon, Sask. was composed of children of all races. The area surrounding the school, that had originally been ranching country, was thrown open by the government to a number of people who had been brought over from many countries in Europe. The teacher, Miss Margaret Lloyd, said she taught English to Germans, Russians, Norwegians, Italians, and wonder of wonders, to a small Chinese boy who had somehow joined the group during their stay in the immigration hall in Winnipeg. Diplomats of the world could have learned much from watching these children playing together in the Stoney Trail schoolyard. The teacher said, "Anyone who says children do not speak a common language should have walked across our playground any recess."

There were few if any teenage problems in the days of the Little White Schoolhouse. The young people were always too busy assisting with the hundred-and-one duties on the farm to have free time in which to get into trouble. The youngsters were also afraid of being punished by their parents. If a boy or girl misbehaved or disobeyed, a discussion in the woodshed and a sound thrashing with a razor or hame strap invariably brought good results. Parents commanded respect in those days. There was no dating and it was rare to see a boy and girl alone together. It was somehow assumed that those who went together were ready to be married and this status was not for the immature elements of society.

Rural children were the acme of innocence. In schools such as Green Lake S.D. (Hamlin, Alta.) and the River Rand S.D. (Rosa, Man.) the pupils of both sexes went swimming together during recess or while on their way home from school. The boys remained in their group several yards from the girls. None owned a bathing suit but all swam or bathed in the nude. The older girls frequently wore their cotton petticoats. There were no incidents and no one thought it was irregular. Manners and morals were taught to the children at home, school and church. The children in a rural school were like members of one big happy family and they conducted themselves in a similar manner.

Many of the children in those pioneer days were rather shy as they did not have the opportunity to travel around very much and see people. One gentleman described going to a home in the Stanley S.D. (Moosomin, Sask.) in 1889 and expressing surprise at not seeing any children around. Upon being asked where they were, their mother pointed to the bed in the corner of the little shack and said, "They crawled under there when they saw you coming!"

Nothing was more distressing or unfortunate to a rural student then to be the sole grade one pupil in the school, or to be the only boy or girl with the rest of the enrollment being of the opposite sex.

In her first year of school in a rural district near Winnipeg, Helen soon found recess something she feared and hated. She was the only grade one student so everyone else was older, bigger and could do many things she couldn't. No one wanted her on his team. The older girls ran away when she came in sight. At one time the big girls built a playhouse at the back of the school with the wood which was drying out for next winter's fuel supply. As usual they didn't want her, so to keep her away, they pushed one wall over towards where she stood and then promptly informed the teacher that she had done it. No matter what the framed grade one said, the teacher didn't believe her, so for a week she lost all her recesses. How she hated school, the teacher and the big girls! Helen cried and cried, but no one sympathized with her. Now she was a cry-baby and that was another good reason for not wanting her on their side. In later years at school, Helen could always tell when she was not wanted right away as her early experiences had given her an insight into the behavior of other people. It served her well over the years. "Believe me I have many friends because I learned to discern people early in life. Cold fact but true and very useful."

Now let's join Patricia at Wilson Hill School No. 2511 (Glaslyn, Sask.). The enrollment here consisted of eight pupils and she happened to be the only girl. The boys were never happy to have her tag along with them at recess or noon hour. They selected their games in such a way as to always exclude Patricia. Hence these activities included drowning gophers, building a hut out of some old boards, curling with old blocks of wood inside the school during the winter or some other purely boyish recreation. It was a lonely existence for Patricia because the teachers that came to teach at Wilson Hill School (generally fresh out of normal school) were not too interested in providing amusement for one lone girl. Such predetermined isolation forced her to seek solace elsewhere. There was a large brown cupboard reaching from floor to ceiling at the back of the room called "the library" and as it contained a number of books, Patricia turned to reading to while away the long hours. In time, she cultivated such a love for books that she became the "brain" in the Wilson Hill School, much to the chagrin of the boys. Yet her secluded existence continued. Even going to the outhouse had its disadvantages for Patricia. The two toilets (one on each side of the barn) were some distance from the school and she used to be deathly afraid of the cattle that grazed between the school and her particular biffy. The animals were there even in the middle of winter, searching for food under two feet of snow. She can still remember the loud thumps of her heart as she plowed through the snow past the cows as they raised their heads and stared at her and then took a few steps towards her out of sheer curiosity. The cattle never attacked her but they made the trip to the outhouse so hazardous that Patricia only went when any further postponement would have resulted in still another calamity. She never appealed to the teacher or to the boys to drive the cattle away for they would have laughed at any such suggestions, and then again, she had a sneaking suspicion that the boys were responsible for the cattle being there in the first place.

Small animals or insect pests of one kind or another were one of the unpleasant sides of attending a rural school. Not that they were frightening in themselves but when a nervous youngster is passed a rather bulky note containing a live grasshopper or when several bees fly out angrily the instant a student opens his prized pencil-box or when a snake or gopher scurries across the school floor, such surprises become nerve wracking. However, after attending school for a time children eventually became accustomed to such incidents. Soon they themselves were able to handle them expertly without any fear or reservation. The rural child became well versed in the world of zoology and botany even at an early age.

One of the favorite spring pastimes in the Eaton S.D. (Craigmyle, Alta.) was snaring, or drowning out gophers—of which there were hundreds. During one expedition the Kingsboro boy caught a gopher barehanded and brought it into the school. Just as he brought it to the front to show the teacher, the gopher bit his hand and he began to bleed profusely. The amazing thing was that the boy didn't drop the offending creature but calmly walked back, took it outside and killed it!

Young frogs were very plentiful in the sloughs surrounding the Independent S.D. No. 3101 (New Dayton, Alta.). Some children liked them; others were afraid of them. It was a sorry time for the timid youngsters for they were chased everywhere by the brave frog-holders. But there's a limit to human fear and patience. One of the abused pupils, a girl at that, got up enough courage to capture a frog and stuff it down the back of the worst offender. She even went one step better—she crushed it.

Practically every rural child has, at one time or another, taken a dip or bath in a slough or pond on a hot summer day. The refreshing experience was short-lived if the rest of the schoolmates shouted out in horrified tones, "Irma, there are three bloodsuckers on your back!"

Wesley Plunkett first started attending Floral S.D. 688 (Saskatoon, Sask.) in 1902 and that was the year that he also learned about skunks at first hand. On this particular day, his brother Edward, who was ten years his senior, was up a ladder painting the schoolhouse and when the children came out at recess he pointed excitedly to a strange looking small black-and-white animal in the corner of the yard and called out, "What's that thing over there?" The group of boys didn't wait to answer but immediately took off in pursuit of the frightened creature. Wes was a good runner but he was not familiar with the habits of skunks when cornered. He soon found out! His parents were forced to bury his clothes and give him several special baths before he could return to school. One pupil remarked many days after the incident that he could still smell skunk whenever Wes came near him.

In the same school there was a boy named Billy Searles who was much enthused about hawks, crows and ducks. His knowledge about these birds, learned at first hand, could best be described as astounding. He used to catch the young hawks before they had learned to fly, pen them up at home and catch gophers to feed them. The lad became known as Pin Tail Billy because he was so well-informed about bird life. It was a simple matter for him to recognize and name every wild duck that ever wandered into the Floral district. In school he often raised his hand to obtain permission to leave the room but instead of proceeding to the outhouse he pursued his hobby of studying bird life. It was his practice to see if there was a gopher in his trap or to dash down to the slough and make a rapid survey of anything interesting happening in the water-fowl kingdom. What a wonderful ornithologist Billy could have become had he been given an opportunity to follow his interests!

The comradeship of rural children and dogs was as inevitable as a haircut and where one was seen the other was not too far away. So it was not surprising to find the odd dog attending school as regularly as his biped friends.

In the Horn Hill S.D. (Penhold, Alta.) the teacher's daughter had a fox terrier that came to school every day and was a model of good behavior. No matter how hard the boys coaxed him he did not pay the least bit of attention to them during school hours but lay quietly by the teacher's desk in the summer and near the stove in winter.

"Bingo" who belonged to the Carter family of the Vernon S.D. 848 (Qu'Appelle, Sask.) became quite proficient in retrieving foul balls for the children during any games they played at noon and recess. He was invaluable, for being fleet of foot he had the ball back in play in a matter of seconds. On one occasion Bingo decided to take the ball home. He led a line of shouting youngsters for three-quarters of a mile before giving it up on the front steps of the Carter house.

A dog at Farrerdale S.D. 3499 (Simpson, Sask.) was more interested in education. He even went on Saturday morning till about 10:30 a.m., then returned home. For some reason or other he never attended on Sundays. During the week he relaxed at the back of the room and watched the classes recite at the front. Sometimes he fell asleep and amused the students with his peculiar snores and strange bodily twitchings. As he was always ready to join the children for any games at recess he became quite popular.

Two of the older girls in the Grandview S.D. (Grandview, Man.) rode to school on a sleigh pulled by a tall powerful dog. The animal reclined by the hot stove during school hours and at noon ate his lunch brought by the girls the same as everyone else. He was an excellent catcher so the pupils used to throw bread-crusts and other left-overs in his direction just to watch him perform. He refused to join in any of the games that the children played but merely went along and watched from a discreet distance.

It never paid the teacher to take a rural child for granted. This was particularly true in the pioneer and depression periods. Often things that the teacher considered commonplace had never been a part of some youngster's life. Blanche Dundas, who taught in the Fry S.D. thirty miles south of Hanna, Alta. in 1914, recalls an amusing but pathetic incident that was related to her by another teacher about "taking things for granted." The primary pupils in this isolated rural school were given plasticine and told to model fruit. One youngster fashioned an object that appeared to resemble a washer. The teacher, a little perturbed, explained to the child that she wanted fruit and nothing else. The little boy replied, "But this is an apple!" It took the teacher a few moments to realize that perhaps this child had never seen anything but dried apples in all his life.

Bananas were more of a novelty than a recognized fruit during the heydays of the Little White Schoolhouse. Mrs. Allen Foster of the Harmer S.D. 415 (Somerset, Man.) remembers the excitement that one teacher created by bringing a banana to school for the students to draw in their art class. Later the fruit was sliced into twenty-three pieces and each child was able to get a taste of this delicacy for the first time. The teacher was also persuaded to divide the banana peeling as well but the students found this to be much less palatable.

The rural child was noted for his ability to initiate recreational activities to fill recesses and noon hours. He could find constructive things to do in the most unlikely places. But sometimes his sphere of action spread beyond the bounds of what the teacher considered as suitable pastime. Invariably such enthusiasm ended in trouble.

The children of the Lancaster S.D. (Bow Island, Alta.) were proud and delighted when their teacher, Miss Southerton, bought a car to drive to school. One youngster, probably scientifically inclined, had learned in town how to get a "spark" from under the hood of such a self-propelled vehicle. Under his expert guidance the pupils were asked to clasp hands and form an arc while the two on either end were told to catch hold of "something" inside the engine. The moment contact was made with the mysterious gadgets every child in the line received an impressive shock. It was fun! The students continued to play this new game until one day the teacher was unable to start the car. Apparently the students became so enthusiastic in shocking themselves that they ran the battery down to a point where it failed to respond when Miss Southerton turned on the ignition. Thus ended the new game.

Barbecuing a gopher could scarcely be described as a pleasant way of spending a recess, yet Charlie, who used to attend the Newdale S.D. (Foremost, Alta.) remembers having to stay in for a month after an unsuccessful attempt at such a venture.

Charlie had caught the gopher, while his friend Martin built a fire in the barn. The school bell interrupted their culinary experiment so they were obliged to hurry for fear of being late. In fact they had forgotten all about their unfinished business until the girls noticed smoke coming from the barn. Luckily the fire was put out before it could do any damage. The boys didn't even get a chance to sample their cooking for it had burned to a crisp in the untended fire.

Sometimes when the boys had nothing to do during recess or the noontime they went down to the barn and lay in the mangers. If they remained quiet and still the mice scurried over their chests and faces. They thought this was fun.

One could not but be impressed with the strong contrasts that characterized the behaviour of pupils who attended the Little White Schoolhouse during homestead days. Great enthusiasm was balanced by deep apathy; deep consideration existed side by side with gross intolerance; crudeness in one pupil was offset by refinement in another. Not all quarrels in those rough and ready times were settled in the schoolyard by fisticuffs. Take for example this refreshing story from the Veteran S.D. (Veteran, Alta.).

During one morning recess the smaller boys got into a big free-for-all fight. Harold Dowler, a fifteen-year-old boy, decided to stop it but in doing so had some harsh words with Frank Martin, a boy of his own age and size. Frank wanted to fight but Harold being of a peaceful disposition said he didn't believe in fighting but would run Frank a race to Coronation and back instead.

The challenge created a good deal of interest in the school so the majority of students went to the station at noon to see them start. The crowd gave the two boys a rousing sendoff as they started down the tracks. By the time Frank had run past Throne and rounded the bend he could just make out Harold far ahead on the long straight stretch of the C.P.R. tracks. In fact he resembled a fly just at the point where the tracks seemed to run together in the distance. Frank turned back. Harold ran on, touched the station platform in Coronation and then beat Frank back home. He had run a total distance of 31.7 miles returning shortly after school closed at four o'clock!

School signified many things to the children who attended the Little White Schoolhouse. It meant a welcome break in the long farm day; it meant an opportunity to play with other children, for toys were rare; it also meant a chance to learn to be a better informed farmer or to be able to choose another career away from the land. Little did it matter that the school was some distance away and everyone walked, winter or summer. Today it is not the hardships, the cold, or the poverty that is remembered. It is reminiscing about the happy times, the pranks and practical jokes. These bring a sparkle to the eyes of former rural students and are remembered and retold over and over again.

North Bench S.D. 4145 was situated near Ravenscrag, in the heart of the ranching country of southwestern Saskatchewan, hence late spring meant branding for most of the residents of the district. So it was not really surprising that the older boys, their thoughts more often on the exciting times at home rather than the dull ones at school, contrived to capture and brand the gophers who made their home in the schoolyard. A length of haywire was easily bent in the form of a Lazy S or T—Down, to improvise a satisfactory branding iron. A small bonfire started in a hollow behind the barn away from the prying eyes of the teacher made the iron red-hot and very effective!

In most rural schools there were one or two pupils who just "didn't belong" and were often subjected to cruel ridicule. North Bench had at least one of these unhappy juveniles—a fat girl named Margaret. It happened that a well-meaning school board, recruited mainly from homesteaders who used to call England their home, had provided the pupils with a croquet set for recess pastime. The youngsters of North Bench found this game rather slow but it became much more popular on the days when Margaret could be persuaded to wield a mallet. As she clumsily bent over to make a shot at the wicket the steels of her corsets had a habit of working out through the back of her loosely knit sweater!

One teacher's dramatic presentation of a history lesson on the Jesuit missionaries and how bravely they bore the torture of the Iroquois created a deep impression on the pupils. What could be a better way to torment poor Margaret than to burn her at the stake. She was securely bound to the flagpole and all the junior scholars were set the task of gathering chips from the woodpile, dead branches from the windbreak, odd scraps of boards and pieces of paper from around the yard. This debris was piled in a circle at the victim's feet. All at once Margaret realized what all this was leading to so she screamed, cried and begged for mercy. No one paid the least attention to her pleas, in fact, they just laughed and enjoyed themselves the more. Margaret indeed was going through the same mental anguish that was probably experienced by the Jesuits. Luckily the bell rang just at the moment when the Iroquois brave was about to strike a flint and start the blaze.

The foundation of the Yale School (Champion, Alta.) was so constructed as to permit cross-ventilation under the building to prevent decay or whatever it was supposed to prevent. The necessary grill-work was put into place over the openings to keep animals (or children) from entering. This did not remain for long as the older boys found it an ideal place to excavate.

An excavation project was begun the spring that Lucille first started to school in 1924. She recalls that the male teacher was closely watched by the students that year and it was the duty of the first and second graders to be lookouts. The primary students didn't question where their loyalties lay for they never thought of crossing the decisions of the older pupils. The following fall the project was taken up in earnest. A lady teacher was no match for the students in laying down the law or perhaps she was easier to fool, but a cellar was scooped out under the front half of the school. None of the young pupils ever knew where the dirt was hidden after it was dug. It was always a mystery to them. Perhaps it was pushed into the small space between the ground and the floor proper of the back half of the building.

The girls were only allowed to crawl into the secret chamber once. They were amazed to find a full room complete with ledges for a place to sit. Someone promptly converted it into a classroom, playing teacher and carrying on lessons and frequently disciplining the rest with a stick during the lunch periods. Perhaps the boys did not care to play school for the girls never saw the basement again.

In time the boys also lost interest in their cavern. The following year, or when it was again the season for excavation, the teacher discovered the undercover workings and informed the board of trustees. As a result the grillwork was fastened in place more securely, the hole filled in and no further entry was made. A few years later a cement foundation was laid and it blocked the grillwork in such an effective manner as to discourage any future entry.

It was a custom among rural students to construct a secret hideout, similar to the Yale diggings, somewhere on the school premises. The youngsters were ingenious in the ways in which they located and built these retreats. People familiar with the once-common rural school and its environs know full well that there were very few places where such a hideaway could be located, yet the children invariably managed to have one somewhere nearby—the barn, the attic, the basement, the shelterbelt, the well, the coalshed, an underground tunnel, the piano box or some such other site.

The hideout at the Burnbrae S.D. (Compeer, Alta.) was really not a hideout in the true sense for everybody knew where it was but the trick was to find the entrance. This particular clubhouse was the property of the boys and the girls were absolutely forbidden to come near it. In fact it was located above the rafters in the barn and had been put together out of cardboard, old fence posts and boards "borrowed" from home and smuggled to school by "cloak-and-dagger" means. The main architectural feature of the hideout and one of which the boys were very proud was the secret trapdoor that led to the inner sanctum. It was an odd-shaped piece of cardboard cut to match and fit snugly into an opening in one of the cardboard walls. The boys considered their jig-saw door a very clever subterfuge but the girls, even with as few brains as the boys credited them with having, could have easily located the entrance without half trying. However it gave the inventors a deep sense of satisfaction to know that they had a secret hideaway.

The main recreation in the secret chamber was playing cards. Parents or the teacher would not have been very happy had they known that the hideout was really a gambling casino with hardened little gamblers playing five hundred rummy. Most parents in those days had very definite views about their children playing cards. The purpose in constructing a hideaway in the first instance was to have a place to do things usually frowned upon by the adults—swearing, smoking, chewing tobacco, gambling, discussion of sex and such kindred subjects. Probably some of the plans and dreams that these youngsters had while hiding in their secret chambers helped them to shape their lives. If nothing else it was their first lesson in designing and constructing a simple room.

Winter-time was probably the best time for fashioning secret abodes. In the first place there was no lack of building material—snow, and secondly, the teacher or parents did not become overly suspicious whenever the students suddenly became interested in constructing snowhouses.

Perhaps the most unique one of the hundreds of thousands that were built during the time that the Little White Schoolhouse reigned supreme was the one put up by the students of Burnbrae S.D. (Compeer, Alta.). It contained a penthouse. Every noon hour found the boys of Burnbrae hard at work cutting out huge blocks of wind-packed snow with an old saw, hauling them into the yard on the largest cutter available and then fitting them together to erect the walls. Old fence posts were placed across the top and then covered over with more blocks and some loose snow. The drinking water that was left in the school fountain at the end of each day was used to wet down the roof until it was firm and strong. A penthouse was built on the top of this. A portion of the lower story was converted into a balcony. Entrance to the penthouse could only be gained by passing through three secret trapdoors. The boys had a good supply of snowballs on the balcony to defend their prized structure in case the girls pulled a surprise attack. Of course the girls always threatened but never did storm the stronghold. The scheming females derived more satisfaction from watching the boys work their heads off for nothing.

Some incidents that took place in rural schools had a singular way of affecting the personal habits of those involved.

During the latter part of the 1917 school term the boys of the Nevis S.D. (Stettler, Alta.) decided that the time was ripe for them to learn how to smoke. They located a supply of tobacco, an old pipe and every time an opportunity presented itself repaired to their hideout to engage in an activity that by some mysterious standard was supposed to attest to their reaching manhood. On the second day of the new pastime, immediately class was called after the noon hour, the teacher asked each boy if he had been smoking as she said she could smell tobacco smoke. Each lad pleaded innocent most emphatically. The next day it was obvious that the teacher had doubted the veracity of her students for she brought her lunch to school. Nevertheless the smoking sessions had proved so intriguing that the participants did not heed the obvious warning. They were caught red-handed. Every mother's son was strapped, his mouth washed out with soap suds and for the next few recesses he had to write out a couple of hundred times on the blackboard the two sentences, "I will not smoke again." and "I will not tell a lie." The punishment must have impressed eight-year-old Raymond Hoff no-end for he gave up smoking there and then and never took up the habit again.

It was remarkable how the fortunes of the children or the adults living on a particular farm had a knack of branding that property with some compatible name. Take the Hoodoo farm of the Potter Creek S.D. (Rimbey, Alta.) for example. It is doubtful whether any other farmstead in Canada could have equalled the many lamentable accidents that occurred within its borders.

After the Dickson brothers, the first settlers, filed on the homestead they unearthed two skeletons while plowing in 1905. It was never established whether the bones were those of Indians or whites but a series of deplorable mishaps continued to hound the farm. Little Kenneth Dickson died of injuries received when he was thrown from a horse. In the same year, 1907, a twelve-year-old girl caught her skirt on a nail while jumping from the top of an abandoned shed on the farm, fell on her head and died a few hours later. Some years later, little Jimmy Fisher was thrown off his horse when returning from the Potter Creek School. He was dragged for a distance and died from the injuries he sustained.

A family by the name of Bower moved onto the farm and one day their small son wandered off. A search party was organized, but if it had not been for William Connors' collie dog, Paddy, the boy might never have been found. The lad was discovered the next morning sleeping at the foot of a large tree apparently not much the worse for being out all night. What had been feared most was the danger from bears and packs of coyotes that roamed the area.

Adults were just as prone to misfortune on this farmstead as were the children.

The Rev. Kemp who was holding church services in the Potter Creek School failed to arrive one morning. Later that afternoon William Connors took a walk down to his back field to bring the cows home. It was a cold wintry day and his dog, Paddy, insisted on leading him to the Dickson farm. Mr. Connors found Rev. Kemp in a sorry condition for he was entangled in the harness and unable to move. His horses had run away, upset the cutter, circled about a clump of bushes enmeshing the poor man. He suffered from innumerable bruises and severe frostbite as a result of the accident.

In the early Twenties a man by the name of Harris, after a quarrel, shot his housekeeper and then committed suicide. About the same time Jack Forge was hunting rabbits on the farm when his rifle discharged and wounded him in the foot.

There were so many mishaps on the farm that a certain school teacher considered it a good place for holding seances. Yet he found it so difficult to entice the people to attend them on this particular tract of land that he finally had to change the venue of his meetings.

Sometimes a tragedy in a district is remembered by the school children for years. In the Glenelen S.D. 1165 (Pine Lake, Alta.) in 1908 while the Clark family were outside working in the garden their four-year-old daughter went into the house for a drink. Before they missed her she came running out of the house screaming in terror with her clothes on fire. The poor tot didn't get very far for the strong wind fanned the flames fiercely and she dropped dead just outside the door in a blazing heap. The little girl's remains were buried in the schoolyard just across from the Clark home. There was a bare spot of ground just outside the

A picture of the pupils and teacher of the Zelma S.D. (Zelma, Sask.) taken in 1913. Notice the short-pant suit worn by the handsome lad at the extreme left.

house on which no grass ever grew and the pupils of Glenelen always reasoned that it was the tragic spot. For years the children kept flowers on the grave. A new school was built in 1945 but the old one is still used today as a community centre. Only the oldtimers and the youngsters who used to do the decorating remember that there is a grave in the corner of the yard.

9

THE ARRIVAL OF THE TEACHER

Teachers, like migratory birds, flocked in increasing numbers to the little one-room schools that had mushroomed all over the Canadian West soon after 1910. These teachers came across the Atlantic Ocean from England, Scotland and Ireland. They crossed the forty-ninth parallel from every part of the United States. They came from the Maritime Provinces. They came in goodly numbers from Ontario and Quebec. They came from the normal schools of Alberta, Saskatchewan and Manitoba. They came across the Rocky Mountains from the Pacific Coast. Some had an excellent educational background supplemented by teacher training courses while others were "permit teachers" with only a grade eight standing and little or no professional training. Some were mere boys and girls leaving home for the first time while others were mature men and women with years of worldly experience behind them. It was not unusual to find a sprinkling of those who had come out of retirement to answer the call of the West for teachers. Yet this vast multitude, different in many respects, had one thing in common. They were destined to be teachers in the Little White Schoolhouse!

The impending arrival of a new teacher always created more than a passing interest in the district. Everyone speculated. What would she be like? Would she be pretty? Would she be a good teacher? Which young homesteader would she like? Could she play a piano? There was a decided shortage of women in the early days so every new girl became a prospective bride for one of the unmarried settlers. Many of these girls found pioneering and farming to their liking. They soon became loved and respected members of the community. Eventually they married and made their homes in the district. The experience that many received as teachers in the one-room school enabled them to cope with the austerity of homesteading. Often the young miss had miles to travel to school in all types of weather, was her own janitor, nursed sick or injured children and had to rely on her own resourcefulness if an emergency arose. More than one rural school district in Western Canada can trace its present high scholastic attainments to these fine and intelligent women. After all there is something to heredity and environment.

Other young teachers found that the lack of modern conveniences, the isolation and the demands of rural life were too much for them. They never became one of the community. They soon left.

The anticipated arrival of a male teacher did not appear to arouse as much speculation as did the female. Perhaps some local girls did envision a life of ease as the teacher's wife and an opportunity to escape from the rigors of the farm. But they kept their secret ambitions to themselves.

Many of these young men were working their way through medical or law school by alternately teaching for a term and then returning to university for a year. Such college students have left their mark on many communities. An outstanding Edmonton doctor and X-ray specialist today taught in the Avonlea S.D. 2868 (Castor, Alta.) during his university vacation months. A young girl while endeavoring to free a horse that had become entangled in some barbed wire cut her hand badly. The potential doctor knew how to treat the serious injury. In the same community a colt belonging to one of the school children had nearly severed a leg while trying to jump a wire fence. Under ordinary circumstances the animal would have been destroyed. But thanks to the skill and the training of the medical student the large wound was cleaned and closed. In a few weeks the pet colt was once again gamboling in the pasture while a young girl was eternally grateful to her teacher and teacher gained stature and new respect in the eyes of his pupils.

Other young men who came to teach stayed and became the business men or held executive positions in the towns and villages that sprang up with the coming of the railroad. Those who remained in the teaching profession eventually became principals, superintendents, inspectors or held top administrative posts in the Department of Education or even became Ministers of Education. Their experience in the rural school gave them the start that sent them to the top. Some chose to remain as rural teachers for the rest of their careers. They dedicated their lives and talents to the children of the Little White Schoolhouse. Monetary gains or prestige were considerations that meant little to them. They were real teachers. Today they are the unsung heroes of the teaching profession.

The district residents may have done their share of speculating about the new teacher but not nearly as much as the teacher was doing about that self-same district after she boarded the bus or the train that was to take her there. The tri-weekly mixed trains (often jokingly misspelled "try weakly") that provided the only means of transportation to her school were not noted for their speed. "Mixed" aptly described them for they carried people, livestock, express, freight and mail. Such a heterogeneous cargo forced them to stop at every scheduled and unscheduled point along the line for anywhere from fifteen to thirty minutes to load or unload. At noon the train made a one- to two-hour stop at some convenient town so the crew and the passengers might have time to eat a leisurely meal at the one and only cafe in town.

These sojourns on the trip permitted the passengers to engage in many diversified activities. If they were so inclined the coach was a good place to rest or sleep. They could get off and throw rocks at the gophers or crows. The more adventurous souls had time for a haircut, a game of pool, or a visit to the hotel. It was possible for travellers to saunter to the head of the train and watch the unloading of the mail and express. The operation of shunting cars was an intriguing one to study. Theirs was a wonderful opportunity for meeting many interesting people travelling on the train with them as there was ample time for visiting.

All in good time the warning whistle from the engine sounded indicating the end to the noon-day respite and that the train was ready to start again. A brakeman passed through the coach and counted the passengers. It was so easy to leave a traveller behind. With a final, "All aboard!" from the conductor the "mixed" gave a few encouraging shudders and then, wonder of wonders, took off. It had backed up so many times previously that the passengers took a second look at the passing fence posts to reassure themselves that they were indeed travelling forward. Soon the rumbling "mixed" attained its normal cruising speed of twenty-five miles per hour and prospects looked promising once again. Now was the time for the teacher to sit back, relax and speculate about the new school. What would the children be like? Would the school building be a good one? Would the trustees be reasonable individuals? What would the boarding place be like?

Most teachers planned their itinerary so as to arrive in the district several days before school started. Unfortunately the arrival times of some trains were anything but convenient for the teachers. The Goose Lake Line of the Canadian National Railways between Calgary and Saskatoon was a good example. Trains numbered 9 and 10 used to leave Saskatoon and Calgary respectively around 6 p.m. so when the teacher was put off with her trunk and suitcases at some lonely prairie railroad station it could be 3 o'clock in the morning—an unearthly hour to expect anyone to meet the new teacher. Besides they were so tired, sleepy and disgruntled that first impressions were bound to brand them as anything but promising teachers. The chilly dawn and the silent, desolate prairies had a singular way of adding to the already depressed school pedagogues. At times like these more than one teacher thought, "Why! Oh Why! did I ever decide to take up teaching?"

Every new teacher was met at the station by a member of the school board or by someone delegated by them. Of course if the train arrived at a reasonable hour all the natives were there too to look for, and over, the new school-marm. If a number of new teachers arrived at the same time a quick comparison of notes was made to assure the right parties getting together. It would never do to interchange teachers. The introductions were usually short and formal with both persons appearing shy and uneasy. Almost immediately the greeting delegate suggested that while the teacher was claiming her baggage in the station he would bring up his team. Soon the teacher with all her worldly possessions was on her way into the hinterlands where her school was located.

Volumes could be written about the various receptions that rural teachers received upon first arriving in the district.

In the Rush Centre S.D. (Esther, Alta.) it was the custom to give the bachelor with the best horse and buggy the privilege of meeting and bringing out the new teacher from Alsask, Sask., the end of steel. Imagine the disappointment of one of these bachelors when he went, and it might be added with a good deal of anticipation, to meet a new teacher from Toronto and saw a little grey-haired lady step off the train. Being a rough and outspoken fellow he immediately blurted out, "Gee, the young fellows are sure going to be disappointed when they see you." Such did not prove to be the case. This teacher, within the year, had married one of the most prosperous bachelors in the Rush Centre District. First impressions can often be wrong!

The chief function of a stoneboat is hauling barnyard manure. Hence one male teacher was more than appalled when a trustee met him at the station in Brooks, Alta., with this particular mode of conveyance. After getting over his initial shock the young man enjoyed the novel trip as the "boat" glided along the snow-covered prairie trail to his school. Nothing more serious happened than that he and his trunk seemed to alternate in falling off. He soon discovered that there was a knack of remaining upright on a moving stoneboat.

A young, handsome male teacher must have been surprised to be met at the station in Tilley, Alta., by two women in a truck. Was he being kidnapped? Or did the women feel that there was safety in numbers where he was concerned? However his fears had no foundation. The women were simply substituting for their husbands who were busy harvesting and, besides, there was always the chance that the young city fellow required some help in lifting his trunk. They were right.

The Conquerville School first opened in 1914 with Miss Susie Finn of Ontario as teacher. Bob and Anna Conquergood were elected to meet her in town when she arrived by train from the east. Bob, always ready for some fun, informed the young lady that they only had a one-room shack and so she would have to sleep with them. To make it look real, on the way home, he drove into Frenchy's place. The shy bachelor lived at one end of an unkempt shack and his horse at the other. When Miss Finn saw the conditions in the shack she began to weep as it was more than her pioneering instinct could stand. Bob immediately realized that his little joke had gone too far so he apologized and told her the truth. The teacher was most relieved and grateful to learn that this was not to be her future home and that she would have a room all to herself.

Miss Hattie Anderson accepted a position as teacher of a new rural school six miles from Netherhill, Sask. The school was to open early in January 1918 so she left Delisle by train expecting to reach her destination that evening. Unfortunately there had been a derailment at a nearby town so her train remained on a side track overnight. To make matters even worse a strong wind had sprung up and by morning, when the train began to roll again, a blizzard was raging across the prairie. The storm was so fierce that it forced the train to slow to a crawl or at times stop altogether. Consequently when Miss Anderson reached Netherhill she was twenty-four hours late and at a loss as to what to do next. A man approached her on the deserted station platform and asked her if she was the teacher for the Muriel School. When informed she was, he nodded and told her that the school board had instructed her to stay at the boarding house that night. Without any further words of explanation he picked up her suitcases and started for the village. She followed stumbling through deep snowdrifts. When they reached a large weatherbeaten building he led the way inside, then up a steep flight of creaking stairs to a small room at the end of the hall. She thanked him and he left. The room was dismal and cold. All she could hear were the loud snores of the male boarders. What a way to welcome a new teacher! She quickly undressed and crawled into the frigid and lumpy bed but could not sleep. It was the longest and most depressing night she had ever spent in her life. In the morning when a board member came for her she felt like greeting him as a long-lost friend instead of a complete stranger.

It was rain and not snow that kept the chairman of the Valley View S.D. No. 666 (Snowflake, Man.) from meeting the new teacher at Manitou, Man., in the fall of 1944. The young lady fresh from six weeks of summer school at United College in Winnipeg had arrived in Manitou by bus expecting to be met by someone who would take her the remaining sixteen miles to Valley View. However the heavy rain had made the roads impassable so no one came to meet her. Outside of the six weeks at summer school the eighteen-year-old teacher had never been away from home before. She was not familiar with hotels yet she knew that was where she had to go. When she enquired at the hotel desk as to whether any messages had been left for the new Valley View teacher the clerk gave her a negative reply and dropped the matter there. An inebriated old gentleman who had overheard the query immediately tottered over to her and volunteered to get in touch with someone from the district and to ask what they wanted the stranded teacher to do.

Her newly-found friend was probably just a kind and sympathetic old man but when she overheard him repeat twice over the telephone, "That if they couldn't come for her he would look after her himself!" she began to realize how sinister it all sounded. She remembered the warning that her mother passed on to her just the day she left Winnipeg to take the teaching job at Snowflake, "Remember, dear, this world is full of evil lurking men. Beware of them!" The girl remained in a quandary until the old man relayed the results of his telephone call. The news was good! The school board had agreed to pay for her hotel room and a livery had been hired to take her to Valley View the next morning. The clerk eventually picked up her bags and showed her to a room upstairs. She was thankful that her benefactor did not attempt to follow but returned to the barroom. And so to bed—but not for a restful sleep that night.

Practically every teacher of those days remembers only too well what a trying experience it was to stay in a country hotel for the first time. Everything seemed to conspire against such unseasoned travellers and made each one feel more lonely and foresaken than ever. No sooner did the newcomer enter the strange and shadowy interior of the hotel than its solitude and vastness enveloped him or her. The hotel apparently didn't have anyone to meet guests who wished to rent rooms during the night so after several purposeless attempts to awaken someone by shuffling around in the rotunda the weary traveller had to resort to other means of getting a room. Sure enough! right on the counter were a few instructions scribbled to guests who wanted rooms. After that it took very little time for the individual to sign his name in the register and forage for the right key but it required what seemed hours to roam up and down every creaky corridor in the hotel in an attempt to locate the right room. Hotel proprietors must have taken sheer delight in fooling the travelling public by thinking up illogical methods of numbering their rooms.

Once the room was found a glance inside was enough to give the bravest teacher the willies. The curtains must have come from the sails of the Ancient Mariner's ship—they were "so thin and sere". The green blind suspended precariously from the upper frame of the one window proved as obstinate as any mule. No matter how carefully it was adjusted it either came down with a crash and stayed down, or else shot up like a rocket and remained at the top of the window out of reach. A corner of the room was furnished with a movable washstand that contained a large porcelain washbasin, a matching pitcher, a couple of greyish-white gossamery towels, a large bar of pitted and rutty soap and a chamber-pot stored in the cupboard underneath. One look at the scum-ladened and rust-colored water in the pitcher was deterrence enough for any city-raised teacher contemplating a wash before retiring. A casual inspection of the bed usually revealed that the mattress was thin, well-worn and lumpy; not to mention the numerous broken springs. The bed wasn't even comfortable for sitting on let alone trying to sleep on it.

There wasn't much an inexperienced guest could find to do, so most nervous individuals turned their attention to the matter of self-preservation. This took the form of closing and fastening the transom, locking the door and propping a chair under the doorknob and finally hiding any valuables.

No item in the room received more attention than the coil of rope that seemed to be so out of place just below the window. It was a fire safeguard and a sign explained how the guests were to use it, "In case of fire toss the free end out the window and climb down to safety." A note of warning was also posted nearby. It read, "Twenty-five dollars fine for improper use of this rope." All this information was quickly noted by the inquisitive guests for they felt that this was a part of the lesson of becoming worldly. Nevertheless there was always one problem that bothered every roomer. The length of rope, even to their untrained eye, appeared much shorter than the distance from the window to the ground.

The hardest task confronting the guest was to find ways and means of passing the time. Reading matter like old magazines or newspapers was never available. True the Gideon Bible could always be found in one of the drawers of the dresser but even the most avid reader gave up after attempting to read by the flickering light of a twenty-five watt bulb or a smoking kerosene lamp. Sooner or later most of these pastimes failed completely and the individual was left to reflect about his poor and unfortunate self. This interlude of indulging in self-pity in a strange environment fraught with imaginary loneliness, frustration, uncertainty, despair and lack of charity was a most unpleasant experience. The author of the fire regulations must have anticipated such a state of mind when he included the note about the misuse of the rope.

Not many teachers could boast of having been met at the train by two delegations when they first arrived in the district. But that is exactly what happened to Miss Hope Taylor who came from London, Ont., in June 1920 to teach at the Melmore School (Pelly, Sask.). Her branch-line train had travelled from Canora to Preeceville, the end of steel, and then had backtracked to Steven. When the "mixed" stopped for water a kindly-looking elderly man entered the coach, wandered up and down the aisle and looked intently at every passenger. He gazed at Hope several times and finally asked her, "Are you Miss Taylor who is to teach the Melmore School?" Then he introduced himself as the secretary of the school district. He asked her if she wished to leave the train and go with him to meet his family at Crystal Lake. The young girl hesitated, but only for a moment. The secretary had his car waiting and in it were his two sons-in-law. Miss Taylor's baggage went on alone to Pelly where, she learned later, a second delegation from the Melmore District awaited the arrival of the new teacher. The attendance at the school on Monday morning was rather poor as word had been spread by the Pelly reception committee that the teacher had not arrived. Yes the teacher had been abducted by three men, taken to a family picnic, treated royally and made comfortable in the home of the secretary. The seventeen-year-old easterner rejoiced in her first taste of western hospitality.

The majority of school boards considered it their bounden duty to personally meet the new teacher at the nearest town. On the other hand a number felt that they had fulfilled their obligations when they had provided the teacher with written directions as to how to get to their isolated school. In the latter case new teachers found it convenient to reach their destination by going in with the rural mail-carrier. There were advantages in doing this. The courier knew everyone for miles around. He was well versed with conditions in all the districts. Sometimes he was a rural philosopher in his own right. Thus, by merely listening and asking a few discreet questions, the teacher became fully informed about the people and the school in the new community. A few words of advice were often passed on to the young teacher before he left her at the appointed farmhouse or teacherage.

Why do teachers retain such a vivid recollection of their first arrival in a district? Perhaps it was the closing of one period in their lives and the opening of another or maybe it was the newness and singularity of the situation that set it apart from others. But whatever the cause, the activities and the people associated with their introduction to the community remained fresh and steadfast for the rest of their lives. Most teachers prefaced these reminiscences with, "Just as if it had happened only yesterday!" when referring to them. So it is small wonder that a teacher like Miss Margaret McFadden can set down her impressions and experiences of first going to teach in the Hillsgreen S.D. (Morrin, Alta.) so graphically although the event took place over thirty-five years ago.

> "The frosty air caught the whistle of the engine as it approached the crossing. Soon the train was slowing to a halt at the little town of Morrin, Alberta, on an afternoon in early January, 1926. There were always a few people who made a practice of walking down to watch the train pull in and depart from the station, but this time there was more than the usual number present. Word had got around that the new Hillsgreen teacher, Miss McFadden, would be arriving that day. So when I stepped from the coach, a curious but not unfriendly group surveyed me.
> "An attractive young lady stepped forward and introduced herself as Harriett Crawford. She indicated her brother Jack, who picked up the suitcases and led the way to a large wagon box mounted on sleigh runners.

There, I was presented to the other members of the family, Mr. and Mrs. Tom Crawford, and the two younger girls Elizabeth and Annabelle, who would be pupils of mine. I had been a bit apprehensive as to the type of home that would be my boarding place, but the warmth with which I was immediately accepted into this family was very reassuring.

"A new district had a bit of the excitement of the unknown. It could be a very pleasant and progressive community, or it could be just the opposite, or even a state in between these two extremes. What I had seen and experienced so far, led me to expect the best.

"Morrin was a small town at that time, with board walks, a typical country store run by the Parry Brothers, a post office attached to the store, Carr's garage, a restaurant, a community hall, some grain elevators, a school, a church and a few other buildings and homes. Everyone for miles around gathered in town on Saturday nights, and the store especially was the meeting place for all. Only when Ossie Parry started sweeping out at 12 p.m. would the crowd begin to disperse. People would slide off counters or rise from the boxes on which they had been sitting, and with reluctance start towards the exit doors. Always, there was a warmth and friendliness, a sense of belonging that pervaded all. The Crawfords called at the store before departing for home and thus I was presented to a new setting, but one with which I became very familiar as I accompanied the family on its weekly outing "to town" Saturday nights. Sometimes there were silent films or amateur drama provided in the community hall. Often a dance was in progress. It was such fun fox-trotting, waltzing and one-stepping to the music of the old-time fiddle with piano accompaniment.

"I was pleased to learn that the Crawfords lived less than a mile from the school. I could easily walk that distance and of course I would take my lunch. The children would need supervision over the noon hour, and part of the time could also be devoted to lesson preparation. I considered myself very fortunate to have a boarding place so near the school, as many other teachers I knew had to either ride horseback or use a horse and buggy for transportation to and from the school."

The first day, or the first night, in a new district was one that was not soon erased from the teacher's memory. Often there was a feeling of inadequacy and uncertainty in the teacher's heart. And small wonder! Many were mere boys and girls not yet out of their teens and away from home for the first time. Surprises and adventures were many.

Take for example the experience of a young city girl going to her first school in the New Dunbow School District near Gladys, Alta., in January of 1930. The district had been settled by several families of Mennonites from Oklahoma in the United States. The teacher had been teasingly told that all her pupils were grown up and the boys had beards. When she arrived at school the first day she was horrified to find the schoolhouse full of men, the majority with beards. All were busy putting in desks and seats as the school had just been newly completed. She was afraid that her friend's joke was well founded. When the work was finished the fathers and the big brothers went home leaving the teacher with her future pupils. True, many were really men in stature but they were without beards. What a relief! These children had been in Canada for three years and as there had been no school in the district they were at least three years older in their grades than they should have been. There was only one family of three pupils who had attended school regularly before and their books were the only ones the school had for two weeks. Of course the students had no idea what grade they should have been in and neither had the teacher.

In the St. Lina S.D. 1642 in Northern Alberta the teacher had reason to scold a half-breed boy of about nine years. The youngster could not defend himself in English so he stood up at his desk and retaliated in Cree. This was the teacher's first lesson in Cree as well as his introduction to a new school.

Follow another teacher as she reached her new school in the West Point District. Her teacherage, which had formerly belonged to a bachelor who had left for parts unknown, was a log shack with a door and one small window. The board member who had met her at the bus built a fire for her and after checking everything returned to his own farm. The fun, if you could call it that, began when the teacher retired for the night. She could hear scratching and unusual noises. Mice were sharing the teacherage with her. She didn't mind them as long as they remained on the floor. However, later on, when she had only a sheet between herself and one of them, she leaped out of bed, lit the coal-oil lamp and decided to sit up for the rest of the night.

A male teacher encountered a problem of a different nature in his first day in the Border S.D. in Manitoba. Sixteen children arrived, ages five to seventeen, but not a single one could speak a word of English. This was a New Canadian district of Ukrainians and English was unknown. The teacher talked all day with five words: school, window, door, teacher, children. That evening he collected all the catalogues available as they were to be his textbooks till Easter.

Not many teachers start their first day at school in a new district with a boxing match. But this happened in Manitoba at the Casimer S.D. in 1934. A six-foot Polish lad in grade four announced to the teacher that he was not going to do what he was told. The teacher grabbed for the strap but the boy took it away from him. Fortunately the man was lithe and quick. He led with a powerful right to the stomach and floored his rebellious pupil. The noise of the scuffle and the agonized cries of the beaten lad produced enough sound effects to stop a horse-and-buggy on the road and cause its occupant to investigate. The teacher had one of the best disciplined schools in the province after that episode and was invited to bring his model class to the teachers' convention at Winnipeg at a later date.

The students of the Concord S.D. 658 (Ponoka, Alta.) were awaiting the arrival of their new teacher. It was a cold morning and the boys were sitting around the old box stove speculating about what the new teacher would be like. They were also planning some new stunts with which to greet the new incumbent. Unknown to the boys the subject of their conversation walked in, hung up her toque and coat and then joined them at the stove. They mistook her for one of the new girls and did not catch on when the other girl arrived. After spending a few minutes listening to the interesting plans and conjectures she stepped to the desk, tinkled the bell and smilingly said, "Let's come to order and get on with the work of the day!" The boys' faces turned red with shame. She probably weighed less than a hundred pounds but after such a surprise introduction she had no trouble from even the big boys.

A mystery can be interesting and exciting when portrayed on the stage or on the screen but when it surrounds a person in real life it can be very disquieting. Anne, who arrived to teach at her first school at Silverton S.D. (Carnduff, Sask.) in October 1921, found herself a part of some profound secret. The liveryman told her that Mrs. X did not want to board her nor did anyone else in the district. Yet, without any explanation, he drove her to the nice white frame home of Mrs. X. After being coldly welcomed she was taken upstairs to her room. Anne had just started to wash her hands when there was a tap on the door. Mrs. X's sister, who also lived in the house, had come on an errand of deep secrecy. Looking very mysterious and bursting with excitement she told Anne that another teacher was still in the house. Sure enough, when she went downstairs for a cup of tea, she met the other teacher of Silverton. Mrs. Hart was a little old lady of sixty-five years or more. She told Anne that she had no idea her services were no longer required. The school it seemed was too hard for her to handle so the trustees decided to advertise for another teacher before letting Mrs. Hart go. At last the mystery was solved! However it did not ease Anne's conscience to know that in an indirect way she was responsible for the venerable Mrs. Hart losing her job.

A prairie wind was almost the sole reason for another rural teacher terminating her contract with the school board in 1927, even before she reached the district. One of the trustees was transporting Lonnelle, the new teacher and all her personal effects to the Alps S.D. (Hanna, Alta.) in a lumber wagon. The vehicle struck a gopher hole and the resulting jar hurled the girl's hatbox to the ground. Unfortunately it happened to be one of those cardboard containers shaped like a cylinder. Just as it landed on its rotund side a gust of wind caught the light box and propelled it like a Russian thistle across the prairie. There wasn't a fence, a knoll or a vale to impede its progress. It rolled merrily on its way over the level terrain and soon disappeared over the horizon. The trustee considering the hatbox of little value made no effort to retrieve it. He wasn't going to "run a mile or two across the prairie in pursuit of no cardboard container". Lonnelle had other ideas. She knew that her most becoming hat, her crowning glory, was in that box. She implored him to go for the box. He staunchly refused. She became adamant. He still held his ground and gave a most emphatic, "No!" Lonnelle broke out angrily, "All right you can have my resignation as teacher of your school, here and now! I'm going back to town."

The school official now realized that the hatbox meant more to the new teacher than her job. He never could understand women! The man turned his team off the road and went grudgingly in search of the venturesome hatbox. The price of education was becoming too high.

Many a teacher was shocked at the complete disregard for any sanitary measures in some of the boarding places to which they had been directed. Muriel McCanus, one such teacher, in 1913 was quite taken aback by the conditions she found in the chairman's home where she was to live. She had just arrived in Round Grove S.D. about fifty-three miles south of Estevan, Sask., near the border of North Dakota. The towel at the washbasin was so filthy that she simply had to forego her desire to wash her hands before mealtime. The teacher lost her appetite when she noticed a home-cured ham being rescued from the dirty floor where the dogs had dropped it. Sleeping conditions were just as bad. It was necessary for her to climb a ladder fastened to the wall to reach her straw-tick bed in the attic. After a sleepless night Muriel insisted on moving to the teacherage in the schoolyard. Things were no better here. The dwelling was infested with bedbugs of which she was completely ignorant until her first night in the new domicile. When she walked across the road to the farmhome where she was to have her meals she noticed four cats under the table dining on their catch of birds and gophers. An Indian mail-carrier visited the district once a week and usually after a drinking bout with some of the men of the district they all came over to the teacherage and knocked at the locked door. This was their idea of a celebration. One night Muriel stayed awake all night with even the windows locked shut because some homesteader had tethered his horses beside the teacherage while he slept in his wagon. The teacher attempted to adapt herself to such a primitive environment but after a couple of months was glad to resign. She accepted a teaching post in Winnipeg.

The young teachers of today have been spared the hardships and privations endured by their predecessors in pioneering education but on the other hand, they never experienced the thrill of opening a vast new country full of unknown possibilities. Take the prairie section for example. The sheer size of the prairies awed early settlers. Today with automobiles

—Mrs. M. V. Hunt

An old Indian mail-carrier has just arrived with Muriel, the new teacher, and her trunk at the Round Grove teacherage, near Alma, Sask., after a fifty-three mile drive from Estevan. This was in May of 1913.

that swish over blacktop highways at sixty miles an hour people are able to traverse as much space in an hour as the pioneers covered in three days. Besides, distances seemed much greater when passed over slowly and longer still when there was nothing to pass or nothing to indicate the progress that was being made across the prairies. The country was just one great emptiness. Yet some teachers chose to endure the hardships of living in such a land to bring education to the youngsters who had no choice where they lived.

Maggie Stevenson was one of hundreds of such dedicated teachers. She describes a journey of a hundred miles that she took in the fall of 1910 over prairie that wasn't even surveyed. Maggie's trip typifies the true spirit of a pioneer rural teacher.

"When my parents left the east to go homesteading on land north of the Hand Hills in Alberta I stayed in Quebec with my grandfather and grandmother until July 1909, then came to Calgary. I took a four-month course at the Normal School and got a school south of Calgary. In the meantime my father was instrumental in organizing a school district which was called Lillico after my mother's grandmother, Elizabeth Lillico. When the Lillico School was ready for a teacher in the fall of 1910 I applied for the position and got it. My folks wanted me with them partly for my company, but I think, mostly because the $25 a month that I was paying for my board would be a great help to a couple of hard up homesteaders.

"There was one serious drawback. Lillico School was three and a-half miles from my parents' homestead and there wasn't a horse on the place nor was it possible to buy one near there. My brother was working on a ranch near High River and he said he could get me a nice, quiet Indian pony for forty dollars. He would have it sent to Gleichen and I could ride it from there — a simple matter of about a hundred miles over prairie that wasn't even surveyed. As my brother had ridden that country he promised to draw a map for me. We had had an old driving horse in Quebec and I had ridden him a few times bareback, so I felt qualified to undertake the trip. "No one took the trouble to tell me that any girl of twenty who would even think of doing a thing like that should have her head examined. No one told me that Alberta weather could be very treacherous, a bright sunny morning could be a raging blizzard by noon. No one told me that even experienced riders had been known to have accidents on a trail like that and lie there for days before anyone found them. No one told me that coyotes in packs had been known to attack humans. And most important of all, no one warned me about two-legged wolves on the prowl. Probably it would have made no difference what anyone told me. I was young, ignorant, very trusting and determined to go ahead.

"In Calgary I bought a cheap saddle, a bridle with a roller bit severe enough to stop any horse in his tracks, a yellow saddle blanket, a quirt, a pair of spurs and a yellow oilskin pommel slicker. When I wrote and told my grandmother what I had bought she had no idea what a slicker was and concluded that it was sort of a dagger for protection. I bought a ticket to Gleichen, but wanted to have my trunk sent to Stettler the nearest railroad station to Lillico. The C.P.R. baggageman took an interest in my problem and offered to check the trunk to Stettler and riding gear to Gleichen.

"On September 10, 1910 I was in Gleichen and down to the livery stable bright and early to get my horse. Fred, named after Fred Hickey who had raised him, was a medium-sized, mouse-colored pony, well trained, but didn't want to be petted. None of this "affection for" or "loyalty to" his mistress for him. Do what was required and let it go at that. As I was leaving the livery barn the man in charge asked, "Would you like a dog?" I thought that would be all right, so I acquired Flossie, a useless little mongrel.

"Five miles from Gleichen there was a set of ranch buildings belonging to a French family. According to my map there wasn't another building until I got to Lawson's stopping house, 35 miles from Gleichen. It was a lovely morning, a little nippy, but the sun soon warmed things up and everything went fine until I stopped for lunch. When I climbed into the saddle after lunch I found that my joints had stiffened, and as I went along I got worse. I tried all sorts of dodges to relieve my aching muscles— leaning heavily in one stirrup at a time, taking both feet out of the stirrups and letting them hang, or getting Fred to alter his gait. But every time the soreness appeared to get worse.

"My map showed a prominent landmark, Dead Horse Lake, ten miles from Lawsons. I watched for that but finally decided that I had overlooked it because I was certain I was on the right trail—there wasn't any other. Hours later I came to what was beyond a doubt Dead Horse Lake and that left me ten more weary miles to go. When I reached the stopping house I ached in every joint. Even my jaws ached but certainly not from talking. "If I had only known I could have had company all that first day. Half an hour after I got to the stopping house Mr. and Mrs. James Smith and their two daughters, Belle and Verna, arrived. Mr. Smith had gone from his homestead in the Hand Hills to meet his family in Gleichen. They had stayed in Ontario until he got a shack built. They had a wagonload of household goods with a lovely soft featherbed on top. When we started the next morning Belle asked me if she could ride my nice pony for a few miles. I gladly agreed but she soon tired. Verna took over and rode the rest of the way to their place. I rode the featherbed all day. That night I stayed with the Smiths and the third day started out on my own again.

"The trail led to the Hand Hills store and as it branched in several directions from there I stopped to inquire which one to take. A young man offered to show me and rode with me for five or six miles. He had a .22 rifle and entertained me by boasting about what a good shot he was.

'See that gopher sitting there? Just watch me pick him off?'

"The first shot raised the dirt to the right of the gopher, the second to the left and so on for five shots. The gopher was quite unconcerned and didn't even move. This was too much for my escort. He whirled his horse around and disappeared in a cloud of dust.

"Twenty miles farther on and many hours later, Fred, Flossie and I reached Lillico. None of the terrible things that might have happened did happen— perhaps just because I was young, ignorant, and trusting. This is September 30, 1960, exactly fifty years since I started my long ride. I am very grateful that I was one of the early rural teachers in Alberta and that I saw this country develop into the prosperous land it is now. I am also grateful that I had a chance to learn about horses from Fred. We had him in the family for twenty years and he educated all of us."

More than one teacherage possessed a "sordid past" that often destroyed the peace of mind of the new tenant once she heard it related.

Kay was a very excited young lady when she reached her new school in the Swedish settlement south of Buffalo, Alta. At all her other schools she had been forced to board out but in this district a teacherage was available. She gloated in anticipation of enjoying real privacy. The summer dust was heavy on everything so just as soon as the mail-carrier who had driven her to the new district departed, she started to clean out the teacherage. Around suppertime, the secretary who had been working in the harvest field nearby, noticed the activity at the school so he came over to welcome the new teacher. The district's child population did not warrant the Department of Education to organize a school in the early years so the settlers had worked hard to purchase an old farmhouse that had stood vacant for some time. The former owner had shot his wife and then himself so no one wanted to live in it. After buying the house it was moved to a central location in the district and converted into a makeshift classroom by removing the partitions. A large section where the plaster had broken off as a result of the shooting in the murder-suicide incident had not been fixed by the trustees but draped over with a large Union Jack. The secretary told her it was cheaper to buy the flag than hire a plasterer. The teacherage had belonged to a bachelor who had hanged himself "from that there beam". So said the official as he pointed knowingly to the fatal spot. No one wanted to live in it after that so the school board purchased it at a very good price and had it hauled to the schoolyard for the use of the teacher.

As the secretary left the yard he called back to say, "You'll have to be careful ma'am, the country is full of rattle snakes". "Snakes indeed!" thought the young girl. "What about the suicides and murders that took place in these very buildings?" Many a night thereafter Kay experienced nightmares in which she invariably saw a strange man dangling from "that there beam".

Sometimes it wasn't the "past" but the "present" of the teacherage that bothered the new teacher. Put yourself in the place of Kathleen as she passed through her initiation procedures in her first evening in the Wintering Hills S.D. (Hussar, Alta.) on January 10, 1928.

As it was rather chilly in the teacherage she decided to start a fire but discovered that there was no wood of any kind either inside or in the snowdrifts outside. Kathleen remedied this situation by unpacking her box of books and breaking it into kindling. After a few unsuccessful attempts she was able to coax the coal to catch fire from the blazing wood. Then she learned that there was no light. The gas lamp was empty and both mantles were broken. A quick search of the teacherage revealed that there were no spare mantles or fuel for the lamp. She next turned her attention to the little glass kerosene lamp. But it was no better. The chimney was missing while the wick was so short that it failed to reach the bit of coal oil in the bottom. By lighting matches Kathleen was able to rummage in her trunk for a piece of flannel and a straight pin to fasten it to the wick. Thus she had a light of sorts, even if it was a smoky one, to see to get supper and sort out her schoolbooks for the next day.

When the teacher attempted to fasten the door for the night she discovered that the lock had been smashed open and the door just wouldn't stay shut. She remedied this situation by wedging it with a butcher knife.

The coal oil petered out at around nine o'clock so the obvious thing for her to do was to crawl into bed and try to go to sleep. Again she was foiled. The ample supply of bedding that she had been assured was there turned out to be a bare mattress and two pillows. Kathleen was still undaunted. She heated a flat iron for her feet, pulled on any clothes that looked warm, and spread her one and only cotton-print quilt and her two coats over herself and finally shivered to sleep.

The below-zero temperature inside the teacherage woke the girl at four o'clock in the morning. She rose quickly, put more coal on the fire and stirred it up a trifle. Since there was no kindling to spare she had to conserve it at all costs.

After daylight she made a thorough examination of the teacherage, both inside and outside, to ascertain what caused it to be so cold. She found that a "refrigeratory cave" had been dug under the building where former pedagogues had stored their perishable foods. None of this nor any part of the teacherage had been banked for the winter. There were chinks around the window-frames and several longer ones extending the full length of the door panels. She was told later that a former male teacher and his pals whiled away their spare time by throwing knives at a target that they had drawn on the door.

Kathleen located a pail but when she trotted outside to get water she noticed that there was something radically wrong with the pump—no handle. A cowboy had tethered his horse to the pump handle at a dance at Christmas and before the evening's entertainment had concluded both the horse and pump handle had disappeared. The teacher was not entirely thwarted in her plans to get water for when she discovered she could not use the pump she took to melting snow to obtain her supply of water. Since one family was in the habit of hauling a can of drinking water to school every morning for the pupils, Miss Ricker used any that was left over for her own purpose.

The teacher kept wondering why the school board had permitted such conditions to exist in the teacherage. She ultimately found out. A private group decided to hold a Christmas party in the schoolhouse without the knowledge of the trustees. There were no lights in the school so the self-invited guests smashed the lock on the teacherage door, expropriated the gas lamp, burned it dry and in the act of returning it in a high wind, lost the mantles. The glass chimney of the coal-oil lamp suffered the same fate. What was left of the kindling wood was taken to make a fire to heat the water for coffee. Miss Ricker was never able to clear up the mystery of who helped himself to the bedding and to most of the coal in the bin.

It was the duty of the secretary-treasurer of the Wintering Hills School to keep a close check on the teacherage and the school. But as he was away for the winter some people probably felt that it was a good time to use public property for their own devices. Often during the period between the time that the former teacher left and the new one took over occasional pilfering or damage took place in rural schools. Those responsible for such isolated incidents probably thought that during the transition period it would be difficult to pinpoint the guilty party. The incoming teacher was the one who suffered most from such lack of consideration.

10

WHERE THE TEACHER LIVED

The simple but age-old question of where the teacher boarded was one of grave concern in many rural districts. So much so that at times it precipitated all manner and conditions of trouble known to man. Feuds have been started, homes have been broken up and homes have been set up, reputations have been made and other reputations have been ruined, some people have stopped speaking to each other and others have spoken rather too much and upon several occasions even physical violence has erupted.

The problem of where the teacher stayed or didn't stay appeared to be the concern of everyone and was a subject of much discussion and frequently, but not always, a little action. Attitudes differed considerably from district to district. In some, nearly everyone wanted to board the teacher while in others no one wanted her. In neither instance was the teacher in an enviable position.

A number of factors contributed to the choice of a particular farmstead as the teacher's official boarding place. A certain family might have had a large house and hence could spare the extra room. If the father and mother were interested in education or were well-educated themselves they had something in common with teachers and so were more inclined to make room for them in their home. Many boarded the teacher for the extra income or the company that it provided. Then there was the usual family that took the teacher in for the prestige it gave them in the community. Although the distance from the school might have appeared to be an important consideration, it never was. The majority of boarding places were anywhere from one to three miles away from the school.

The introduction of the Divisional System of School Administration towards the latter part of the history of the Little White Schoolhouse made it even more trying for the teacher to secure a boarding place. The district didn't have a part in hiring her so they were not concerned whether she had a place to stay or not. This attitude was exemplified in the oft-repeated remark, "Let the divisional board find her a place, they hired her." It was also in this type of district that the teacher felt stunned and baffled at the reply she often received at some prospective boarding place to her query as to whether she could stay there. "We don't want to take you, but we will if we have to, although we don't want to!" The district had lost its personal interest in what was formerly "their teacher" but now was only a part of the huge political machine known as the Divisional Board.

In a few districts the local boards were loath to surrender their power to the divisional authorities and hence tried to assert themselves by attempting to show the teacher, the tool of the Division, a thing or two. In a situation like this it didn't make much difference where the teacher boarded because it became impossible for her to please everyone anyway.

The most promising type of boarding situation for a teacher to meet with was where tradition had established one and only one home in the district as the teacher's boarding place. Then the community as a whole expected her to stay there. If she did, everyone was happy. But even here as sometimes happened for various air-tight reasons the only boarding place could become no longer available. This news always had the effect of throwing the district into a state of confusion.

Here is the typical manner in which such bungling episodes ran their course: The former landlady would send word to the secretary-treasurer of the district that for reasons of health it was no longer possible for her to board the teacher. Of course no action resulted until a day or two before the teacher was to arrive in the district, then quite suddenly the residents woke up to the inevitable fact that something must be done and done posthaste.

Now the plot began to unfold. Mr. Z being a sympathetic individual, decided that it was his duty to go over to see Mrs. Y and ask her if she could board the teacher. In the meantime Mrs. Y, another kind soul, drove into the yard to inquire from Mr. Z about this boarding business. No, she couldn't possibly take the teacher but what about Mrs. Z? No, the Z's had talked it over just that morning and it was out of the question.

Mrs. Y told the Z's that she had gone up to see Mrs. X a day ago but as the X's were milking too many cows the idea of taking the teacher was dropped. The Z's and Mrs. Y discussed other possibilities. Mrs. W had a spare room so she might consider the proposition. Yes, Mrs. V used to board the teachers before her husband began to imbibe too freely, but—. Then there were the U's. Not a hope here. Yes, there was a good granary in Mrs. T's yard that could easily be converted into a good teacherage.

The discussion between the Z's and Mrs. Y resulted in Mr. Z riding over to interview Mrs. W. Yes, Mrs. W readily consented to board the teacher. Mr. Z was flushed with victory as he turned his horse homeward. His elation was short lived when he met Mr. Y. Mr. Y told him with a sense of pride that he had found a place for the teacher. Mrs. X was going to take her in after all for the X's had found a boy who was willing to help with the milking. The two men felt dejected after listening to each other. Under the circumstances they decided to let matters rest for a while.

Shortly afterwards Mr. A met Mr. U in the field. Mr. U had some important news to relate. The new teacher was going to board with them. To further complicate matters, the former landlady had reconsidered her decision not to board the teacher and was quite willing to accept her now. By this time everybody was so utterly confused and upset that any choice the teacher made was readily acceptable to all with no questions asked. The teacher went to live with the V's.

The homes in those days were very crowded but as the teacher was a special person everything was done to make her comfortable. The teacher's room was usually upstairs where a partition, open at the top, had been erected to provide privacy but at the same time permit heat and air to circulate overhead. The furnishings were few and simple but the best the household could afford. They usually consisted of a bed, a dresser that could double as a desk, a chair or two, a kerosene lamp, a homemade rug, a towel, a washstand with a matching water pitcher and basin, and a set of shelves. Drapes were often strung from the topmost shelf to fashion a makeshift clothes closet with the wall.

These upstairs bed-sitting rooms could get very cold in the winter so it was not unusual to find a feather tick on the teacher's bed. As many teachers from the city were not familiar with this type of bedding they did not know whether they were fortunate or not. Later they learned to bless it for its heat and curse it for being so unmanageable while they were making their bed.

One standard method of heating the upstairs was to string the stove-pipes from the heater downstairs through the bedroom. The more length of pipe circulating about in the room the warmer it became. This arrangement always left the teacher with the impression of a lost stovepipe wandering through the bedroom looking for the chimney. The pipes often glowed red-hot when the drafts on the heater were left open too long. The stifling smell of overheated sheet metal is not soon forgotten. Nor were the grating sounds that accompanied it. More than one teacher has awakened to the smell of smoke or the sight of a blaze caused by a blanket or some clothing coming to rest against the hot stovepipes. Eyebrows and hair were often casualties in these superficial fires.

It was so cold in these upstairs bedrooms that many a teacher had to forego the nightly ritual of curling her hair. The usual practice was to dampen the hair and then put it up on hairpins. In the cold temperature the moist hair froze stiff and no teacher ever liked to sleep with a crown of ice on her head.

Plumbing facilities were non-existent in the farm homes in the early days. The outhouse located some twenty to thirty feet back of the house served the purpose during the day, while an earthenware pot stored inside the washstand or under the bed took care of any emergencies during the night. All water had to be carried whether it was for washing, drinking or bathing. The reservoir at the back or the side of the cookstove and the kettle on top were the only sources of hot water. There were two ways for the teacher to take a bath. Either she took a sponge bath in her upstairs boudoir or else she splashed around in a washtub behind the kitchen stove. The ordeal was enough to reduce it to a Saturday night effort unless an important social function was scheduled during the week.

No favoritism was shown. The teacher ate all her meals with the family. Whatever they had was shared with her. Wherever they went for a visit or a ride she accompanied them. She shared both their joys and sorrows. In short, she was a member of the family. An occasional teacher refused to join the family circle and instead isolated herself by staying in her room most of the time. She acted like a guest at a hotel. Such teachers found it too distressing to remain in the district for any length of time and soon left.

Most teachers didn't take too long to adapt themselves to the daily routine of a rural family. The weekend was always special. Saturday was shopping and mail day. The family rushed through the chores in the morning and went to town for the afternoon or the evening. On Sundays, after attending the church service in the schoolhouse, they usually went visiting or had company over to their place. On occasion the family took in a sports day, a ball game, a concert, the local fair or a movie in town. These diverse activities gave the teacher an opportunity to become better acquainted with every family in the district as well as a little time to relax. It was always pleasant for her to hear the cheery invitation, "Don't forget to bring the teacher!" when the family was asked to a chicken dinner or a berry-picking party.

Many a teacher's memory of a boarding place was associated with food. Farm women are expert cooks and have the ability of converting common-place foods into unforgettable delicacies. Each rural housewife was known far and wide for her competence in preparing some special mouth-watering dish. There could be simmering baked beans and brown bread, beef and Yorkshire pudding, johnnycake and corn syrup, sliced potatoes fried to a golden brown, cabbage rolls in onion sauce, spring chicken fried in butter and deep apple pie topped off with mounds of homemade ice cream. Teachers often ate so much that sighs of gratification mingled with sighs of satiety. And still the hostess pleaded with the pedagogue to have "just a little more".

There was much to do on the farm particularly during the busy days of harvesting and sowing. The teacher, male or female, who pitched in and helped with the work was considered a gem. It took a while to learn how to harness and drive a team of horses, to operate a mower or binder, to stook, to help with the threshing, to take a load of wheat to town, to milk cows, to clean the barn or to do the hundred-and-one other tasks that were just a part of the job of farming. But once mastered it gave the teacher a personal satisfaction. They could be of some help now. Besides, they were beginning to acquire an insight into some of the problems that were confronting the farm folk and this helped them to become more effective in their profession.

A good deal of credit must be given to the homes that took in the teacher. Not only was the family privacy invaded but they were obligated to remain more or less at home during the period that the teacher stayed with them. On rare occasions the farmer and his wife found it necessary to go away from the farm for a day or two. Perhaps it was the farm-organization convention, the need for medical attention, a wedding or funeral of a relative, or a shopping trip to the city that took them away. Then the teacher, if he was worth his salt, assumed the responsibility of doing the necessary chores about the farm. Of all these routine tasks the milking of the cow for some reason or other always proved to be the bugbear. Here is how Pete Lyle, a former rural teacher but now a realtor in Calgary, described the operation.

> "Well night came and the cow must be milked. I put on my overalls, took down the milk pail and went out to meet my cow. I fed her as per instructions, but I must admit I didn't like the look in her eyes. You don't milk that end so I nonchalantly started to sit down on the stool. Before I could get comfortably seated she let out with her right foot and caught me on the shin. That made me angry. I let loose with my right foot to get even. But before I could get it away she caught me again, stool, pail and all. That settled it! I finally got her milked by tying her legs together. I don't think she liked it for she gave about a quart of milk and I had been instructed to get two. From then on I always made inquiries about any cows which I had to milk."

Many of the places where the teachers boarded could best be described as primitive. It is indeed difficult for the present generation to even imagine what some rural teachers had to endure.

Take the experiences of Kathleen who taught from 1934 to 1936 in the Shining Bank School, an isolated district some fifty-five miles northeast of Edson, Alta. She lived with a widow and her two grown sons. The meals were good but the sleeping conditions were far from satisfactory. There was just sufficient space in the bedroom to accommodate a double bed, an orange-crate washstand and the teacher's trunk. Kathleen shared the bed with her landlady, a very large woman. The mattress was so thin that a lumpy moosehide had been placed underneath to provide a more comfortable sleeping foundation. Kathleen always doubted this logic. The bedroom side of the house adjoined the chicken and pig yard, so often the teacher was wakened by the sounds of pigs and chickens at the window over her bed. One night she was aroused from her sleep by the peep! peep! of baby chicks. The landlady had taken some hatching eggs into bed with her as it had turned cold outside. Another time the woman brought some baby pigs into the house and Kathleen fully expected to have them for bedfellows. Luckily it was found that they could be kept warm in a satisfactory manner by placing them in a basket on the open oven door.

Another rural teacher not only shared a bed with the mother but also with her eight-month-old baby. Not a happy arrangement for the teacher. Some mornings found her soaking wet up to her shoulders. There was no other boarding place in the district and since the landlady was kind she did not complain. In fact the young miss stayed on from March to May enduring her occasional nightly drenching.

Which is preferable—the odor of liniment or barnyard manure? Jennie, who taught in the Willowdale S.D. during the 1926 school term, had no choice in the matter. She boarded with an old farm couple, which was fine, but unfortunately the husband was badly crippled with arthritis. He spent most of his nights rubbing his body with liniment as this treatment provided him with a measure of relief from the agonizing pain. The odor of liniment permeated not only the entire house but every article of clothing that the teacher possessed. Even her books smelled like a dispensary. She made a single attempt to provide a little ventilation through the one and only window in her room. Immediately she had to reconsider her decision. The house had been banked all around with manure so when the window was opened the stench that accompanied the influx of fresh air was anything but pleasant. She soon discovered that she preferred the smell of liniment to that of manure.

One of the most suitable boarding places to be found anywhere was the Big Briscoe Home located in the Fertile Valley S.D. (Moston, Sask.). When Mr. Brian Briscoe a former chairman of the school board built his house he made it large enough to include a special teacher's room. It contained everything for the extra comfort and convenience of the teacher. After World War I as many as three teachers, who were teaching in nearby schools, came to board at the Briscoe home as it was such a good place to stay.

A former teacher of the Valley View S.D. when recalling her boarding place in the district some twenty-one years ago could not understand why the chairman of the board, a seemingly understanding individual, compelled a seventeen-year-old girl to live in such a place. The lady of the house was but two weeks a widow and living with her in the three-room shack was her subnormal nineteen-year-old daughter and her definitely abnormal twenty-year-old son. In fact the son had spent two years in a mental institution and had at one time become uncontrollable. The three were all extremely neurotic and the two young people were very jealous of everything the teacher was, or had, or knew, or said, or did. The teacher's room was half the living room curtained off with sheets, while the other three grown-ups shared the one bedroom. When the cow had a calf and died they brought the calf into the house as well. The daughter contracted ringworm and passed it on to the teacher with the result that she had to extend her Christmas holidays by several days to permit her hometown doctor to clear up the infection. Nothing more serious than being shouted at actually happened to the teacher. She often feared the worst and to this day still thinks that given the right set of circumstances a tragedy might have occurred.

Joan Wigby, a teacher in the King S.D. (Kelloe, Man.), found the meals at her boarding place were good only if visitors were present. She often had to force herself to drink milk that had fragments of straw floating in it. Joan was more fortunate than most teachers for she had a room to herself. Once during the winter when it was around thirty degrees below zero she objected to having to use the outdoor toilet. The landlady solved the problem very simply by placing a pail with a cutting rim in her room. This indoor convenience remained in her bedroom and it was the teacher's responsibility to empty it. Miss Wigby walked home every weekend a distance of nine miles. She was disgusted to learn that during these periods when she was absent the hired man or any other visitor who happened along was given the full use of her bed and room.

A teacher in the Clydebank S.D. (Eriksdale, Man.) best remembers her boarding place for the many games of five hundred that were played there as everyone waited patiently for the one goose to lay her egg. If the egg was nipped by the frost it became useless for hatching purposes so a constant vigil had to be maintained on cold evenings. While waiting for the blessed event to take place the family and the teacher played five hundred. There would be great joy if one of the players returned from the barn without the egg, for it meant that the game could continue. It often did until far past midnight to the accompaniment of merry shouts of "Good Old Goose" by the winning players until the egg was finally tucked away in an alcove in the warm kitchen.

When Mr. C. D. Denney taught in the Poe S.D. (Ryley, Alta.) in 1923 he stayed with Mr. and Mrs. Kerr who were refugees from the civil war in Ireland. He recalls that Mr. Kerr was a strange man. Frequently he undertook to support some exaggerated statement or position by swearing on a stack of Bibles—four or five feet high if necessary. The Kerrs also ran a small country store, where he refused to sell tobacco. The couple was very kind and generous. One day when Mr. Denney said something about Bendicksons in Ryley having a Ford car for sale for one hundred and five dollars and he wished he had the money to buy it, Mr. Kerr produced the necessary cash and insisted that the teacher get the car. Mr. Denney recalls that he was a long time saving any money after the purchase.

To reach his school in the St. Lina S.D. (St. Paul, Alta.) Philios Durocher, the teacher, had to cross a large creek. One morning in 1916 after it had rained steadily for a week he discovered that the bridge had been washed out. He stood on the bank of the swollen stream and wondered what to do. In casting about for ideas he spied a large pig trough in a nearby farmyard. The farmer was quite willing to loan it to him, so Mr. Durocher, after a few unsuccessful bids, managed to pole the strange craft to the other side. He used this ferry for a whole week until the flood waters had subsided and the bridge was restored. Mr. Durocher's solution to the problem served as an example to other adventurous souls. Soon anybody who wished to reach the store and post office took the "pig-trough" ferry.

In 1919 when Hilda taught school on a permit in the Wildflower S.D. (Sedalia, Alta.) she boarded with a French-Canadian family. The husband didn't believe in banks so he buried his money in a hole after putting it in a protective glass sealer. One day a badger dug the jar out and the teacher found it. When she gave it back to him he extended her no thanks but scolded her for snooping around his pasture and farmyard.

Not many teachers have had the experience of attending a wake but Mary Dickie did so in the Greenock S.D. (Pinkerton, Ont). One of her students died and the people with whom she boarded took her to the wake. She didn't know what it was all about but soon found that it was a watch held over the body of her former pupil prior to the burial. Board seats were arranged in the kitchen and everyone sat around and talked and prayed in low voices. Miss Dickie left at eleven o'clock but she guessed that the wake continued for many hours thereafter. She would have missed this moving experience if she had not roomed with this particular family.

The boarding places in rural districts were just like the teachers—some were good and others extremely poor. The meals served at some of these homes were so inadequate that at times a compassionate family in the district made a practice of sending a note to the teacher, saying—"Cooking a roast tonight. If you can come plan to stay the night!" There was no second guessing. The teacher always thankfully accepted such invitations. In time this practice initiated a friendship that grew firmer with the years. Most rural teachers can point with gratitude to some such family that exhibited a solicitude for their personal welfare.

Money was so scarce during the hungry Thirties that it became a Herculean task to finance the operation of a rural school with any degree of success. The farmers did not have the wherewithal to pay their school taxes, the district as a consequence found it impossible to pay the teacher's salary and the teacher in turn could not pay for her board and room. The net result was that many districts became insolvent and were forced to close their schools. A number of rural communities however, came up with unique solutions to this problem of "no money" in the economic cycle and in some instances never closed their schools. The Newheim S.D. (Medicine Hat, Alta.) was one such district. Here the women took over from the men and solved the impending financial crisis by introducing what they called the "itinerant boarding of the teacher" method.

The scheme, as explained by the inspired female economists at the well-attended annual ratepayers' meeting, appeared to be simple enough. Each family in the Newheim School District would board the teacher for a month and the expenses of her board and room was to be deducted from the farmer's taxes as well as from the teacher's salary. In this way the teacher managed to satisfy her indebtedness for her board, the school district a goodly portion of its salary commitment to the teacher and the farmers some of their taxes to the municipality. The salient feature of this plan was that no money every changed hands as all business transactions were consummated by simple bookkeeping entries.

So much interest was engendered at the gathering that unanimous approval was given to the adoption of the ladies' unique proposal. So while some neighboring districts closed their schools, the Newheim School continued to provide education for their children for another year or so. In addition, the scheme had certain worth-while social implications for everyone in the community. For the teacher it also meant numerous bizarre experiences as she was shuttled back and forth from one home to another like a switch engine.

The hosting home was a hive of industry just prior to the teacher's monthly sojourn. It was like preparing for Christmas or Easter. There was an endless round of scrubbing, washing, baking and rearranging the furniture in the home. Even the children were instructed as to their standard of behavior during the teacher's stay in their midst. The boys and girls, although proud to have her in their homes, were scared of her. The older ones often felt a little ashamed when using "ain't" or when dad sipped his hot coffee or soup accompanied by sharp sibilant sounds. The living room was heated continuously for the first time during the winter months as the "spare" bedroom was just off from it and of course had been reserved for the teacher. Breakfast during the teacher's stay was served in the living room to her and to the school children in the family. During these breakfasts the youngsters partook for the first time in their lives of such novel foods as shredded wheat, cornflakes or grapenuts. The introduction of such new items of nourishment was a mark of respect for the teacher in this German community. The rest of the family had an earlier breakfast in the kitchen with the usual uninspiring menu of rolled oats, bread, jam and coffee.

Since lunch was taken to school it left only the problem of providing supper at home. This was served at the long table in the kitchen with the entire family present. It included the shy school youngsters, a number of embarrassed older brothers and sisters who had left school earlier, and the parents and the grandparents who spoke very little English. The food was simple but prepared in a manner that reminded the children of a festal occasion. The elders spared no time or effort to make the meals attractive.

Usually it took a month before the family began to feel at ease in having the teacher in their home. But by this time she was slated to move on to the next home. The people of Newheim who shared their homes with the teacher were agreed that their lives had been enriched by her presence. She, in turn, respected the efforts of these people who, under trying circumstances, were doing their best for her. It must have been an inconvenience for her to be passed on from home to home yet she never complained. The parents and teacher of this small German community typified the true spirit of education in the pioneer days when they co-operated with each other for the ultimate benefit of the children.

The residents of Rocky Coulee S.D. (Granum, Alta.) also initiated such a practice of boarding the teacher from home to home. It was said that the roosters of Rocky Coulee literally "went to pot" during this period. Every household wanted to treat the teacher just as well as their neighbors had done. This friendly competition was hard on the teacher. After being on the receiving end of a continuous royal diet of chicken she was heard to remark, "I would give up my kingdom right now for a nice piece of beef or pork!"

An opportune time for the nomadic teacher to arrive at a new boarding place was when the farmer was butchering. It was then that the teacher could enjoy a feed of fresh meat whether it was pork chops, spare ribs, juicy steaks or tasty morsels of liver. Due to a lack of refrigeration in those early days it was necessary to salt, smoke, pickle, can, or prepare the meat in some other way to prevent it from spoiling. Rural teachers of that era still make mention today of the huge slabs of fat salt pork, the massive legs of smoked ham or the endless array of sealers of canned meat that used to embellish the pantry shelves, the cellar larders and the utility sheds on most farms. The introduction of "beef rings" and the advent of the refrigerator in later years made fresh meat available at all times. So was it any wonder that the teachers of yesteryear looked ahead with as much anticipation as a gourmet towards the occasional butchering day!

Contrary to common belief milk, eggs and vegetables did not make up a substantial part of the teacher's bill of fare during the depression or drought periods. The sale of cream and eggs was often the only source of ready cash for many of the poverty-stricken farmers so it was only on rare occasions that these foods found their way to the dinner tables. It was true that such common vegetables as potatoes, turnips, beets and cabbages were an integral part of most meals but during the very dry years there was seldom enough of these stalwarts to go around.

Since no two rural homes hosting a teacher were ever alike each new boarding place plunged the teacher into another drama of life dictated by a different set of circumstances and new characters. Some of these experiences stood out in a steacher's memory like eminences of land on the prairies.

Stella F. Johnston, an Edmonton housewife and a grade three teacher for the Edmonton Public School Board, recaptures much of the pioneering spirit of this singular custom of "boarding the teacher".

"My hostess was an overworked young woman with four little children, ranging in age from three months to five years. Her greatest culinary achievement—teacherwise—was to buy a large can of pink salmon (twenty cents in those depression days) and make it do for my sandwich filling from Monday through Friday. Spread lightly between two thick slices of coarse, dry, homemade bread and buttered as lightly with off-flavor butter — well, it wasn't too appetizing. And when the second can made its appearance the second week and I had manfully eaten my way through it, I rebelled, and pleaded for a change. I got it in the form of blueberry jam sandwiches! Never will I forget the sight of those soggy, blue-soaked slabs of bread that confronted me when I hopefully opened my lunch pail on the Monday of the third week. I must admit their taste was better than their bilious appearance; but they were not sustaining and by the time I had taught thirty-five active youngsters all day and walked a mile-and-a-half home to my boarding place my appetite was ravenous. I was ready to eat anything."

"Returning to the prairies — perhaps one of the worst experiences I suffered through was when I was boarded with a shiftless, happy-go-lucky family who subsisted mainly on flour which they ground themselves. That, in itself, would not have been too bad. In fact, I used to be very fond of brown and whole wheat bread, but not any more! The sacks of flour, for lack of a better storage place, were lined up starting at the kitchen door, all along one wall and were used as seats. When anyone came in, family or friend from the barn, pigpen, garden or field, he perched on a sack of flour while he removed his gum boots, overshoes or overalls. Walking along the top of the sacks of flour without falling off was a favorite game with the younger members of the family.

"Once, while I was staying with a young Ukrainian couple, all three of us were stricken with a severe case of flu. The wife's father came to our aid—

with a bottle of moonshine of his own making and honey from his own beehive. After downing my share of the concoction, which he brewed on the old cookstove, I was barely able to stagger into bed, where I 'sweated it out' all night long. Next morning I walked the mile to school — a little shaky, but the flu was gone."

Mrs. Everatt, another former rural mentor, likes to recall her experiences while boarding with a singular but certainly the most benevolent landlady any teacher could wish for.

"My proprietress was a jolly fat woman, who was so kind hearted that she wouldn't hurt a fly. The flies must have known this for they came from miles around just to visit her house. I was everlastingly buying fly-paper to wage my own personal war against these unwelcome guests. At home in the city I used to cringe at the mere sight of my mother disposing of one of those sticky, fly-laden and buzzing serpentines in the kitchen stove, but here I delighted to do the cremation with my own hands.

"Confusion seemed to be the keynote of this household, as my landlady was a very disorganized person. In the morning when I'd be anxious to be on my way to school, she would be racing around the kitchen frantically trying to get the kettle to boil. Finally in desperation she would fish a dirty old pie plate out of the greasy warming-oven and boil the water in it to prepare my coffee.

"Last minute rushing was also the rule in this household. Once she had promised me for two weeks that she would have some strawberries for me to take home to my mother. Ten minutes before I should have left to catch the bus to the city on this particular Friday, my benefactress was still boiling strawberries and shoving kindling like mad into the roaring cook stove. To this day I can remember running down the dusty country road with a shopping bag full of newspapers and a asealer of hot strawberries.

"In the evening I felt it was my duty to help with the supper dishes. As her cupboards were kept like the rest of her home I was not surprised to find everything imaginable packed into them. One night as I was attempting to put a cup in its place on the top shelf, out popped a vanilla bottle and landed on my head. Why remember such a small incident? The stopper had only been resting on the bottle!"

The accommodation for the teacher rather than the provision of meals was the principal problem encountered by most districts. The majority of homes were built only to take care of the immediate needs of the family of the settler. Hence comfort was not always the objective nor was the construction of a spare room considered a necessity. Take the case of the teacher in the Leamington S.D. (Pasqua, Sask.) who shared her bedroom in a farmhome with four children separated from them merely by a sheet strung on a clothes line. Certainly not a very substantial partition. It must be remembered that the exigencies of the day necessitated the introduction of a rapid and inexpensive method of dividing the existing bedroom into two or more roomettes. It was a common practice to fashion these temporary cubicles by the simple expediency of suspending sheets, blankets, a piece of canvas, a rug, or even a hide, over a convenient two-by-four, a

A basement suite for the teacher of the Chain Lakes School (Hanna, Alta.)

rope, or a wire. This method of providing some measure of privacy was the rule rather than the exception.

In later years the question of providing living quarters for the teacher became so acute in many districts that a number of school boards went to the trouble of providing one of those mixed blessings called "a teacherage". The decision to build one of these monstrosities may have stemmed from protests rather than actual need. In a school district near Blackie, Alta., the board decided to construct the teacherage only when the newly-hired teacher from Edmonton arrived with a dog. No one wanted to board a teacher with a dog. The district had boarded teachers without too much inconvenience from 1908 to 1926 but it took a canine to alter the tradition. Up went the teacherage at a cost of $150 to the ratepayers. They had only one terse comment to make, "It was an expensive dog!"

Teacherages were simple structures built to suit local conditions. Some were residences apart from the schoolhouse while others formed an annex to it. Many were glorified granaries, bunkhouses, sheds or even barns. At best they could be described as mere shacks. In the Chain Lakes S.D. (Hanna, Alta.) half the basement was partitioned off to make the teacherage. It consisted of two rooms eight feet by twelve feet. One had a tiny basement window near the ceiling but the other boasted of a large picture window. This was possible because the cement basement extended some three feet above ground level on one side as the school had been built on a sloping piece of land.

The school board of the Pobeda S.D. 1604 (Two Hills, Alta.) had the school attic renovated to provide living accommodation for their teacher in 1908.

—Mrs. Thomas Hrapko

The trustees of the Pobeda S.D. 1604 (Two Hills, Alta.) looked up rather than down when contemplating living quarters for their teacher when the school first opened in 1909. The school attic was transformed into a cozy teacherage. In order to enable the teacher to reach this lofty perch outside stairs were built and anchored to the end wall of the school. They extended all the way from ground level to the attic door. As an after-thought a flimsy guardrail was provided to lend assurance to any teachers who had an aversion to height. The teacherage was complemented by a small rectangular opening cut in the wall beside the doorway and a window installed to permit the entrance of a little light and even still less fresh air. It was impossible for the teacher to stand erect in most parts of this teacherage due to the low ceiling. Any time she forgot this and raised her head, "Boom," it came in contact with a rafter and sharply reminded her of the limitations. Eventually the teacher developed a habitual stoop and even became cognizant of nine-foot ceilings.

At that the teachers of Pobeda were more fortunate than the one who taught at Cuthbert S.D. 633 in 1892. The Cuthbert teacher lived at Melita, Man. sixteen miles away. He came on Monday and "bached" in the classroom until Friday. This teacher slept in a bed that had been placed in one corner of the room.

A number of teachers taught in schools that operated only during the summer months and they found it convenient to live in tents. The first teacher in the Wavy Plains S.D. 2511 (Oyen, Alta.) along with her brother and sister and two neighboring boys lived in two such tents during the summer of 1912. Pioneers of this district still remember the sign affixed to one of the tents. It read, "Fair View". This probably had reference to the commanding view of the rolling prairies that the site offered since it was the highest point for miles around. It also could have referred to the pretty school teacher who lived therein.

—Mrs. Bishop

The teacher in the Wavy Plains S.D. (Oyen, Alta.) during the summer of 1912
lived in a tent.

The Cambachie S.D. 2264 (Moose Jaw, Sask.) built a twelve-by-eight-
teen-foot teacherage on skids so it could be readily moved from one farmyard to another, wherever a family was willing to serve meals to the
teacher. This "home on skids" was quite comfortable. It was furnished with
a good bed, a small coal heater, a dressing table, an armchair, a table, a
set of cupboards and a limited supply of dishes and cooking utensils. The
only sign of luxury in the portable home was an attractive piece of
linoleum that graced the floor. All in all the teacher was provided with a
living space that gave her a sense of privacy.

Such a portable teacherage had another advantage. In the Alpha S.D.
2338 (Hanna, Alta.) the hosting family became involved in a school row
and this attained such a pitch that the farmer ordered the school authorities to haul the shack off his place with "the damned teacher in it". The
teacherage was moved to another farmyard. Before long it had to be
shunted again. Ill feelings had developed betweeen the teacher and the
head of the household when the son was strapped for a grave misdemeanor
at school.

The majority of teacherages were small and very poorly equipped.
Outside of a bed, some form of dresser, a table, a couple of chairs, a
cookstove, a cupboard, a coal-oil lamp, some cutlery and tinware there
was very little else in the way of furnishings. The teachers provided their
own bedding, curtains and other clothware. The advertisements in the
newspapers under the heading of, TEACHERS WANTED always con-

cluded with a statement like, "A fully furnished and comfortable teacherage is available on the school grounds. In lieu of rent the teacher will be expected to do the janitor work." The words "fully" and "comfortable" meant one thing to a hiring school board and something else to the teacher moving into the teacherage. Mr. William Hay, an inspector in the Hanna area of Alberta, was instrumental in persuading his school boards to adopt a policy whereby each teacherage was furnished with a certain minimum amount of household equipment. The idea was to supply not only the essentials but at the same time enough luxury items to enable the teacher to entertain at least one guest. Like providing two knives and forks rather than one or two chairs in place of one. Coal and wood were usually supplied free by the district. Unless a nearby well and pump were available the water supply for the teacherage had to be hauled and stored in a barrel or cistern.

There was no getting away from the fact that many of the teacherages were cold places in which to live. It was not unusual to find the walls, the doors, the windows and the floor not fitting together at all. At times it was possible to see the blue sky through the resulting chinks. Outside of one layer of tarpaper there was no other insulation between the walls. These huts lacked a solid foundation as the majority had been placed on blocks of wood. Floors consisted of a single thickness of rough-hewn boards which soon dried to leave hideous gaps between them. To the tenant these accidental ventilators had one advantage—no dustpan was ever required. It became easy and convenient to sweep the dust and grime down through these openings, the wind took charge of the refuse after that. The slightest stir in the atmosphere during the winter-time carried fine snow and silt into the holey teacherage. And as if by magic small drifts mushroomed all over the floor, the windowsills and the furnishings. At times like these one was apt to remember the haunting words found in the title of the old western song, "The Shifting Whispering Sands." Everything froze whether it was the water in the pail or the food in the cupboard. Even the teacher's clothes congealed to the wall. Hoarfrost formed on the floor, the walls, the table, the blankets and pillowcases and on the bottom of the mattress.

Getting ready for bed in a cold teacherage or in an upstairs bedroom in a farmhouse, implied putting on clothes rather than shedding them. Stella, a nineteen-year-old teacher, who taught in the Fife S.D. (Carnduff, Sask.) back in 1922, aptly describes her routine of beating the implacable cold.

> "I wore about all I could put on at night — the undershirt of my long underwear, a flannelette nightgown, a sweater, and finally a kimono. My feet rested on my fur muff or on a pre-heated flatiron, or on a hotwater bottle, but still I shivered from the cold many a night."

Isabel of West Union S.D. (Leduc, Alta.) had her own way of keeping warm during the cold winter nights of 1914.

"I found I could not sleep in the bedroom of the teacherage as it was too cold. I used to pull the lounge up in front of the stove in the kitchen, wrap up warmly, and pile everything possible on top of me to keep warm. My sleep would be broken several times during the night as it was necessary to refuel the small cookstove. However, by strategically placing the sticks of wood and lumps of coal near the lounge I was able to fire the stove without the necessity of getting out of bed."

Teachers considered themselves fortunate if their dwelling contained one stove in good working order, yet Kay's teacherage south of Buffalo, Alta., had three different stoves installed on the same day. This is Kay's story of "The Three Stoves".

"The first fall (1934) was quite cold with early snow. The stove in the teacherage, a huge old range, had no grates so I was forced to light the fire in the ashpan. Unfortunately there was a hole in the oven wall so a good deal of smoke sifted into the room. At night I pulled the table in front of the oven, put my bedding on the make-shift bed, crawled aboard with my little fox terrier and tried to sleep. By morning I was so cold, stiff and tired that I could scarcely get mobile. At last I faced the board members when they brought their children to school and told them that I had had enough. If something wasn't done about a stove that day I would leave the next morning if I had to walk into town. I meant it too, even though I needed the job. When school was dismissed at 3:30 I saw three outfits coming from three different directions each with a stove in its sleigh box. "The first, an enormous range, would not go through the doorway and would have taken up most of the room in the kitchen anyway. The second went in but the pipes would not fit so it was carted out. The third was a camper's stove about eighteen inches high with an oven just big enough for a cakepan. It was put up in the bedroom. The doorway between the two rooms was closed off with a heavy blanket so my bedroom became my living room and kitchenette. The former kitchen became the storage bin for winter fuel. Frequently it doubled as a good refrigerator. The four years that I stayed there were made comfortable by that little stove; and like Robinson Crusoe, I became so attached to it I hated to part with it when I left the district."

Teacherages on the prairies were never made completely weather resistant. The wind lashed about the little shack, rattled the windows and door and left a thick mantle of dust over everything. To keep out these chilly or dust-laden winds, the teacher soon learned to stuff rags or old newspapers into the places where the windows or the door did not fit their frames. An old coat or rug was also pushed up against the base of the door to stifle any drafts. The matter of entering a teacherage on very cold days was no longer a simple operation for it had to be invariably accompanied by pinching the rags back into place about the ill-fitting door. As a dull table knife proved to be the best tool for doing this particular job one was always found somewhere quite handy to the door. It gave the visitors unfamiliar with rural living the impression that the knife was there for self-defense against would-be assailants. A few teachers became such experts in this art of "stuffing" that evidences of their work may still be seen in a few deserted and dilapidated teacherages. True the newspapers are covered with dirt and are weather-beaten but they still retain their original places by the window-frames after being buffeted about by winds, snow and rain for well nigh twenty-five years.

The incessant bombings of teacherages by dust storms and skipping Russian thistles during the dry years will not soon be forgotten by teachers who taught on the prairies during that time. All night long the thump, thump, thump, accompanied by grating sounds told how the thistles struck the building and then rolled along the wall until set free again by the wind. At odd intervals gusts of dirt-laden wind blasted the teacherage until it shook, to be followed by a parting shower of pebbles, sand and other grit as it swept by. During these windstorms the cottager always feared that at any moment the shack itself might break loose from its foundation and follow the Russian thistles across the prairie. It was also common practice during the worst parts of these black blizzards for the teacher to keep a damp towel over her mouth and nose so as not to inhale too much dust. On odd occasions it was also terrifying to be wakened in the night by the sound of scraping horns against the walls of the little teacherage indicating that stray cattle had wandered into the schoolyard. Sometimes it was the weird howling of the coyote that disturbed the teacher's slumbers.

Chinook winds often melted the mounds of snow that frequently gathered about the teacherage so rapidly that in a matter of hours the rural pedagogue found herself completely isolated by a moat of considerable depth. Not being versed in irrigation she experienced some difficulty in digging the proper ditches to drain the water away from her domicile. Meanwhile the inside was deluged.

The teacherages had no facilities whatsoever for keeping perishable food from spoiling. The common method was to store it down the well where cool temperatures prevailed.

Living in a rural area had some advantages. Fresh milk was always available. While treats from the gardens, the kitchens and the butcheries of the district often found their way to the teacher's table. Rural people cannot be equalled for their generosity. It used to be a common sight to see some youngster with a bulging parcel sidle up to the teacher some morning and blurt out, "Mother asked me to give you this." The "this" turned out to be anything from a piece of liver to a bowl of fresh strawberries.

Four Representative Teacherages

Arethusa S.D. 4449 (Cereal, Alta.)   Southview S.D. 3489 (Oyen, Alta.)

New Brigden S.D. 2751   Lanfine S.D. 2640 (Lanfine, Alta.)
(New Brigden, Alta.)

For the most part the teacher living in a teacherage did not find it too difficult to obtain supplies from town. The neighbors were most considerate in shopping for her. Besides, Saturday was a good day for her to go into town to replenish her larder, to visit, to get the mail, or to transact business. If there was no need to go into town she could do the washing, the cooking, or tidying up generally. The problem of how to get to town six to seventeen miles away was always present. She could walk, borrow or buy a horse, catch a ride with a family or ride a bicycle. Some school districts, like Dundee S.D. 4326 (Hanna, Alta.), were very thoughtful and made arrangements for her transportation into town.

> "A motion was made by Mrs. Grimes and seconded by Mrs. Hemstock that the parents of the children going to school be responsible for taking the teacher to town on such occasions as Saturdays, holidays, conventions, etc., same to run alphabetically. The party taking the teacher in will not be responsible for the teacher's return, but the next party in alphabetical order shall be responsible. Carried."

Since the teacherage was a convenient place in which to prepare lunches for the various gatherings held in the school the teacher on such

—Mrs. M. C. Farwell

A teacher's first car bought in 1923 from Vickers in Drumheller, Alta. for $700.

occasions found herself dispossessed. Hordes of women, or so it appeared, surged into the little kitchen to heat gallons of water, make coffee, cut cakes, sort out sandwiches and talk. Knowing eyes took in every corner of the shack and the teacher's reputation as a housekeeper suffered or attained status. It behooved the teacher to have everything neat and tidy when these infrequent invasions occurred. There were advantages however. Any extras such as cream or cake were left for the teacher. Besides, some influential or sympathetic woman might spot the lack or poor state of the furnishings and set about rectifying the matter. It was a wonderful opportunity for scheming teachers to exhibit their leaky kettle, the cracked pitcher, the broken-handled knife, the smoky stove, or any other item that required replacing or fixing. These items made wonderful conversational pieces for the ladies.

It was a tough life for the young girls who came out from the city to teach in these rural school districts. In the Wolf Willow S.D. (Alsask, Sask.) for example, the chairman of the school board met the new teacher in the dead of winter at the Alsask railway station and then drove her in a horse-drawn sleigh six long cold miles to the lonely shack in the schoolyard. School terms in those days commenced early in the year so most teachers, who so far had spent their lives in comparative comfort in the city, learned for the first time how miserable a winter could be.

Nature's old law of the survival of the fittest was pretty much in evidence in the country.

The Wolf Willow teacherage was a one-room hut fourteen by sixteen feet. It was heated by a far-from-adequate coal stove that had the habit of petering out every night. The teacher rose early in the morning in a frigid room, lit the coal-oil lamp, started a fire in the stove and then hopped back into bed until the temperature of the room reached about ten degrees before she began dressing. Soon it was time to make a dash over to the schoolhouse to kindle yet another fire.

There was no well at Wolf Willow. In the winter, the teacher melted snow for washing, while in summer she carried water from a nearby slough, or prevailed upon a friend to haul her a barrel of water. An alternative plan was not to bother washing. Combine these inconveniences with an outdoor toilet, no telephone and the nearest neighbor an old bachelor and "baching" could be pretty grim for a city bred eighteen-year-old girl.

Teacherages provided their occupants with privacy but in turn were so isolated that it took a special breed of teacher to live in them. The loneliness and the liability to peril from one source or another discouraged the wholesale use of teacherages. Records indicate that teachers have been beaten, robbed, insulted, subjected to personal indignity, intimidated, raped and murdered in these solitary dwelling places.

Margaret Lloyd, who lived alone in the Pinto Creek S.D. (Aneroid, Sask.) teacherage received a real scare one night. The foreboding sound of loud knocking at her door in the middle of the night was frightening in itself but it was even more alarming to open the door and discover two Royal Canadian Mounted Policemen standing outside. The officers informed Miss Lloyd that they were looking for a dangerous criminal and had reason to believe he was heading for the United States border sixty miles away on the road that went by the school. They stayed the night as they were concerned for the safety of the young teacher.

Not many people today have heard of "The Strangler". Back in 1913 this brute strangled a young girl who was teaching in a rural district in Southern Manitoba. He cornered her in the out-of-the-way teacherage and after raping her, choked her to death. Rural teachers throughout Manitoba spent many anxious days and nights until he was safely lodged behind prison bars.

One teacher in the Menzie S.D. (Oakburn, Man.) thought that the strangler had come to dispatch her when a strange man walked into her school just about the time the murderer was still at large. The girl's mother had written to her describing the sordid doings of the strangler. She informed her daughter that the authorities did not know where he was and that it would be advisable for her not to stay at school after the children had gone home at 3:30 p.m. The girl had received the letter the evening before so her mind was heavily weighed with tales of horror surrounding the activities of the killer. Nevertheless she remained in the school to put some extra work on the blackboard. She was nearly finished when a man walked in without even taking the trouble to knock. The teacher was terrified! She realized that it couldn't be anyone else but the hideous strangler. She started to go around the desks towards the door. Yes! she must get to the door somehow. This was the only avenue of escape. The strangler seemed to anticipate her strategy for he moved straight towards her to cut off her path of flight. She could almost feel his cold, steely fingers clutching at her throat as he came near. The teacher was too frightened to scream. Besides, who would hear her? She wished she had taken her mother's advice and gone home with the children. Too late to be sorry!

The girl made a final desperate lunge toward the door. Merciful heaven! she made it. She was free. Now to run away as fast as she could. The "strangler," instead of pursuing her, asked, "How old are you?" She hesitated a moment in her dash for freedom and replied, "None of your business!" Now the "monster" was enticing her to return she thought. She had better be wary. He appeared to be very uncertain and puzzled about something so when he said, "I am the census-taker and you have to answer my questions," the teacher realized for the first time that she had mistaken the rural enumerator for the strangler.

The census-taker graciously accepted her explanation so she felt relieved on that score but the shock of such a nervous ordeal left her in tears and with a bad case of tremors. The young teacher had never been so scared in all her life and for years thereafter never stayed in after school.

Being lonely was almost as terrifying an experience as being stalked by a murderer. Take this story of Cyprienne Jolly, (today Sister Victor-de-Milan), an eighteen-year-old teacher who was hired in December 1913 to teach in the newly-formed Belzil S.D. 2979 (St. Paul, Alta.).

Cyprienne decided to live in the school instead of walking the three-quarters of a mile to and from school every day. Not to be alone she persuaded her ten-year-old sister to stay with her. The first three nights were not too bad for they had the company of Maria Doucet, a girl of Miss Jolly's age and then Felix Berlinquette, a nearby farmer, was kind enough to visit them during the evenings. The fourth night was different. For the first time they were left on their own resources to spend the night and sleep alone in an empty and unfurnished school. It turned out to be a cold, windy and stormy night. Many noises, both real and imaginary, disturbed the slumber of the two girls: the cracking of the fire in the box-stove, the howling of the wind in the chimney, the creaking of the unfinished building and the weird yelpings of the coyotes. They were too frightened to sleep. What could they do? Stay alone with these hideous sounds of the night or brave the blizzard and the wild animals outside? They chose the latter course of action. The two girls ran the three-quarters of a mile to the Doucet home as fast as their legs could carry them. By the time they reached their destination they were completely exhausted and nearly hysterical. At first, Mr. Doucet was tempted to send them back so they would get used to spending the night alone but seeing how over-wrought they were he decided to let them remain.

The sad experience convinced Cyprienne that it was much wiser to board with the Doucet family than attempt to live alone at the school. She did this for the four years that she taught in the Belzil School.

The Glen Echo S.D. (Conquerville, Alta.) was one school district that did something towards making living in a teacherage less lonely. In 1938, when Blanche McLean was teaching there, she was able to enjoy radio music by remote control. It was piped into her teacherage via a barbed wire fence and received by means of a "His Master's Voice" loudspeaker.

It wasn't the isolated living in a teacherage that troubled Mrs. Cecile J. Paul. Her problem was having too many visitors. This was in a newly-formed district in northern Saskatchewan where people had been reha-bilitated from the Dust Bowl in the southern section of the province. Little did the teacher realize when she accepted the position on a temporary basis that the place bore a marked similarity to the fairy tale where the footprints all pointed going into the fox's den but none returning. As she was travelling to this isolated district by bob sleigh over corduroy roads, around stumps and sloughs, across fallen trees and through thick bushes, Cecile began to have misgivings as to whether it would be a simple matter to get out again. It wasn't. She spent a couple of happy years there. At least they were happy to a certain point for she did encounter some unpleasantness while residing in her newly-constructed log teacherage.

There was an Indian reservation right across from the school and for the most part the squaws were always underfoot. One day she had given them some tobacco and from that time on her teacherage was theirs. She had a good hook on the inside of the screen door but that meant nothing to the Indians. Whenever she came home from school she was certain to find four or five large Indian women seated on the floor with their voluminous skirts covering most of the area. It did no good to ask them to leave. They couldn't understand English. Only when she reluctantly took the crumpled package of tobacco from her pocket and gave each of them a pipeful did they disappear. Even then they stayed until they were good and ready to leave. Almost every evening found Mrs. Paul stepping gingerly over purple and red dress tails as she went about her task of preparing supper. Sometimes they arrived early in the morning long before the teacher and her family were up. There appeared to be no way of stopping these persistent visitors.

And then there was the smell of smoked hide. She eventually knew without looking when an Indian was in the house while she was still several feet away from her door. Of course Mrs. Paul received expert advice from everyone on how to get rid of the human pests. "Don't give them tobacco or anything!" was the the wise counsel. The frenzied teacher tried this as well as saying "go!" and pointing most emphatically in the direction of the door. The squaws stayed. Cecile received some respite from her silent guests during the blueberry picking season. But they returned soon after, offering their blueberries in exchange for her tobacco or old clothes. The teacher finally accepted the Indians as a cross she had to bear. Any time the the squaws failed to show up she appreciated the freedom of such a "red letter" day.

Indians were not the only ones who visited Mrs. Paul in her teacherage. There was a mental case in the form of a burly ex-trapper who found her company rather relaxing. While she did enjoy unusual characters she did not feel an affinity for such people. Cecile always felt that he might go berserk at any moment. He did, but fortunately for her, she had left the district by that time.

Why the teacherages possessed a special fascination for wandering animals was an enigma that the school authorities were unable to explain. Yet birds and animals of all types were impelled by some unseen force toward the teacher's residence. They had the habit of appearing at the doors, the windows, inside the chimney or stove, under the floor, on the roof and once in a while gained entrance into the teacherage. They did not respect any visiting schedule but came at all hours of the day or night. It seemed that the more inconvenient the time for the teacher the more likely were the visitors to appear.

Mrs. Olive Parkes, who taught at Clarkleigh S.D. 1909 (Oakes, Man.), lived in a very old teacherage with creaky floors, poorly fitting doors and windows, and topped off with a dilapidated chimney. Such a draughty habitation had a special appeal to skunks. One night after the children were in bed and everything was quiet the teacher heard a noise in the outside porch. She thought it was the neighbor's dog so she opened the door quickly to frighten it away. Imagine her surprise to discover a large fat skunk sitting on the inside doorstep. Olive instantly shut the door rather rudely in the visitor's face and to be doubly sure placed a chair against the door. The latch did not work properly and a slight push against the door would have opened it. The uninvited guest made his presence felt in the only way he knew how. The archaic teacherage was not impervious to this type of treatment. In the morning, Mrs. Parkes went out the front door and around the building to the back to see if the visitor was still there. Mr. Skunk had left without resorting any further to his nauseating chemical warfare for which the teacher was most grateful.

It wasn't a skunk but a large police dog that annoyed Ida when she taught in the Three Hills Rural (Three Hills, Alta.) in 1939. The section foreman from Twining often drove his little girl to school by car. On such occasions their giant-sized police dog followed the model-T Ford to school. The animal always gave the teacher a start by bounding up against the teacherage door. If the door wasn't securely fastened the canine darted inside and into the bedroom where Ida was usually getting ready for school. The first time this occurred the youngsters were highly amused. They chanted gleefully, "The dog went in and the teacher came out!"

Yet it was a dream about that selfsame dog that saved the teacher from being burned to death. Prior to retiring for the night she was in the habit of placing her one-dollar Big Ben watch on the floor beside the bed along with three or four matches. When she woke up at any time during the night she struck a match to see what time it was. Clocks or watches in those early days did not have luminous dials.

One night she dreamt that the police dog had come into her room. She reached out and touched him. To this day Ida still remembers the feel of the dog's coat. As she rested her hand on the dog she reasoned that if he was in the house the door must be open and she should get out of bed and close it. At that instant she woke up. The mat was on fire. Ida had dropped a lighted match on it while looking at the time-piece earlier in the night. If she hadn't had that dream her bed would soon have been on fire. When Ida's parents heard of the near cremation they presented her with a novel gadget called a flashlight.

A locked teacherage was no deterrent to some animals. Shortly after returning to his teacherage in the Pakan S.D. 1175 (Smoky Lake, Alta.) Mr. C. D. Denny put on a fire in the stove. Soon he and his friend John heard the most weird and agonizing sounds. Mr. Denny, on the inside, thought they were coming from the outside; John, on the outside, was just as certain they originated on the inside. Finally they decided that the cries were coming from the chimney. Surely such eerie sounds were never broadcast from a chimney before! The two grown men were more or less transfixed with fear. Finally reason held sway. They concluded that some creature was in the chimney and was being destroyed by the heat and the smoke of the fire. The two teachers were hearing its death cries. Acting on this premise they doused the fire with water, removed the pipes from the chimney and found a flicker pretty much the worse for wear from the smoke and heat in the chimney.

Teacherages were normally out of bounds to yet another type of animal —young homo sapiens. In the Aurora S.D. 1050 (Winnipeg, Man.) there was a time during the late Thirties when all the children used to troop

Most teacherages, like this "three-in-one" in the Dundee District (Hanna, Alta.) were erected quickly by fitting together several surplus parts of farm buildings found in the settlement.

over to the teacherage to listen to the teacher's battery-operated radio and the government-sponsored school broadcasts.

To the older girls the teacherage was something special. Caroline Barnes of the Moose Hill S.D. (Thorhild, Alta.) gives the feminine point of view.

"The teacherage used to be a haven of beauty for us country girls. In one way or another we used to wangle some way to visit the shack and then stand inside the door with our mouths open and bugging at the dainty clothing, lovely pictures and brightly colored nicknacks that our lady teachers had gathered around themselves. Our whole being would long for the same sort of things and I'm sure many a young girl's heart was turned to teaching as a career by what she saw in the teacherage."

Most rural teachers found it a trying experience to get back to the city for the Christmas or Easter holidays. Kathleen, who taught in the Shining Bank S.D. 4034 (Edson, Alta.) between 1934 and 1936, describes one such trip.

"At Easter I decided to go to Edmonton for the spring convention. An old bachelor of the district kindly offered to take me by democrat to Peers, some thirty miles away, to catch the train. The drive took all day. In some places the road was icy and in others muddy. The bachelor's horses had lived on straw all winter so after twenty miles of rough going they collapsed. A fresh team took us the rest of the way. When we reached the McLeod River we discovered to our dismay that there was a foot of water on the ice, but we made the crossing without any mishap. I managed to catch the train and wondered why all the passengers stared at me as I made my way to an

The simplest type of teacherage possible — a granary. (Bullpound S.D. Hanna, Alta. in 1936).

empty seat at the far end of the coach. I soon found out. My face had broken out in blisters while my eyes had turned scarlet from sunburn. I was a sight to behold!

"For the return trip I made arrangements to travel with the mailman. The ice had broken up in the river and it was necessary for us to make the crossing in a row boat. It was a nerve wracking experience to dodge the large pieces of ice flow as well as the other debris that was coming down the river. On one occasion we were caught up in the ice and taken downstream some distance before we were able to break loose from our undesirable mooring. We lost one bag of mail in the process.

"I wonder how many present-day young teachers would have been able to cope with the conditions that prevailed in rural areas in those days. Luckily I loved the outdoors and my parents had taught me how to adjust myself to any conditions. My father, who was an early pioneer, said, 'If a daughter of mine can't put up with such conditions for a year, I would disown her.' "

THE RURAL TEACHER

The children who were educated in the Little White Schoolhouse in the early days have memories of many teachers—they came so often and stayed for such a short time. There was no security of tenure for they could be dismissed on the slightest provocation or by any personal whim of a school trustee. Hence the turnover was rapid in those days, the average rate being about one per year with an occasional district recording as many as two or three such changes.

The School Act attempted to lay down some hard-and-fast rule with respect to the termination of teachers' contracts but in actual practice these measures proved to be very indefinite and could easily be circumvented. No one understood the problem better than the officials in the various Departments of Education. Periodically they attempted to improve security of tenure as well as protect the school boards from the necessity of retaining poor teachers.

An example of one such directive was issued on June 2, 1932, under the signature of J. T. Ross, the Deputy Minister of Education, to all school boards and teachers of Alberta.

> "There appears to be some uncertainty about the provisions of The School Act with respect to the termination of teachers' contracts. For your information the Department has prepared the following statement:
> The board may terminate the agreement by giving thirty days' notice to the teacher at any time during the month of June without obtaining the consent of the inspector to do so, but if it wishes to terminate the agreement at any other time during the year it must secure the inspector's consent before giving the thirty days' notice. The teacher may terminate the agreement by giving thirty days' notice to the board at any time during the months of June and July without obtaining the consent of the inspector to do so, but if the teacher wishes to terminate the agreement at any other time during the year he must secure the inspector's consent before giving the thirty days' notice."

Teachers who had planned to make teaching their life work rather than a mere stepping-stone to something more lucrative, realized that one way of improving their lot was to organize themselves into an association.

STANDARD FORM OF CONTRACT

BETWEEN

TRUSTEES AND TEACHER

This Agreement made in triplicate.

BETWEEN—

The Board of Trustees of .... *Spondon* ....

School District No. *3375* .... of the Province of Alberta, hereinafter called "the Board"

— and —

.... *Janet Isabelle Ellis* ....

of .... *Drumheller* ....

the holder of a .... *2 nd* .... *Permanent* ....
(Insert class of certificate)

Certificate of qualification as a teacher in Alberta, hereinafter called "the Teacher."

WITNESSETH :—

That subject to the provisions of *The School Act, 1931*, and the Regulations of the Department of Education, the Board hereby employs the Teacher, and the Teacher agrees to teach and conduct school for the Board on the following terms:

1. The annual salary shall be $ *400.00* , and subject to the following schedule of increases :

2. The period of employment shall be from and including the *third* day of *September* 193 *5*

DATED this .... *third* .... day of .... *September* 193 *5*

Signed on behalf or the Board [CORPORATE SEAL].

....
Witness to Chairman's signature.

T. H. Crego
Witness to Teacher's signature.

John Quast Jr.
Chairman.

Janet Isabelle Ellis
Teacher.

No. of Teacher's Alberta Certificate *474-*

Spondon
Teacher's Address in School District.

NOTE:—Refer to The School Act, 1931, and Amendments thereto:
    For engagement and contract, see Sections 155 to 158 inclusive.
    For minimum salary, see Section 161.
    For method of payment of salary, see Sections 161 to 164 inclusive.
    For method of terminating an agreement, see Section 157.
    For information regarding vacation periods and holidays, see Sections 144 and 145.
    Teacher should sign with Christian names in full.
    In absence of Chairman, any other Trustee may sign (Section 158).
    One copy of this Agreement should be retained by the Board, another by the Teacher, and the third forwarded at once to the Department of Education.

A form of contract between the trustees and teacher.

One such person was J. W. Barnett. He travelled the length and breadth of the province of Alberta over poor country roads putting up with discomfort and hardship to visit as many individual teachers as possible learning about their problems at first hand and explaining to them the aims and objectives of the budding Alberta Teachers' Alliance of which he was the first Executive Secretary. Teachers who wished could join this organization on a voluntary basis. The patience, courage and labor of this dedicated man laid the foundation for better days for all teachers. Yet the dawn of this new era came too late to benefit many of the pedagogues in the Little White Schoolhouse.

The method employed by some rural school boards for selecting their teacher may sound fantastic today. For instance, Hilda was the successful applicant for the Georges S.D. 1386 (Qu'Appelle Valley, Sask.) because her letter was the easiest to read. The next board hired her by flipping a coin to decide between her and another good candidate. When she took over this school they gave her the coin to keep as a good-luck charm.

The school board of Moose River S.D. (Smith, Alta.) received so many applications in the summer of 1935 that they were in a quandary as to the best method to proceed. The four trustees first read all the letters. This in itself was quite a task and took days to accomplish for each referral contained a handwritten application, copies of several recommendations, maybe a picture or two as well as transcripts of a number of inspector's reports. Next, each member selected an applicant he liked best. Unfortunately there was no agreement, as each one picked a different teacher. Seeking to break the stalemate they finally decided to hold a lottery. The four letters of application were placed under a blanket and an outsider called in to make the draw. Miss Laura Scott was the lucky lady.

Teachers must have been very scarce between 1909 and 1914 for the minute book of the Fordville S.D. 1908 (Midnapore, Alta.) contained a motion passed unanimously to the effect "that the teacher was not to be more than 70 years of age".

When Mr. F. D. Patterson, a board member of the newly-formed Bally Hamage S.D. (Priddis, Alta.) was sent to interview two prospective teachers in the spring of 1919, he agreed to pick the prettiest. Thus Miss Ruth Baker became the first teacher at Bally Hamage.

It wasn't a matter of promoting a beauty contest to expedite the selection for the Brandland S.D. (Camrose, Alta.) in 1917. Here the school board was uncertain whether to hire a schoolmaster or mistress. The members considered their dilemma with so much fervor and at such length that the school failed to open on time for the summer term that year. In the end they could have saved themselves all the trouble, for by the time a decision had been reached the only teachers still available for Brandland School were of the sex they had decided not to employ.

Is it possible today to imagine any school board receiving five hundred and seventy-five applications in reply to a simple "Teacher Wanted" advertisement in the Edmonton Journal? Yet the Big Coulee S.D. 4497 (Athabasca, Alta.) did in 1931. Their method of selecting the first teacher for their new school from such an astounding number of applicants was relatively simple. They sorted, sorted and then resorted and resorted until they picked the two best writers. Out of the two, Violet Reynolds was given the preference because they were certain "Violet" was a girl's name and they were not so certain of "Leslie". The family that had promised to board the teacher had stipulated, "We will take only a schoolmistress!" Quite an achievement to be selected from five hundred and seventy-five applicants but Violet's fitting comment was, "Such is fate!"

The name of the teacher, the place of her residence, her picture, or the occupation of her father often brought a wisp of nostalgia to some trustee and this in itself often determined whether she was selected or not.

During the 1930's when there were hundreds of applicants for any vacancy a number of teachers "bought" their jobs. The teacher offering the highest bid became the successful candidate. Usually it was the local secretary who was the recipient of these unprincipled payments. Some teachers after getting the job under such a scheme experienced a twinge of remorse and refused to make any payments. In a number of such cases the matter was forgotten discreetly but in other instances the righteous teacher was dismissed for reasons other than the little matter of non-payment of the bribe.

No matter on what basis the final selection of a rural teacher was made the trustees felt that picking a teacher was like "buying a pig in a poke". You never knew what you had until you accepted delivery of the "goods".

It took the general public many years to learn that normal schools were colleges for training teachers. So it was not uncommon in the early days for a trustee to approach, rather warily, a prospective teacher and question her about the implication that she attended a "normal" school in some far-off city like Regina, Cedar Falls or Camrose. There was a strange "something" in the meaning of the word "normal" that caused people to associate it immediately with a mental institution. No school board wanted to hire a psychopath, who, through regular attendance at a normal school for several months, had been able to regain some degree of normalcy. One just couldn't be too careful whom one selected to teach his children. There was always the chance that she might go berserk again and murder the children. It was always with a feeling of relief and diffidence that the uninformed trustee accepted the explanation that a "normal" school was a teachers' academy.

The teachers over the years in any particular district varied from the very good to the very poor. Parents were always grateful for the good ones and simply tolerated the poor ones and hoped for the best. Good or bad the rural teacher was an exalted being in the community. Since the majority had come from the city and on occasion went back to visit with their relatives and friends, they brought in new ideas, new fashions and trends. In those days people didn't travel too far or too often, so they looked to the teacher for information and guidance.

In many cases the teacher was a confident seventeen-year-old miss and the proud possessor of a third-class, or grade-ten certificate. Yet to the parents she truly represented the books of knowledge. If she was worth her salt at all, she made sure that the children of the homesteaders learned to read, to write and do arithmetic, as well as say the ABC's in their proper order. Most of these girls were wonderful young people and a good example for the local girls to follow both in dress and behavior.

These early school teachers need a historian to glorify them. The majority were teenage girls living away from home for the first time. They worked amid loneliness that defied description. They were forced to live under conditions that were far from ideal. The least that could be said of them was that they were true Canadian pioneers. In addition to their teaching duties they acted as school janitors, stoked fires, diagnosed illnesses and applied first aid. They counselled, scolded, played games, umpired, cut the children's hair, settled disputes, learned to ride skittish horses and drove to school in all types of weather. They taught Sunday school, played the organ for church services, trained the choir, helped at social functions and organized such cultural activities as debates, plays and concerts. These teachers worked hard to make their particular rural community a better place in which to live. In fact some of the fairer sex often ended up marrying one of the numerous bachelors in the district. One instructor in the old Calgary Normal School used to drum it into the minds of the would-be teachers that, "It is the duty of every teacher to participate in the work of the community as it is the price they have to pay to occupy their three by six plot of ground for eternity".

Teachers who taught during the "dirty" Thirties also deserve a good deal of praise. The hardships they endured can never be known. Their wages were mere tokens. No doubt, even today, there are many such teachers who still have I.O.U. slips as grim reminders of that era. Some teachers, like Hilda who taught in the Twin Gate S.D. 4841, were forced to cash in their life insurance policies in order to pay part of their board bill, or to obtain enough money to buy a ticket to get home for Christmas. A teacher in the Hexagon S.D. (Bengough, Sask.) wore hand-me-down

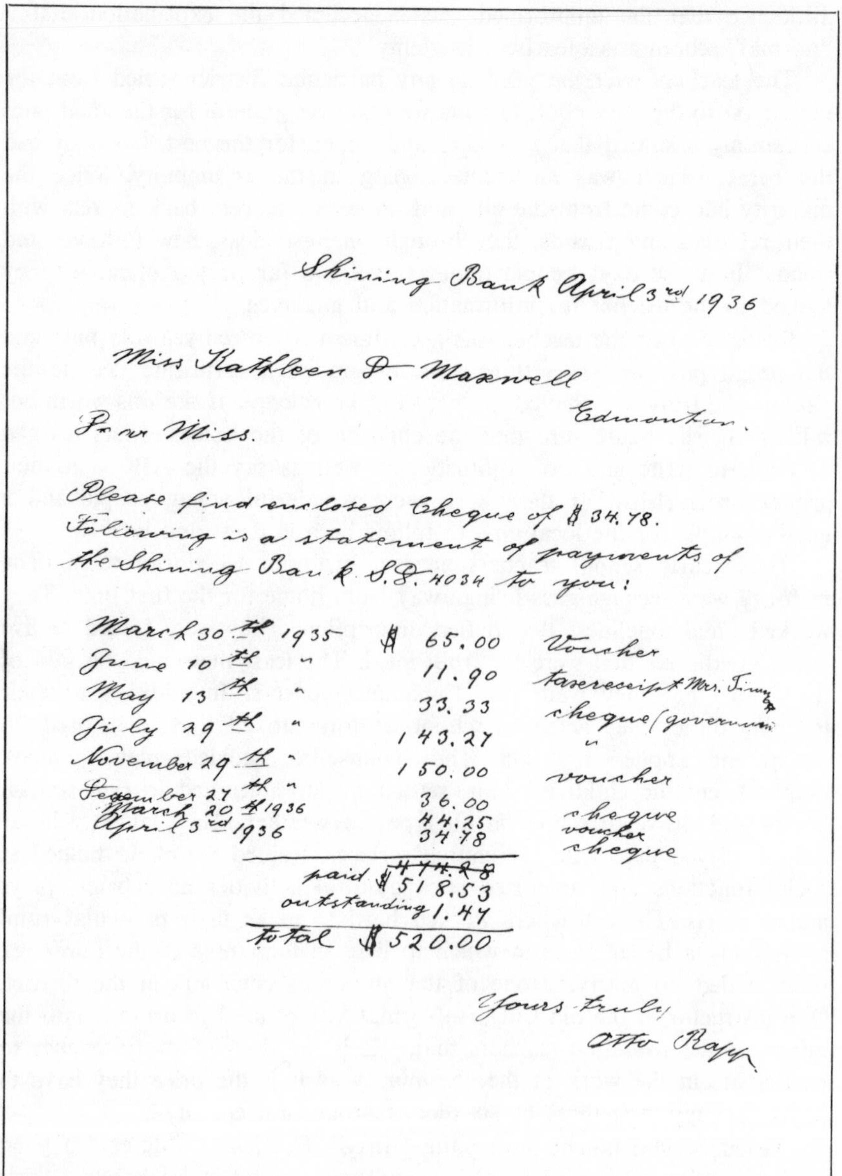

Shining Bank April 3rd 1936

Miss Kathleen P. Maxwell
                                            Edmonton.
Dear Miss.

Please find enclosed Cheque of $ 34.78.
Following is a statement of payments of
the Shining Bank. S.S. 4034 to you:

March 30th 1935	$ 65.00	Voucher
June 10th "	11.90	taxreceipt + Mrs. Jimy
May 13th "	33.33	cheque (government
July 29th "	143.27	"
November 29th "	150.00	voucher
September 27th 1936	36.00	cheque
March 20 1936	44.25	voucher
April 3rd 1936	34.78	cheque

                        paid $ 518.53
                  outstanding 1.47
                  Total $ 520.00

                            Yours Truly
                            Otto Rapp

—Mrs. R. Christie

In the early days the teachers' salaries were not only low but they were paid irregularly and in driblets. The salary statement shown above was issued to Miss Maxwell in 1936 while she was teaching in the Shining Bank School (Edson, Alta.)

clothes and had to depend on her parents and friends for a little spending money. Her home was only forty miles away yet she seldom got there as it meant begging someone to provide transportation for which she could not pay.

The Kipp S.D. 1589 (Davidson, Sask.), a good representative school, had 39 teachers during its half-century of operation from 1907-57. It is interesting to peruse such a list of teachers as it gives one a better idea of what the average rural teacher was like, her qualifications, and her salary down through the years. The written records of the majority of rural schools, like Kipp, have carefully preserved all official documents since the date of their inception. Mrs. Dorothy W. Willner, a 1918 pioneer of the Kipp district, has in her safekeeping all the copies of the teacher contracts since 1907, the minutes of all the meetings since 1906, and all the registers 1918-57 with the exception of one.

TEACHERS OF KIPP SCHOOL 1907-57

Name of Teacher	Date of Contract	Class of Certificate	Annual Rate of Salary
W. A. Gilchrist	May 1, 1907	Third	$ 660
James Brown	April 29, 1908	Third	792
James Brown	May 3, 1909	Third	792
Arnold Brammer	April 1, 1910	Second	720
James Brown	October 24, 1910	Third	770
Beatrice Lick	April 1, 1912	Third	720
Wilfred Traynor	April 1, 1913	Third	840
Wilfred Traynor	April 1, 1914	Third	840
Hugh McIntyre	January 4, 1915	Second	780
Samuel Platt	May 3, 1915	Permit	780
R. H. J. Roberts	March 13, 1916	Third	780
Martin Stonehouse	March 19, 1917	None stated	840
A. E. Todd	September 24, 1917	Third	840
Mildred DeWolfe	April 30, 1918	Second	1020
Virginia Longpre	January 13, 1919	Second	1020
Virginia Longpre	January 13, 1920	Second	1050
Olive Jenkinson	January 10, 1921	Second	1200
Olive Jenkinson	January 10, 1922	Second	1200
G. W. E. Wood	January 12, 1923	Third	1000
Gladys Ames	January 2, 1924	Third	1000
Gladys Ames	January 2, 1925	Third	1050
Edgar Filby	January 4, 1926	First	1200
Ella Morrison	August 16, 1926	First	1050
Ella Morrison	August 16, 1927	First	1050
Ella Morrison	August 16, 1928	First	1100
O. M. McCreary	August 12, 1929	First	1050
O. M. McCreary	August 12, 1930	First	1100
Margaret Law	August 24, 1931	First	600
Ann Goodwin	August 15, 1932	Second	500

TEACHERS OF KIPP SCHOOL 1907-57

Name of Teacher	Date of Contract	Class of Certificate	Annual Rate of Salary
Amy Stewart	September 1, 1933	First	200
Mrs. Alice Hill	August 20, 1934	First Grant + $5 per month	
Mrs. Alice Hill	August 20, 1935	First Grant + $5 per month	
Stella G. Marvin	August 17, 1936	First	350
Stella G. Marvin	August 17, 1937	First $350 + any taxes paid	
Mary V. Beckie	August 15, 1938	First	400
Louise F. Hooper	August 14, 1939	First	500
Thelma G. Renaud	August 15, 1940	First	700
Iris W. Old	August 18, 1941	First	700
Iris W. Old	August 18, 1942	First	850
George H. Bessey	August 16, 1943	First	900
George H. Bessey	August 16, 1944	First	1000
*Dorothy M. Holder	August 20, 1945	First	1100*
Olive Lucille Eddie	September 2, 1946	Permit	1150
Olive Lucille Eddie	September 2, 1947	Permit	1200
Olive Lucille Eddie	September 2, 1948	Permit	1300
Shirley L. Harris	September 1, 1949	Supervisor	None stated
Jean P. Buitenhius	August 21, 1950	First	1400
Mrs. Lucille Ames	August 21, 1951	First	1650
Mrs. Lucille Ames	August 21, 1952	First	1900
Lois Gould	April 20, 1953	Int. Sup.	2200
Dorothy I. Haas	August 24, 1953	Int.	2000
Mrs. Lucille Ames	August 23, 1954	Int.	2500
Mrs. Lucille Ames	August 23, 1955	Int.	2500
Susan Heinrichs	April 30, 1956	Perm.	2500
Janice Dixon	August 21, 1956	Int.	2200

*Administration of school taken over by the Division in January 1946.

There can be few rural students who look back without having warm memories of some teacher who took the time and the patience to help out when the going became tough. The slow students received extra help, the brilliant ones encouragement to use their God-given talent and the unruly ones discipline from a firm hand.

The teaching in the rural schools was of varied quality. Very few timeservers were found, but because of varying degrees of training, experience, aptitude or zeal there were great differences in the quality of work done. In general, the qualified teachers were reasonably efficient but in the schools with permit teachers the character of teaching could best be described as indifferent. Although the number of permit teachers in any province during the history of the rural school never reached beyond the 40 per cent mark it was a serious problem at all times.

Indiscriminate promotion of students was probably the greatest weakness exhibited by most rural school systems. In schools where the teachers remained for more than a year, the inspector's visit served as a deterrent, but in others and in the short-term, or summer schools that operated from April to December, it was seldom that the teacher left the school without promoting nearly every pupil in attendance. There were many cases, too, in which oral reading was made the sole basis for such promotions. Instances of self-promotion on the part of the pupils at the change of teachers were also quite common. Not very many rural teachers had the necessary fortitude to stand up for their rights and the pupils' welfare by not promoting or putting the pupils back a standard or grade to where they rightfully belonged. All in all the results of such wholesale promotions were bad and the task of each succeeding teacher made progressively more difficult.

Classification, or the act of placing a child in the proper grade, was another problem that created many difficulties for early rural teachers. As the pupils had come from many of the states of the United States, from the various provinces of Canada and from the British Isles, it was not easy for the inexperienced teacher to effect a satisfactory grade placement. The non-English-speaking students, no matter what their ages, were always put in grade one. That part of the task was easy, but once they learned the English language the question of where they should be put was a difficult one. Today, the experts in the Department of Education have assumed the responsibility of dictating the grade placement of any student entering a school from another Canadian province, or from a foreign country. In yesteryears, when the tide of immigration was sweeping Western Canada, the lowly and poorly-trained rural teachers handled the onerous task by themselves.

Every rural school district, as can be seen from the list of teachers of the Kipp School, had many teachers during its years of existence. Yet in this group were teachers who stood out among the rest like banners in a parade. People of the district liked to recall and talk about them for they were like little slivers of memory sticking into them.

It could be the old Ontario teacher of the Ridgeway S.D. (Carmangay, Alta.), who had at least twenty years' experience behind him. He was a real schoolmaster! His use of words was wonderful to hear, but oh, so very, very boring to the younger students. He had four boys in the higher grades and how he loved to teach them! Thelma, being the only beginner, was more of a nuisance than a joy to him. He taught her phonetics and then allowed her to take all the subjects with the higher grades. The little six-year-old acquired knowledge by leaps and bounds.

This teacher appreciated a child's need for movement. If they raised one finger they were permitted to move about, even all around the school-yard if one happened to be only six. Two fingers allowed the youngsters to talk to anyone they wished. He had a full slate of signals for all the common exigencies that could beset the pupils in the classroom, to which he gave his consent with a nod of the head.

Every mid-morning and afternoon the need for a nap overtook him. He tilted the swivel chair, placed his feet upon the desk and dozed off comfortably. The few stray locks that were usually combed carefully over his bald spot fell slowly away exposing a shiny surface that seemed to entice the flies in the room. Either the talking or the movements of the students that gradually increased in crescendo, or his own snores which seemed to keep pace with the increasing hubbub, eventually wakened him. Soon the order of, "Places everyone!" was given and the classroom settled down to work again.

Eccentric as the old pedagogue appeared, he had the ability to arouse a desire for knowledge. The four senior boys were the only pupils in the district who aspired to a university education. However, after a few months, the school board suddenly decided that he was too old. They gave him his notice. He next tried his luck in a mining town in northern Ontario and taught for at least another twenty years.

Another old teacher in the Ridgeway S.D. had a peculiar habit of taking out all his money and dashing it to the floor any time he was displeased with the way the students behaved or responded. While doing this he repeated over and over again, "I don't need to teach school! I don't need to teach school!" The Ridgeway school board took him at his word and dismissed him.

The Clover Hill S.D. (Irvine, Alta.) seemed to have had more than its share of unusual teachers. One was a civil engineer from Quebec. He always swam smoking his pipe and wearing his hat. Another teacher had ambitions to become a real Westerner. He wore a fancy shirt, a ten-gallon hat and cowboy boots. In fact when he came to school he looked like Tom Mix or Hoot Gibson of cowboy movie fame. Somewhere in this procession of educators was a male teacher who had skin you loved to touch. His hands and face were an effeminate white and the pupils had a sneaking suspicion that he used coldcream. He always smelled as though he had just stepped out of bubble bath. Then there was the long-distance runner who held several medals. This teacher influenced Tom Wood, one of his pupils, to become a runner as well. The two often took off across the prairie after school for a practice run. They jogged along until suppertime making certain that they completed their practice race at some home in the district where there was a good chance of getting supper.

Next came a teacher who had a checker-complex. Recess extended into an hour and the noon hour into two in order to complete the finals of the checker tournament. Then all the students made up the lost time by staying in after school. By a strange coincidence there was a school district in Saskatchewan, near Kindersley, that also bore the name Clover Hill. Like its name-twin this school also had an unusual teacher, one who strongly advocated checkers as the chief pastime for his students. Unlike his prototype in Alberta, Mr. Bachus the teacher also introduced the game of football. He was a great hand at having the whole school play football during winter even though the schoolyard was covered with a foot of snow. He always played with the girls against the boys. Since Mr. Bachus was a trained football player his tackling was rather vicious and the boys soon found it convenient to be elsewhere when a football game was in the offing. When the weather became too severe for football he organized a checker tournament. Everyone, including the children in the primary grades, was required to play. The ultimate winner played Mr. Bachus. Again as in football, he demonstrated his superiority over his students.

The most unique teacher that the Alberta Clover Hill had was a man named Babington. On the first morning of school he took the strap and burned it in the stove before all the students and then warned them with these words, "If any of you misbehave, what will happen to you will make you wish I had kept the strap instead". No one was ever brave or inquisitive enough to find out what the new punishment was. Then he took all the textbooks and stacked them away in the cupboard with the explanation that they were no longer required. He did permit each student to retain his reader and exercise books.

His "different" method of teaching was to give a lecture on some topic to each of the seven grades in the school and then write thought-provoking questions on the blackboard for the students to answer. The man had a wonderful memory and anything that had to be copied by the students flowed off his chalk like magic. He never referred to textbooks but geared his lecture topics to the actual needs of the students. The children became so interested in their work that three-thirty didn't mean too much to them. Around five o'clock Babington would say, "Well children its about supper time. I guess we'd better break it off for today."

Everything went fine until the inspector made his annual call. When the official entered the school he found the teacher with his feet up on the desk reading a newspaper. Outside of a few magazines and current newspapers Babington's desk was as bare as Mother Hubbard's cupboard. It was almost too much for the inspector to discover also that all the prescribed textbooks had been piled in the cupboard and were never used. He angrily paced up and down the classroom all the while making uncomplimentary remarks about the teacher. Eventually, Babington broke in quietly with, "Sir! Let me say something now. Would you ask any or all the pupils the hardest questions you can think of for each grade?" The inspector agreed. He tested every pupil, grade by grade and subject by subject in rapid succession but no matter how difficult he made the problems the youngsters came up with the right answers. After half an hour of such questions the surprised official threw up his hands almost in despair and said, "I simply can't believe it!" He stamped out of the room still shaking his head and never returned as long as Babington taught in that school.

Ada vividly recalls a number of teachers who taught her in the Eagle S.D. (Airdrie, Alta.).

"I started school at the age of seven in 1910. My first teacher was Miss Annie Yuill, a Scottish girl. I believe she was the first to teach in the newly formed Eagle School District. She was followed by a Miss Maud Stewart, also Scottish. For a short time Mrs. Drake taught, followed by Miss Dorothy Atkinson who was with us for several terms. My last teacher was Miss Hattie Deller, a Canadian girl.

"I remember Miss Yuill and Miss Stewart but vaguely. They were good-natured and kind and I always looked forward to school. Mrs. Drake on the other hand was very cranky and disliked by the pupils. We found out in later years that the poor woman had a heavy burden to bear. She had a large family, her husband was an invalid, and they were endeavoring to farm in an adjoining district. Besides she had a long way to travel each day to teach. I recall one day she slipped up behind me (I was whispering in class) and hit me across the shoulders with a long wooden pointer with such force, that I was rendered breathless.

"Miss Atkinson was a jolly buxom English girl and a very good teacher. Our parents were inclined to think her too unorthodox at times. She would play games with us at recess and noon hour. Since she was engaged to be married at the time to a French artist, she talked of him a lot and also about art.

"Miss Deller, my last teacher at Eagle, was a shy, sweet little girl and also a very good teacher. I recall the school inspectors always appeared to 'bully her a little'. She died during the influenza epidemic of 1918. I shall never forget her as she was so kind to me."

The first teacher in the Stonelaw S.D. (Monitor, Alta.) was an old English schoolmaster. He had not taught school for a number of years and although he managed reasonably well with the older children, he was completely lost with the younger ones. The master had the habit of taking things easy in the classroom. He would put his feet up on the desk, light his corn-cob pipe, and become engrossed in some book. He was an avid reader and had a good collection of literature, history, and the classics. His favorite pastime was playing cards and many a game was played at the school until some of the mothers became suspicious as to why their sons had so much spending money. The master had introduced the game of poker to three of the older boys. At the outset the teacher was the winner but in a comparatively short time the students were relieving their teacher of around five dollars a month. That was big money in those early days.

Another Stonelaw teacher was a George Blocksome from Erskine, Alta. He was a presentable young man but very shy with the little children. His interests seemed to be confined to radio and all his spare time was spent in building and tearing down radio sets. As he boarded with the Partridge family their children were the first to hear a radio program. If they were very good Mr. Blocksome divided his second pair of earphones and let them listen.

Then came Miss Hutchinson, a maiden lady from England. Right from the start she had a problem in the person of Alice, a beginner. The little girl had memorized the grade one reader from one end to the other, The Little Red Hen, The Three Pigs and so on. Miss Hutchinson did something extraordinary for teachers of that day. She procured an entirely different set of primary books and used them in teaching Alice how to read. True, Miss Hutchinson was old-fashioned and very strict, but she was a wonderful teacher. Everyone liked and respected her. She taught the students to sing "The Beautiful Isle of Somewhere" and today, without exception, this is the favorite hymn of those who attended Stonelaw School back in 1918. She also started home economics classes and had each youngster make a Christmas present for his parents. One oldtimer proudly said, "I still have a sampler that Miss Hutchison showed me how to make."

Thomas Kennedy was recognized as an outstanding teacher when he taught in the Fleetwood School in a rural area near Bowmanville, Ontario. Yet the familiar rhyme that the children recited about him could scarcely be termed very uplifting.

> The devil flew from north to south
> And took Tom Kennedy in his mouth,
> When he found he had a fool,
> He dropped him off at Fleetwood School.
>
> Oh! Lord of Love look from above
> On all your little scholars.
> We have a fool to teach our school,
> We pay him four hundred dollars.

The departments of Education of the Western provinces and the Midwestern United States instituted four-month courses at their teacher training institutions—the normal schools. Yet owing to the rapid settlement and the consequent opening up of hundreds of new rural schools each year, there was still a shortage of teachers. University students from eastern Canada, particularly from Queen's University of Kingston, Ontario, came to the rescue. Each spring hundreds of them came west and taught until such time as they had to return in the fall to register at their universities. There were potential engineers, doctors, lawyers, veterinarians and university professors among these itinerant teachers. As a whole they

Queen's University undergraduates at the Winnipeg C.P.R. station, April, 1910, waiting for a train to take them to Saskatchewan and Alberta to teach from May to October in prairie "one-room schools".

—Earl W. Van Blaricom

proved to be good teachers and the West owes a lot to them for the service they rendered in the rural schools of that period.

Arthur Elson, the first chairman and trustee for three years and secretary-treasurer for thirty-nine years of the Fartown S.D. 1857 (Marshall, Sask.) gives first-hand account of these university students who doubled as teachers soon after 1908.

> "Mostly throughout our existence as a School District we have been fortunate in the matter of teachers. For a period of five years we were lucky enough to secure the services of Queen's men and we always look back to that period as the highlight as regards teachers.
>
> "The first of these students, Bert McDougall, taught during 1911. He was followed by Robert McGregor, who was with us in 1912, and came back again for 1913. Incidentally, I might mention that it was Bob who first brought us the news of the Titanic disaster. We, of course, had no radios in those days. Willard Holmes followed for the next two years, 1914 and 1915.
>
> "All three gained their B.A. degrees at Queen's. Bert McDougall left us to take up an engineering position with the Federal Government. Robert McGregor taught for a time in the Saskatoon city school system and when the Provincial Government erected the Provincial Technical Institute at Saskatoon it was Bob McGregor whom they chose for its principal. Willard

Holmes joined up with the Air Force in the First World War and later took up the study of medicine. He became one of Saskatoon's better known medical men.

The three teachers gave us splendid service and proved themselves wonderful citizens. We older members of the community like to look back to the days when they so truly made themselves one of us."

A teacher in a rural school in those days was a person to be looked up to and followed. They had to be cautious of what they said or did both in and out of school. But once in a while a district had the sad experience and misfortune to end up with nothing better than a wench for a teacher. Even in school she wore her dresses short and her bloomers long. Any time she stood writing at the blackboard her pettipants showed. She habitually kept company with people of ill repute and stayed out late at night or all night. The district gossip variously branded her as: fast, tough, flapper, a homebreaker, a drinker, a flirt, a heartbreaker or a loose woman. No man escaped her wiles, no, not even the inspector. The children showed no esteem for her whatsoever and as a result all her attempts to maintain discipline suffered accordingly. As one oldster put it:

"We had no respect for her and often played run-sheep-run over the surrounding hills when we should have been in school. Out of a class of about 28 only one child passed that year—the teacher's pet."

Such teachers often left the district in disgrace in the middle of the term, or they lasted the year largely due to their ability to beguile the male members of the school board.

The teacher in the Saskatchewan S.D. No. 2 (Fort Saskatchewan, Alta.) in 1932 must have aspired to become a professional baseball player. Whenever a pupil annoyed him he flung whatever he happened to have in his hand at the youngster whether it was a piece of chalk, a yardstick, a book or a brush. There were eight grades and fifty-three youngsters crowded into the small schoolroom so the young man had plenty of opportunity to practice his pitches and nasty temper. The children learned quickly when it was safe or dangerous to misbehave by merely observing what he had in his hand at the moment.

Paradoxical as it may sound some teachers were remembered because of some malady they suffered. The interesting fact about the first teacher in Circle S.D. (Barons, Alta.) was that she was an epileptic. Yet no matter how closely the children watched her she was never considerate enough to have a seizure in school.

The teacher at Endcliffe, Man. in 1943 was subject to migraine headaches which left her incapacitated for hours at a time. The days she had one of these attacks her mother substituted for her. The youngsters liked the daughter but hated the mother. Every morning the children gathered on the school porch and gazed wistfully up the road to catch a glimpse of the person at the wheel of the model-T Ford. If it happened to be the young lady herself they smiled and jumped with glee, but if it turned out to be the "old lady" everyone turned away grumbling. "Well anyway she'll be back tomorrow for sure!" was their only comment.

A quirk of fate sent the headmistress of a Scottish girls' school to teach in one of the prairie rural schools of Alberta. She had given up a good position to come to Canada to keep house for her brother and his four motherless children, but when she arrived she discovered that he had married again. She wore her hair peculiarly for those days, in rolls about her face. The general comment in the district was, "She isn't very young, you know. Did you see how grey her hair is beneath those rolls?"

The former headmistress had three after-dinner stories at which she excelled, but they never varied no matter how often she related them. She brought a breath of the Old Country to the lives of these prairie farmers by telling them about the Highlands, the city of Edinburgh, Balmoral Castle, and of seeing the Royal Princesses running and playing about like ordinary children.

The pupils of the Fertile Valley S.D. (Moston, Sask.) liked their new teacher. She was young and pretty and even taught them how to shimmy. The school board members were divided in their opinion of her. Every time Mr. Brian Briscoe, the chairman, with whom she boarded, asked her for her teaching certificate she said it was at the school. Yet every time the inspector wanted to see the document she confided in him that it was at the Briscoe residence. In spite of this apparent discrepancy the young lady continued to teach in the Fertile Valley for at least another three years. Later the school board discovered that she was a swimming instructress in the city of Ottawa and had never been a teacher. At one time during her tenure she had confidentially advised Mrs. Briscoe to send her daughter to the town school to take her grade eight rather than attempt it at Fertile Valley. The advice was taken and the girl passed. The other four grade eights failed. It is not difficult to guess why?

Some teachers had the knack of being able to upset the even tenor of a rural community by their antics. The residents of the Eaton S.D. (Craigmyle, Alta.) became greatly alarmed on the last day of the 1930 school term. Their teacher had been found in the school basement, unconscious from a suspected beating, and tied up with barbed wire. The police were called in on the case and made a thorough investigation but apparently never did find the person or persons responsible. Some of the oldtimers in the district, who had been concerned about the singular actions and attitudes of the teacher, were convinced that she had manipulated this situation upon herself to gain attention. Regardless of how the incident happened the people of the Eaton community, particularly the children, lived in a state of terror for many weeks thereafter. The teacher recovered and moved elsewhere to do her teaching.

In the Ridgeway S.D. (Carmangay, Alta.) it was a Scottish surveyor waiting for a job who kept the district in a state of anxiety. He was a dour young man, except over the weekends when he was apt to imbibe too freely. Then things began to happen. His capers ranged from becoming madly infatuated with the most-unlikely females of the district to a firm resolve to ride a vicious bronco. He had to be restrained in both of these activities. He could consume quite a quantity of liquor neat, until he attended a wedding dance where they served a vitriolic concoction of homebrew. He was never quite the same man after that. The community breathed much easier when he gave up his teaching post and joined a government survey party in northern Alberta.

One of the first teachers in the Skipton S.D. (Leask, Sask.) was an Irish lady of uncertain age. She was the essence of neatness and her clothes were the envy of all the bigger girls. She was only the size of a minute but she could handle the thirty or forty youngsters with ease. This teacher really knew about discipline. Years after, oldtime residents remembered her and said, "Now there was a teacher!"

Spoonerism, the accidental transposition of sounds, made two teachers in the Fartown S.D. 1856 (Marshall, Sask.) quite distinctive. A pupil named Garnett had left the room and on returning had gone to his seat leaving the door wide open. The teacher, looking up from her desk, surprised the pupils by saying, "Go back and shut the goor Darnet". She wondered why the pupils smiled at her simple command. On another occasion, the young lady wanted Jack Bicknell to give the large chunk of coal a "crushing blow" so it would fit into the stove. Instead out came, "Jack, give the chunk a blushing crow". Then there was the teacher who on a rather cool fall day asked one of the pupils to go down to the basement and "Fight the lire", when of course she meant, "Light the fire".

When a certain Mr. Currie first came to teach in the Krydor S.D. (Prince Albert, Sask.) in 1912 he wore a thick black beard of such luxurious proportions that it completely hid his face. One day towards the end of the term he decided to shave it off clean. That morning the youngsters vowed that a stranger had come to teach them. They failed to recognize their beardless teacher.

Every parade of rural teachers in the district had its Mabel—a good conscientious teacher but possessed of little idiosyncrasies that at times endeared her to the community and upon occasions caused tongues to waggle.

Mabel was the answer to a landlady's prayer for she loved food and ate everything. But this same trait often became very embarrassing when

Mabel went visiting. She ate so ravenously and became so grateful to her hostess it was thought that her landlady did not give her enough to eat.

Mabel appreciated music or at least that was the impression she attempted to convey. She collected all types of classical music scores and then merely piled them on the piano. She never looked at them again. Mabel loved to visit, but no sooner had she crossed the threshold than she proceeded directly to the piano to play over and over again and sing in a doleful voice the same few bars of "Why Do You Do Me Like You Do?" The performance was enough to make one believe in justifiable homicide.

The homes without pianos did not escape Mabel's musical treats for she played the guitar too. Like Mary's little lamb everywhere Mabel went, that little guitar was sure to go. Like a wandering troubadour she played and sang for her supper. It took countless hints and almost downright rudeness to finally persuade her she was more welcome without her guitar.

This teacher was the essence of generosity and if someone merely mentioned anything they wanted, say a necklace or an evening dress, she insisted on giving it to them. Mabel had an aversion to old apparel. She had trunks of pretty clothes but that did not mean she wore them. If one garment appealed to her, she wore it everywhere, no matter how soiled it became, or what the occasion. A hideous mustard-colored jersey dress was her favorite for months. She wore it to school, for visits and finally to a dance. She had taken her slippers along to change for her moccasins but had failed to do so. Mabel's feelings were hurt for the first time at this dance as the people actually referred to her as their hillbilly teacher.

Some memories of teachers have the habit of clicking through one's mind like slides through a projector. Levering of Conquerville S.D. (Foremost, Alta.) wore a very waxed mustache which quivered dangerously when he was annoyed or angry. McIntyre's peculiar practice in the Kipp S.D. (Davidson, Sask.) was to bump the boys' heads together and then walk away grinning. Longpre of the same school used to sit and crochet for her hope chest instead of helping the children with their work. The man teacher in the Alps S.D. (Hanna, Alta.) always drove his Model-T car backward up the hills. He was enough of a scientist to realize that since it was gravity that forced the gasoline from the tank to the engine, the horseless carriage would stall on the slope of a hill in the forward position but was less likely to do so if turned end for end. He found this method especially effective when the gasoline tank was almost empty. A young man in the Gumbo S.D. (Twining, Alta.) often displayed a lack of the judgment expected of a teacher. On one occasion he kept the pupils working at the blackboard so long that a girl ran crying from the room leaving a pool where she had been standing. One teacher in the Arethusa S.D. 4449 (Chinook, Alta.) introduced a somewhat unorthodox method of gaining a measure of popularity with the larger boys in the school. She permitted them to enter and leave the schoolroom through a window. So, while the girls and the little boys made their exits and entrances rather easily through the doorway in the accepted manner, the privileged characters raised a window and scrambled in or out with much difficulty and little dignity.

No person can be more dedicated to his task than was the rural teacher. Pearl Shandro, who taught in the Carvel S.D. (Stony Plain, Alta.), exemplified this characteristic to a high degree. Her 1930 school register showed an enrollment of 45 pupils distributed among all the grades from one to ten. To teach so many students and grades was a gigantic task in itself. Yet, as if this wasn't enough, this little paragon of diligence conducted extra classes. She taught Ukrainian twice a week after school, English to the mothers and fathers two evenings a week, and thrice a week for an hour at a time she supervised her students as they prepared their various entries for the school fair. In addition Pearl spent a considerable amount of time each evening planning and preparing her work for the next day. In those days duplicating facilities were very limited so the seat work for the primary grades was laboriously transcribed on the blackboard. Every morning the blackboards in the Carvel School gleamed white as a result of the numerous exercises written on them. Pearl assigned the seat work for the higher grades from the various textbooks or on occasions duplicated them on the messy; awkward and sometimes obstinate hectograph. No one who has ever used this slab of gelatin and glycerin will ever forget what a boring task it was to run off even five copies!

Then came Pearl's most arduous duty—the marking of the endless stream of student books and exercises. When one considers the extra time and work that she expended in preparing for the Christmas concert, the school picnic, the Hallowe'en party and other similar extracurricular activities one wonders how one human being could manage to do it all. Pearl did!

Not all rural teachers were as devoted as Pearl but the majority rendered reasonable service and proved themselves to be good citizens. They were always ready to turn their hand and ability to anything or any job that required doing. Take the preparation for the grade eight or nine final Departmental Examinations for example. Many gave up their Saturdays and evenings to assist students in getting ready for these important tests. Whatever their faults the grade eight examinations of former years were unequalled as a means of developing the ability to get down to business. As a result there developed a comradeship between the teacher and pupil that has never been equalled. They became a busy, happy family and these extra coaching sessions were among the most cherished memories of both. Clifford West, who passed his grade eight

examinations in 1914, reflects in this manner about the teacher in the
Lathom S.D. 1538 (Osage, Sask.).

> "That teacher certainly worked hard to get the four of us through as we
> did not attend school as regularly as they do now. I remember that teacher
> with gratitude. I know I would never have passed if she had not put in
> a lot of extra time with us after school hours."

Whatever knowledge or skill the rural pedagogue possessed, he or she
was willing to impart it to the interested pupils or adults in the district.
A number gave private music lessons or organized and trained choral
groups. Others turned their attention to such activities as dramatics, art,
handicrafts, tumbling, soccer, hockey, public speaking, field trips and
literary societies. The list was endless. One teacher who had taken
commercial training taught a number of students how to type. Of course all
the practicing was done on the only typewriter available—the teacher's.

Teachers had more than school problems to cope with in those years.
Salesmen made themselves a nuisance by calling at rural schools at any
time of the day. The inexperienced youthful teacher was no match for the
highly-trained and persistent salesman. There was no one to whom the
young lady could turn for guidance or escape. Some teachers ordered goods
or services for which they had no use whatever mainly to get rid of the
agent. Then came the perplexing puzzle of how to meet the payments
demanded by a binding contract that had been signed under duress.

This practice of salesmen visiting schools could be quite distasteful and
troublesome as illustrated by a couple of incidents in the Strathcona S.D.
(Canora, Sask.) in August 1926.

On Miss Clara Johnson's first day in the school she was visited promptly
at the three-thirty dismissal time by an encyclopedia salesman. At six
o'clock he was still extolling its virtues. She finally signed his offered
contract just to get him going. A letter home caused her irate father to
write to the company to the effect that a contract signed by a minor was
not legal and would they please not allow their salesmen to bother busy
teachers in the future.

About two weeks later an equally persistent insurance agent called at
the Strathcona School. Again Miss Johnson signed, desiring a policy but
resenting the browbeating tactics of the salesman. After this second episode
the teacher's heart became hardened and it was short shrift for any future
salesmen.

The doggedness of travelling salesmen was just another tribulation
tolerated by rural school teachers. However, a better day was dawning on
the horizon. A government regulation was eventually introduced which
forbade door-to-door selling at schools.

The rural teachers carried more than their share of philanthropic
responsibilities. When the deadly influenza epidemic struck Western

Canada in 1918, Donalda McIntyre of the Friendship Hill S.D. 3137 (south of Moose Jaw, Sask.) like so many of her colleagues did not wait to be asked but closed the school and went nursing, caring for the sick and dying with no thought of her personal safety or recompense. Not many people today can remember the mine disaster at Hillcrest, Alta., in 1914 when 189 men were killed in the explosion. Yet it can be told that rural teachers from Burmis S.D. and other districts in that area rendered many valuable services in the sorrowful aftermath.

A teacher was awarded the George Cross for her act of heroism in a rural school yard near Calgary, Alta., during World War II. Jim Robinson, an officer in the R.C.A.F. stationed at No. 2 Wireless School, and a Wireless Air Gunner student were making a routine training flight one morning. Due to some unknown reason the pilot experienced difficulties in controlling the aircraft and crashed in a schoolyard. The aircraft caught fire on impact and Jimmy Robinson was pinned in the front cockpit beyond any chance of rescue. The student in the rear seat was still conscious but in a helpless position. The teacher, disregarding entirely the risk to herself from the holocaust and the still more serious danger of an explosion, proceeded to drag out the wireless air gunner. She saved his life.

The following incident may not have saved a life but it illustrates how some teachers made life more tolerable for their students.

There was a little seven-year-old in the Angle Lake S.D. (Vegreville, Alta.) who used to walk three miles to school in the winter carrying nothing for his lunch but a few frozen potatoes. Times were hard for most of the families in that district in 1922. In the cold weather the potatoes froze as hard as bullets. Even with his dinner pail next to the heater they failed to thaw out in time for him to eat lunch at noon. One cold day while the hungry tot was sitting by the stove trying to crunch the frozen potatoes the teacher's heart went out to him. Georgina gave him half her lunch which consisted of a couple of dried-up cupcakes and four slices of bread sweetened with a trace of syrup. The boy's clothing was very poor. He wore a coat so patched that the teacher wasn't sure if it was originally dark grey patched with light-colored cloth or vice versa. The unfortunate youngster used to come to school crying bitterly as his cold feet pained him so much. When Miss Connors received a payment on her salary she sent his mother three dollars and asked her to use it to buy the lad some overshoes.

Today there are special schools for children who are retarded, or deaf, or have speech defects, or are abnormal in one way or another. But in the days of the rural school every child, regardless of aberrations, was sent to the Little White Schoolhouse. These sad cases not only took up much of the teacher's precious time but contributed to her discipline problems as well. A few conscientious teachers, in spite of their lack of training in such matters, attempted to assist these unfortunate members of society to attain some measure of success and become independent.

One such teacher was Miss Vernette Akeley.

During the 1924 term, while teaching in the Wild Rose Valley S.D. (Eston, Sask.) she encountered a seemingly unconquerable problem in the person of Wray. This seven-year-old boy had been rejected by his two preceding teachers as unteachable. He possessed a bad speech impediment and was the butt of his schoolmates' good-natured but ill-advised teasing. Wray's biggest drawback was that he had no concept of numbers beyond four. Miss Akeley found this incredible as farm children were always in the habit of counting things like eggs, chickens, cows, horses, bushels and stooks. Somehow or other the teacher penetrated that particular blank by the use of numerous concrete examples and Wray learned to count.

Then she dealt with his stutter. First she let him listen to the recitations of the other children. Then prepared special seatwork for him and encouraged the other students to keep straight faces when Wray labored with his speech. Miss Akeley was sympathetic to a degree but the day came when she had to draw a firm line. Wray had the habit of struggling with his s's and then dissolving into tears. Soon he started again, and again ended up in a fit of weeping. This time the teacher drew from its hiding place the strap, that medieval instrument of torture, and placed it in plain sight on the desk.

"Now, Wray," she said, "you have turned on the tears often enough. I am sorry that you have a little trouble but if you cry again I shall have to use this." She ominously pointed to the strap.

Wray's tears vanished as if by magic and somehow he conquered his difficulties. Spelling became his favorite subject and he was on the way to normal study habits when Miss Akeley left Wild Rose.

The case of Teddy was more serious. Jennie knew that he was "different" from the moment she started to register the students of the Pathlow S.D. 58 (Pathlow, Sask.) for the 1927 term. He was seven years old, badly retarded, and unable to talk or concentrate. His parents sent him to school with a younger sister just to make him appear normal. Time and again the teacher was stymied by his bizarre behavior. Here is an example.

Jennie had originated a novel scheme of signalling to the students when it was permissible for them to leave the room. The device consisted of a piece of cardboard suspended on the inside of the front door by a string. The word "OUT" was shown on one side of the tag and "IN" on the other. Whenever a pupil left the school he turned the card to read "OUT", indicating that no one else had the privilege of going out until he returned and changed it to "IN". The plan eased many of the problems that materialized when two or more spirited youngsters found themselves beyond the restraining presence of the teacher for a few minutes, but on the other hand it provided Teddy with an opportunity of trying out a new idea. This day he left the room and after one hour the teacher asked one of the big boys to bring him back. The lad returned alone. He whispered to the teacher that Teddy had removed all his clothes in the toilet and refused to put them back on. Jennie took a small stick and briefed the boy not to use it but merely to threaten the stripper with it. The scheme worked. In a few minutes, Teddy, quite unconcerned, took his usual place and went back to his routine of grinning and blankly gazing into space.

Inspired teaching has left its mark on many a rural child. A grade eight girl who attended the Kincora S.D. (Kindersley, Sask.) back in 1917 reminisces about her teachers in this manner.

> "I have always owed a debt of gratitude to my eighth grade teacher. She believed in spelling drill. This included not only the correct spelling and pronunciation, but a concise dictionary meaning as well. We vied for the 'top of the class' as we stood in line and spelled each other down each day.
> "We were introduced to Shakespeare through 'As You Like It' and I can still recite 'the seven ages of man'. Another gem memorized then that has stayed with me through the years was the passage from the Vision of Sir Launfal which starts, 'What is so rare as a day in June'.
> "While I have always loved the written word and have lived with books all my life, I know that my life has been the richer for the devotion that those early teachers gave to the task of bringing a little learning to the pioneer children."

Madeline, a student in the Westmoor S.D. 2010 (Punnichy, Sask.) became a teacher because she was so impressed with the respect and honor accorded the teachers in her own district.

> "It was an event of great importance to have the teacher stay overnight. The best dishes were brought out, and there were preserved peaches for supper — very rare in our home. Dad had to sleep on the lounge that night while teacher shared the one big bedroom with mother and us girls.
> "I recall watching our teacher daintily pouring her tea from a thermos bottle—surely a thing of wonder to us. She also had one of those watches on a long neck chain with a slide. My! how I pictured myself teaching one day in the distant future. I would have a thermos and a watch which I could tuck in at my tight waist. I would doodle with my slide as I read to my class. Alas! by the time I had a class of my own, the wrist watch had appeared and all my dreams had crumbled."

Not infrequently some ex-rural teacher succeeded in making a name for himself in a field of human endeavor other than education. The district residents were quick to claim him or her as their own. They pointed proudly to the particular accomplishments of their native son or daughter, or else said, "I bet you didn't know that he taught in our school in 1913?" At the Lifford School, S.D. 5 Manvers (Bethany, Ont.) one early teacher was Sam Hughes, later Sir Sam Hughes—the Minister of Militia (National Defense) in the Borden Cabinet during the World War I. He married one of the local girls and years later brought back her body for burial in the St. Mary's cemetery, adjacent to the school.

A pioneer teacher of the Alpha S.D. (Osage, Sask.) was James Gardiner, who ultimately became Canada's renowned Minister of Agriculture. He also taught in the Wermley S.D. (Kisbey, Sask.) at the age of nineteen.

Solon Low, for years the National Leader of the Social Credit party, started his teaching career in a little rural school in south eastern Alberta.

How did the rural people show their deference to a teacher for a job well done? No! It wasn't money. They couldn't afford it. It was the kindly little gestures that sing on in the soul forever.

A tradition in the Fair Valley S.D. (Glenbow, Man.) was to honor the teacher at the end of the school term by presenting her with a wild orchid. A couple of the older students made their precarious way down into the nearby tamarack swamp. There in the heart of the luxuriant wilderness grew the orchids—fresh, dainty, and so lovely. The youngsters brought the orchid directly to the teacher's desk at the last recess. No speeches were ever made. The orchid itself conveyed the sentiment that was overflowing in the hearts of the children. Nor was any reply ever given. The two or three tears that the young teacher brushed away from her brimming eyes meant more than any "thank you" speech possibly could.

It was gratitude to a teacher that prompted Harry Partridge of the Stonelaw S.D. (Monitor, Alta.) to name his firstborn daughter, Louise. When Harry first started school, a Louise Whitesides had been kind, considerate and devoted to him. The passage of fifteen years or more had failed to dampen his appreciation of a fine teacher.

Time and tide do not dim the work of a good teacher. James Bond Steele was such a teacher. He started to teach in the old Belmont School (where Swift's Edmonton Packing Plant now stands) immediately after the Riel Rebellion in 1885 and stayed on until 1889 when he was enticed to the newly-formed Beaver Lake School No. 222 some 50 miles east of Edmonton. He remained there until 1900. Mr. Steele had the reputation of being an excellent teacher and today, some seventy years later, any of his pupils still living all agree that "he was one of the best teachers they had ever met". Steele Heights in northeastern Edmonton was named for this outstanding early teacher.

Perhaps the most touching gift ever presented to a rural teacher was proffered by a Metis child in the Patterson S.D. (Alonsa, Man.). The inhabitants of that district in 1928 were poor in material things but rich in the offerings of simple kindness.

One morning the tiniest girl in the school, a mere baby, stood at the teacher's desk and picked the precious currants from her dry bannock for a treat for her beloved teacher. Currants were something she had tasted per-

haps once or twice in her short life and they were very special. The teacher
was to have them. She offered them with love in her shining dark eyes.
Truly it was a great gift!

The life and work of a good teacher lingers long in the affections of his
pupils. In fact these entities have a way of becoming a part of the fabric of
a child's very being. This is probably the greatest reward that a teacher
can ever hope to reap for "To live in the hearts of others is not to die".

"Ferg" James of Hanna, Alta., in his Tales of the Pioneer Days pays
tribute to the rural school teacher in a poem that he composed in 1922
entitled, "The Rural School Teacher".

> In the world's mightly race for existence,
> There are some who don't get their just dues,
> The doctor can write his prescriptions,
> The druggist can fill them with booze,
> The garage man can gas to advantage,
> The butcher can "beef" till he dies,
> But the Rural School Teacher
> Is one little creature,
> Who never comes in for a prize.
>
> The lawyer can write out his "quit" claim
> And a "quit" claim it is without a doubt,
> For a lawyer will ne'er think of quitting
> As long as the claim will hang out.
> The merchant can pull off his "Big Sale",
> And his goods and the "people" are sold,
> But the Rural School Teacher
> A cute little creature,
> Is always left out in the cold.
>
> The dentist can pull out your "eye teeth",
> And charge you for giving you pain,
> The teacher goes on with her labors,
> The nerve wracking labor of brain.
> She "pulls down" a meagre existence,
> Must always be "pleasing and prim",
> And next to a preacher,
> The Rural School Teacher
> Keeps on when the going is "slim".
>
> They come from their homes in the city,
> From the farmsteads far over the land,
> They toil in the Little White Schoolhouse,
> They are guiding the little brown hand,
> They are moulding the men of the future,
> And the future's demand will be great,
> And the Rural School Teacher
> Is fitting them each year,
> To fill every office of state.

And yet there are those who will grumble,
"Their salaries are always too high!"
But those kind of folks always grumble,
So grumble away till you die.
But some people boast for the teacher,
The bachelors think she's a charm,
So don't be a piker,
You know you should like her
And welcome the little school-marm.

Practically every school district that ever existed could lay claim to fame for one reason or another. Some event invariably occurred in the course of its history that enabled the inhabitants to boast of its importance.

The people of the Floral S.D. (Saskatoon, Sask.), for instance, maintain that their school district is the best known of any in Canada as it was the birthplace of Gordie Howe, the most famous hockey player in the world.

The citizens of Kenlis S.D. 6 (Abernethy, Sask.) on the other hand point to 1890 as a year of accomplishment. The poetess Pauline Johnson visited the district at that time. She put on a concert in Kenlis School and held her audience spellbound with her repertoire of dramatic readings. George Ismond, an early resident of the district, makes this observation about the eventful evening.

"This took place twelve years before I was born, but I have often heard my mother and others in the community speak of the occasion as one of the highlights in the history of the district. The poem that apparently impressed the settlers the most was, The Legend of the Qu'Appelle. The year 1889 was almost as noteworthy for our district as Hannah, the sister of the authoress Nellie McClung, taught our school for one term."

The oldtimers of the Scotfield area in Alberta always speak proudly of a letter that their secretary-treasurer, T. J. McKeage, received from the provincial government to the effect that the Scotfield Consolidated School District No. 26 (Lanark, Gordon Park and Plover Dale) was the only school district in the province of Alberta in 1926 in which every resident ratepayer had his taxes paid up. This was such an unbelievable achievement that forty years later Mr. McKeage writes, "I wish I had a copy of this letter today for there are so many people who think I am stretching the truth when I tell them about Scotfield's perfect record."

Dame Fortune smiled on some rural schools and made them widely known. May 5, 1960, was such a day in the history of the Coates S.D. (Outlook, Sask). Georges Vanier, the Governor-General of Canada, was on his way to see the South Saskatchewan River Dam on that particular day, when he caught sight of a lonely little rural schoolhouse basking in the prairie sun. He wanted to know its name. Nobody knew! Immediately His Excellency expressed a desire to visit the school. As if by magic the scene of solitude was transformed. A scarlet-coated Mountie stood in the middle of the highway halting all traffic. The Governor-General's limousine and the accompanying cars turned into the Coates schoolyard until the dusty ball-diamond was covered with glistening cars, naval officers in gold braid, television cameramen, newspapermen, radio announcers, R.C.M.P., aides and secretaries.

His Excellency, moving with slow dignity, mounted the rickety steps and made his way into the school. The children and the teacher, Lynn Price, were speechless. The Governor-General proceeded down the aisle and then took up a position behind the teacher's desk. He surveyed the sixteen students of the Coates School with a keen eye. There was a hushed silence for a moment and then His Excellency asked, "Well then, who am I?" There was an embarrassing pause until one or two hands edged up into the air. A voice piped up as His Excellency nodded in her direction. "You're the Governor-General of Canada!" the student said. "You're right!" was the cheery reply. Then the Governor-General proceeded to walk about the little room patting heads and shaking hands. Then he was gone .

The dust in the schoolyard settled and the sun streamed down on a little group of students huddled on the school-steps wondering just what quirk of fate had brought a Governor-General into their little school. Eventually all Canada was to hear about the Coates School.

THE DAILY ROUTINE IN A RURAL SCHOOL

The Council of Education for the North-West Territories and later the Departments of Education of the western provinces emulated the Ontario system of education. Classes were not known as "grades" but as "standards". Grade one was known as Junior Standard I, grade two as Senior Standard I, grade three as Junior Standard II, grade four as Senior Standard II and so on. Standard V, or grade nine, was the entrance to high school. It was referred to as Fifth Class Leaving as the majority of the students had little opportunity or desire to go beyond this grade. The high school consisted of Standard VI as grade ten, Standard VII as grade eleven and Standard VIII as grade twelve, or equivalent to senior matriculation standing. The change to "grade" classification came in 1910 along with making grade eight the high school entrance year. It wasn't until 1936 that grade nine was again restored to its former status as high school entrance. Whether the high school entrance came at grade eight or nine level it was certainly the most important year as far as rural teachers and students were concerned. It meant writing the all-important Final Examinations set and marked by the Department of Education. Rural teachers soon became aware of the fact that their competence was judged on the ability of their students to pass these examinations. For many students it was the end of their formal education so the examination meant a good deal to them as well.

If the entrance examinations were passed, what then? Prospects for a higher education in those early years were dismal. High schools were few and far between, the boys or girls could not be easily spared from the farm work, and not many families could afford the added expense of sending the children away. Sometimes a student was able to take a high school grade in the local school if there were not too many other grades and if the teacher was willing and able to teach it. In 1923 the Department of Education of Alberta organized a Correspondence School and this enabled ambitious rural students to receive some or all of their high school education by mail. Occasionally parents banded together and were successful in operating a private high school. M. R. Morrison of Vulcan, Alta., describes one such endeavor.

> "In 1918 when I was manager of the Bank of Hamilton in Cayley there was no provision in the district whatsoever for higher education. At that time there were about fourteen students in the area who were ready for high school and they would have to go to High River or Calgary to attend high school. The expense to the parents to send their boys and girls away was beyond the means of many of them. A committee from these parents was formed to investigate the possibility of hiring a teacher and operating a private school in Cayley.
> "Consultation with A. J. Watson, the Inspector of Schools at High River, took place. It was agreed that if the parents could find a satisfactory teacher and undertake the financing of the school a government grant might be obtained by turning over the teacher's salary each month to the local board so they would actually pay the salary.
> "The Committee, of which I acted as secretary, was successful in securing the services of Miss MacMillan of Toronto. She held an M.A. degree.
> "The town hall was obtained for a schoolroom. These pupils were provided with a high school education without having to leave home. A great deal of satisfaction was derived from this effort. The outstanding part of this project was that at the end of the year it was found that the total cost per student paid for by the parents was approximately $95.00. Think of how this figure compares with today's costs?"

Another such "little high school" was organized in the hamlet of Watts, Alta., in 1938 through the efforts of interested parents in the St. George S.D. Here the people converted a railway sectionman's two-room shack into a schoolhouse, hired a dedicated teacher in the person of Mrs. M. D. Cook, and provided higher education for at least fifteen grade nine students who otherwise would have left school. Even a piano was purchased on time with everyone helping to pay for it through concerts, raffles and teas.

The Ellisboro Rural High School in Saskatchewan was still another school born of necessity. In 1934 there were families around the Ellisboro District with children ready for high school, who could not afford to send them into the town of Wolseley and pay tuition fees and board. To drive them back and forth daily was out of the question because the roads were not sufficiently all-weather to make regular attendance possible.

An idea was developed by Messers McLean, Banberry, Thompson and Olive whereby they hired a teacher and opened a high school, using the vacant United Church manse at Ellisboro for a school. The Minister and Deputy Minister of Education in Regina were sympathetic but rather amazed at the audacity of the idea. These officials advised the organizers that one of the rural schools in the area with an enrollment of at least twenty students had to apply for a second room before they would give their approval. Ellisboro S.D. 228 did this, while two other districts offered to help absorb any loss of grant which the local might sustain.

In the next few days the building was cleaned up. A teacher hired, who with his wife and son lived in the manse and in addition to teaching supervised the students who stayed in residence from Monday through Friday. Parents of the students provided wood and coal for heating the building. Each student brought a small table and a chair to be used in place of a desk. A blackboard, chalk, a few maps and other essential items were provided by the participating school districts. The students who intended to set up light-housekeeping brought beds and bedding and whatever else they wanted for their room. A coal oil stove (wick type) was set up in a small alcove for any cooking the students might do. Tuition fees were set at fifteen dollars per year for each student.

Mr. A. Taylor of Carlyle accepted the position as teacher. His salary was to be $400.00 plus housing, fuel, no tuition fees for his son, and a bonus at the end of the year if funds permitted. He received a $50.00 bonus. In the light of today's salaries such an arrangement seems preposterous but it should be remembered that in the depression period many schools were so short of money that teachers often received notes in lieu of cash. There were also many teachers who could not get a school so remained at home with their families, living off relief. So what the board offered Mr. Taylor was much more attractive than it appears today. He stayed at Ellisboro Rural High School for three years.

The Ellisboro Rural High School opened on Tuesday, September 4, 1934, with eleven students registered, just sixteen days after Messrs. McLean and Banbury discussed the idea with Mr. Olive. Mr. W. H. Olive, who was chairman of the school board of this unique school throughout its ten years of existence, sums up its success and the hard work of the board in this way.

> "Financing the school without any tax levy was often very difficult. Many times when the Board met, the report of the Secretary-Treasurer seemed to indicate a hopeless situation, but after hours of hard thought and calculating, a ray of hope would glimmer through the clouds, and like the knight of old after lying down and bleeding for a while, the Board would rise up and fight again. Looking back it was all worth it.
> "Here may I emphasize the success of the whole undertaking by recording that of fifty-two students who attended the Ellisboro Rural High School during the ten years it was in operation, not one failed to pass his or her Departmental Examinations."

The pupils of the Little White Schoolhouse came by their education with much greater difficulty than do the students of today. They rode or walked miles to school over poor roads, through the rains and mud of spring, the heat and dust storms of summer, and the snows and cold of winter. It was common to take students out of school for a month or so during the busy spring or fall season. Frequently the pupils lost a few days of school when blizzards or cold spells made it impossible for them to attend. The teacher shortage became so acute in the postwar period that many rural schools were unable to hire one and had to resort to the use of "supervisors". It worked like this. The entire enrollment in the school registered in correspondence lessons and the supervisor assisted the students with their difficulties and mailed the lessons in on time. There was no teaching as such. These supervisors were high school students who had completed their grade twelve or were within a couple of subjects of doing so. The standard of education under such a stopgap arrangement deteriorated noticeably. It became difficult to obtain a grade eight much less a high school education. The surprising fact was that in spite of the many imperfections and the vicissitudes attending the rural school, every district could boast of university graduates or others who, in one way or another, made a valuable contribution to mankind. Not forgetting the hundreds of thousands of men and women who just by doing their daily tasks and living as God had intended, were fashioning a great Canada.

Teaching in a rural school was challenging. There were so many organizational and teaching problems that special techniques had to be devised to overcome them. The average school had fifteen students and six grades, although this could go as high as forty students and nine or ten grades. Teachers combined classes in certain subjects, or taught them concurrently, in order to cover the prescribed courses of study. Time was precious. The beginners or grade two or three students could not be expected to work by themselves for any length of time hence the teacher scheduled her periods so as to meet with them at frequent intervals. The classes were so small that it was not unusual to have just one student. Competition under such circumstances was out of the question. Accordingly schemes were introduced to motivate the child to improve upon his own work. Samples of his writing or composition were saved and compared to some of his later efforts. Progress charts, presentations of gold or silver stars, granting of special privileges, all inspired the youngster to compete with himself or attempt to outdo some other grade. The timetable was made flexible enough so when a time-consuming introductory lesson had to be taught one day the follow-up lessons on succeeding days could be brief and reduced to review and drill.

There was a decided lack of textbooks in the schools during the early years. Outside of readers, provided by the Department of Education, there were practically no other books in the hands of children below grade six. Few parents could afford them, and if they could, it took weeks for a book-order to come through. As a result of this nearly all the assignments were laboriously copied on the blackboard by the teacher. This extra chore necessitated many hours of tedious work after school. It wasn't too bad during the summer but in the late fall and early winter when the days became

—Mrs. David Grisdale

In 1946 the Dunwell S.D. 4857 (Weekes, Sask.) had one teacher and—
too many students.

shorter, many a rural pedagogue finished his transcribing task under
the uncertain gleam of a borrowed coal-oil lamp.

Writing paper was made to do until every square inch of blank space
had been filled with figures or words. One mother in reminiscing about this
practice said, "When I see the sheets and sheets of paper our children of
today use and frequently waste, I realize how times have changed. We made
the most out of every piece of paper, in fact we got into the habit of saving
blank sheets no matter where they came from—calendar pages, order forms,
pieces of cardboard, brown wrapping paper, paper bags or used envelopes.
Furthermore, we wrote on both sides."

Every piece of blackboard chalk was used to the very last mite, no
matter how badly the teacher's finger nails suffered in the ordeal. Colored
chalk was a luxury that very few schools could afford, most teachers bought
their own.

It was common practice to bring the classes to the front for recitation.
While the pedagogue taught one class the members of the other five or
six classes worked and studied by themselves at their desks. The teacher
expended considerable time and effort to plan the seatwork for each class.
Her success as an educator depended on whether the students understood
the various assignments and the degree to which they applied themselves.

The pupils of the Red Rows School illustrate a singular characteristic exhibited by most rural children: that is, they liked to play in, on or about a school barn.

The boys and girls were not spoonfed as they are today. They ordinarily worked quickly so as to be free to listen to what the next grade was being taught. The "listening-in habit" accelerated these children and very often they became advanced. The buzz of classes in session never appeared to distract the seatworkers any more than the record player and radio distract modern children doing their homework at home. The teacher's desk was always piled high with scribblers and pages of assignments that had to be examined. The marking or the correcting of the seatwork exercises was a necessary and a never-ending chore of the rural teacher. They never quite kept up with the demand.

Drill and memory work characterized all the studies. The blackboards gleamed with arithmetic tables, history dates, the names of countries and their capitals, definitions of parts of speech and labelled diagrams of all sorts. The students were expected to know them by heart. They also memorized poems, prose parts and gems of thought. The latter consisted of choice maxims that were intended to instill certain virtues in the one who committed them to memory. The mottoes were written across the top of the blackboard, or else painstakingly reproduced by painting or gluing letters on art paper or white bleached-cotton sheets. The Clarendon S.D. 9 in the Ottawa Valley for example featured such sayings as "Kindness is nobler than revenge", "Let love, purity and truth always reign here", "Shun evil companions", "Wine is a mocker". After fifty years or more many students still remember them. Lengthy poems like the "Ancient

—Mrs. Carl Runyan

A class "in recitation" at the front of the room in the Westmoor School 2010 (Punnichy, Saskatchewan). Note the pinafores and the braids of the girls. The wood stove seen in the picture is still in use today in the basement of a home in the district.

Mariner" or the "Holy Grail" were memorized in their entirety by the students.

Although all the courses as prescribed in the Programme of Studies were taught in the one-room school, emphasis remained on reading, writing and arithmetic. The belief was that a good grounding in these "tool" subjects enabled a student to educate himself up to any level, including university. At present the logic of the knowledge explosion is obliging some educators to say what we need in the schools is a narrowing of the program—reading, writing and arithmetic, and little else.

The readers supplied free by the Department of Education contained selections suitable for silent reading, oral reading, study as literature, scanning and memorizing. The material was somewhat macabre in nature. The poems in particular were mainly of death, disaster and misadventure with a fair sprinkling of patriotic themes.

Oral reading received more than its share of class time. It was a common sight to see some youngster struggling painfully through a literature selection with the teacher following him in a half-hearted fashion and at the same time marking some arithmetic exercises. A few teachers had the unsettling habit of halting the reader in the middle of a paragraph or sentence and then asking another pupil to continue reading from there.

More than one pupil after being called upon to do this blushed, rose slowly but remained silent. He had lost his place! The teacher was a genius in spotting those not following the reader.

The beginners in those days started with a phonic primer and then graduated to the primer. Many people can still remember the brown Alexandra reader with the big Union Jack in the frontispiece. It introduced the would-be reader to a colored picture of a big red apple, a little girl, and some mysterious markings that were purported to say, "Apples! Apples! Fine red apples. Will you have one? Will you have one? See the apple. It is a red apple. This is Helen. Helen has the apple."

Penmanship was practiced daily in all grades. The prescribed writing texts were pamphlet-like booklets that contained samples of good penmanship and numerous exercises in writing. Students wielded their straight-pens in free-arm movements to produce page after page of impacted straight strokes, clockwise circles, counter-clockwise circles and various combined circles. While all this was going on, the teacher with a yardstick in her hand, paced up and down the aisles checking each student's writing posture and arm mobility. Woe betide the youngster who slumped at his desk or used finger movements! The ruler descended smartly across his shoulders or the back of his hand. The grading of penmanship was not the hit-and-miss proposition that most people considered it to be. It was possible for any student to evaluate or to note any improvement in his writing by matching his specimen with one of the rated samples shown on the Standard Writing Scale.

If a person learns to write compositions well by repeatedly writing them the rural children should have excelled in this field. The favorite assignment was: Write a composition on Champlain, or the meadowlark, or the Great Lakes, or Marquis wheat. No matter what subject was being taught it ended in the same prosaic fashion, "Write a composition!" The primary student wrote his single sentence, the intermediate his paragraph, and the senior his essay. The first composition topic in September was; "How I spent my summer holidays" and the last one in June was, "How I expect to spend my summer holidays". Rural students never had an opportunity to enjoy holidays for they stayed at home and worked harder than ever. However, when the topic was assigned they fabricated a holiday story of some sort. No wonder their compositions were listless.

The ideal seatwork for the students was using the dictionary. Every day without fail the students were given ten to twenty words to learn to spell, to look up their meaning, pronunciation, their derivation and to find a synonym for each one. They also had to use each word in a sentence. The ability to spell was held in high esteem in the rural schools. If students made mistakes in their daily orthographic tests they wrote out the correct spelling of each such word as many as one hundred times.

Spelling bees were held on certain Friday afternoons and it was not un-common for schools to compete against each other for the spelling championship of the inspectorate. People used to pack the community hall in a central town or village to watch these spelling competitions. The matches themselves took from one to two hours to complete. Even-tually a bright youngster spelled everyone else down and became the champion. Words like miscellaneous, feasible, ostentatious, heterogeneous offered no difficulties to these spellers. Many people wish it were so today.

A good deal of significance was placed on rapid calculation in arith-metic. Students were given a daily test, usually of twenty to thirty minutes' duration, to work through a rapid calculation exercise. It consisted of questions in all the fundamental operations with emphasis on speed and accuracy. The tests, which became longer and more difficult as the year progressed, were contained in a pad that bore the title "Exercises in Rapid Calculations". The result of this constant drill in computation accorded the students added facility in handling arithmetic problems.

The arithmetic problems characteristically involved the characters "A" and "B". Here is an example: "A and B engage in a wholesale business. A invested $6000 to B's $4000. They gained $1250. Find their profits." After working such problems for a number of years the students became quite familiar with the antics of A and B. "A" was crafty, wealthy and an extrovert, while "B" was his complete antithesis. In sharing property or profits, "A" always managed to receive the lion's share. When it came to work, wily "A" contrived to do less than "B" yet received a higher wage. Any time the two travelled "A" rode and poor "B" walked. If circumstances forced both of them to walk "B" was assigned the longest stretch of the road. The sympathies of the boys and girls were continually with down-trodden "B" and they gleamed with pleasure if in the occasional problem "B" succeeded in outsmarting "A". "C" and "D" were brought in to help out "A" and "B" any time the work increased or became too difficult. When the business enterprise flourished to the point where enor-mous profits resulted "C" and "D" were invited to join the firm to share the profits. It was better to divide the benefits four ways than to pay the high income tax. Sad to relate they also participated in making up any deficits that the company incurred.

Many methods employed by the rural teacher would be viewed as obsolete today. Map drawing was highly regarded. Once a week at least, a map was unrolled and the students copied it with the required details on drawing paper or in their scribblers. Nowadays ready-made outline maps are supplied to the students. In grammar the student spent consid-erable time in learning definitions, parsing parts of speech and analyzing phrases and clauses. The modern school dispenses with the mechanics of grammar and concerns itself with usage. Art classes in the Little White Schoolhouse included the detailed study of the world's masterpieces and their artists. The grade eights were required to have comprehensive knowledge of the following pictures for their final examination in art:

The Horse Fair	Bonheur
Aurora	Reni
Avenue of Trees	Hobbema
Dance of the Nymphs	Carot
By the River	Lerolle
Pilgrims Going to Church	Boughton
Sir Galahad	Watts
Joan of Arc	Bastien-Lepage
The Madonna of the Chair	Raphael

The students owned miniature reproductions of these pictures. It was also customary to have large copies of one or two hanging on the walls of the classroom.

Mrs. Helen Penner, who attended the Balfour S.D. 4151 (Blumenhof, Sask.) for over six years in the early Forties, gives her impressions of the type of learning that went on in the rural schools.

"In a little prairie schoolroom
So many years ago.
'Twas easy then to quickly learn,
At least it seems so now!
Eight grades crowded in one room
Still, desks there were and to spare;
And teacher gave to every child
The help that was his share.
Of course it wasn't all easy as pie
And teacher, at times, was quite stern.
Yet, I cherish the memory of the prairie school
Where it was so easy to learn."

The school day commenced at 9:00 a.m. and continued until 12:00 noon with a fifteen-minute recess at 10:30 a.m. The hour between 12:00 noon and 1:00 p.m. was allotted to lunch. The afternoon session lasted from one o'clock until 3:30 p.m. with recess at 2:15 p.m. The only change from this routine occurred during the winter term when the school-opening was delayed until 9:30 a.m. There was no elaborate system of time signals. The teacher took a step or two just beyond the door and rang the handbell to call the students into session, while a few taps on the deskbell, or a verbal command dismissed them. The beginning or the end of a class period was communicated to the students by a few words of instruction from the teacher. "Grade Six! bring your arithmetic exercise books to the front," or "Now you can go back to your seats, Grade Three, and finish the questions on page sixty-five."

In days when there were no radios or telephones to give the correct time it was remarkable that so few children arrived late. This was because an important errand performed for the entire district by anyone going into town was to obtain the correct time at the railway station. Only the older boys in the school carried pocket watches. These time pieces could be purchased for one dollar and were jokingly referred to as the Big Ben or the Massey-Harris. There were no wristwatches. Often the teacher was the only person in the school with any type of watch. Nevertheless the students soon found ways of telling when it was time for the two recesses, the noon hour and three-thirty. Take this example from the Botany S.D. (Prince Albert, Sask.)

There was a small window in the south end of the school and as the sun shone through, it cast its beam in a big arc on the floor as it moved across the sky. The students scratched marks in the floor to indicate when it was time for recess and the noon hour. This sundial worked well.

The first few minutes after school was called were devoted to saluting the flag and repeating the Lord's prayer. Schools in those days prominently displayed the Union Jack on the front wall just above the blackboard. The students remained standing at attention by their desks, saluted the flag, and repeated, "I salute the flag, the emblem of my country . . . and to her I pledge my love and loyalty", or else they sang, "The Maple Leaf Forever". The children of some newly-arrived families from the United States or Continental Europe often staunchly refused to salute a foreign flag. No international incidents were precipitated but it created much unpleasantness in some school districts.

Once the patriotic exercises were completed the children bowed their heads and repeated the Lord's prayer. The occasional teacher also read a passage from the Bible. Then the routine of the day began as the teacher made her first round of all classes assigning work for each group. In the meantime one class had made its way to the front ready for the initial lesson of the day.

The rural teacher did not concentrate on textbooks exclusively. They watched carefully and patiently for learning opportunities beyond the narrow confines of the classroom.

One teacher was instrumental in inducing radio station CFAC of Calgary to broadcast a half-hour program direct to his school. He wrote in and asked whether such an undertaking was feasible. The manager replied that not only was it possible but that he would be glad to do so. The date and time were given. Since radio was still in its infancy this was quite an undertaking. A battery radio was hastily rigged up in the school and the teacher and students were thrilled when the manager of CFAC talked to them. He said, "Hello, Mr. . . . and the students of . . . school! How is our program coming in? Please wire or phone and let me know." He apparently was unaware that the school was so small, having an enrollment of only 13 students, or that they were some twenty miles from the nearest phone. In the opinion of the students of that school, they had at last gained world-wide recognition.

Science excursions were not new or unique. The teacher of the Forks S.D. usually squeezed her students into an old model-T Ford on suitable Friday afternoons and went on science-discovery expeditions. The school was located near the junction of the Bow and Red Deer rivers so the area teemed with wildlife of all sorts. The children attained scientific understanding through their own observations. One grade eight student, who was gifted in art, reproduced colored sketches of the living organisms that the students studied.

Consider how thrilled the students of Corner S.D. must have been to study a herd of antelope at firsthand. The teacher happened to glance out of the window and spied these animals standing outside, evidently pondering whether the schoolhouse was a point of danger. She beckoned to the pupils to come very quietly and look at them. They did, but only for a couple of minutes. Someone moved. The entire herd vanished into the distance almost before the children realized that the graceful creatures were moving. The beautiful sight left the youngsters overwhelmed with wonder and surprise. It was a nature study lesson made to order.

The pupils of No. 1 Woodyatt, on the banks of the Rainy River near the village of Devlin in Ontario like other rural students used to bring a great many living specimens to school for study. Jessie brought a yellow-shafted flicker with a broken wing and Jenny carried a snapping turtle for two miles in a dishpan. The Barley boys caught a brown mother bat and her two babies and put her in a honey pail with a handkerchief tied over the top. The students kept the turtle around the school all day, testing him out on pencils which he snapped in two with no trouble at all. In the end they let him loose in a nearby creek. The bat lunged at the children any time they came near and bared vicious little teeth while the frightened babies clung tenaciously to her sides. At four o'clock the boys left the honey pail tipped on its side so she could get away in the night. The flicker ripped the teacher's hands with his beak and claws but there wasn't very much she could do for the injured bird. Beatrice Fines, the teacher, taught her students a lesson on the survival of the fittest and the balance of nature and then permitted Alfred to take him home and put him out of his misery with a shot from his twenty-two.

At times the learning experiences were tinged with real adventure. Take the example of what happened in the Gooseberry Lake School in the fall of 1929. It is certain that the young teacher never forgot the selection, "The Lotus Eaters". She was teaching this literature selection to two girls in grade eight when suddenly Louise looked up and yelled,

"Fire!" As far as the teacher knew fire drill had never been taught or heard of in that school. In a matter of seconds the building was emptied. She followed and dazedly looked at a fire started by a whirlwind from the ash pile. The children crowded around her and said that they must fight it. The inexperienced teacher did not have a clue. However the youngsters were resourceful and knew what to do. They ran to the barn for the horses' feed sacks, dipped them in water and started beating at the flames. All available cream cans and pails in the school were filled with water and carried along by the fire-fighters. Occasionally the gunny sacks were soaked in the water, but the flogging of the advancing line of fire continued unabated. Teacher and students fought the trail of prairie fire for almost two miles—just short of a granary of wheat. Not a single adult came to their assistance as everyone had gone to an auction sale in Coronation. The victory was theirs alone! The teacher had some doubt in this regard. As she trudged wearily back to school she discovered that somewhere along the line of battle she had lost both her three-inch spike-heels.

The desert-like area north of Medicine Hat was known to harbor rattle-snakes so teachers who taught in that part of Alberta were nervous when they saw the children running into the Russian thistles at the edge of the schoolyard to retrieve a ball. Kay Beirbach and her pupils had a brief but terrifying experience with one of these snakes.

"Once on a very hot afternoon the class sat on horseblankets in the shade of the school for their lessons. I looked up to see a very large snake creeping behind them. I cautioned them to remain perfectly still, and for once they really obeyed. As the big fellow crawled away to a safe distance, the big boys were after him with sticks and stones. The students held a funeral at recess, burying the rattlesnake in the fireguard. They erected a cross and sang, O Canada."

Sometimes an amusing incident occurred in the school to provide the students with a moment of relaxation. Most were of the homey type. One such incident happened in the Glendale S.D. (Cochrane, Alta.) while school was being held in the Frank Hanes house. The Glendale School had burned down in December 1932 and the various homes in the district took turns in hosting the classes. It was a sunny morning, so the teacher, Miss Zella Olivier, had left the door open. A leghorn hen wandered in and upon seeing a drawer open in Don Brown's desk, she climbed in on top of his books and laid an egg. The children enjoyed the unexpected diversion. The hen returned on the following day and Don obligingly pulled out the drawer. She repeated her performance. This went on for a number of days until the teacher figured enough time had been wasted watching a chicken so she put an end to the entertainment by keeping the door closed.

Most rural teachers made brave attempts to teach the social graces to their students by both precept and example. It wasn't easy. Life was hard and rough in a new land and the pioneers spent all their waking hours wresting a living from the soil. They didn't have the time or the desire to enlighten their offspring about anything cultural. It just didn't fit in with the tough life they had to lead.

Miss Rebecca Maxwell of Hainstock S.D. (Olds, Alta.) was one teacher who was successful in inculcating a sense of propriety and pride in her pupils. She was always polite with her students. "Please", "thank you", "excuse me" and "pardon me" were in constant use. She also taught the proper use of "was" and "were"; "did" and "done"; "went" and "gone"; "may" and "can"; "she" and "I"; and "have come" and "have gone." In fact Miss Maxwell set aside fifteen minutes each day in which she had all the students participate in activities designed to provide them with cultural training. She also promoted what she liked to call "Gems of Thought" when the students and the teacher discussed the practical application of such mottoes as:

> "Handsome is as handsome does."
> "Make haste while the sun shines."
> "The longest way round may be the shortest way home."
> "Every cloud has a silver lining."
> "Many hands make light work."
> "Truth is honest, truth is sure, truth is strong and must endure."

The method of registering new students in a rural school was a far cry from the present-day procedure of filling in a multitude of forms. It wasn't a paper war. Violet (Reynolds) Carr remembers seeing two white shapes in front of the Big Coulee S.D. 4497 (Athabasca, Alta.) as she approached the school one fall morning in 1931. When she came a little nearer she made out two ladies with white kerchiefs on their heads— a headgear she had never seen before. Each of the women held a child tightly by the hand. They tried to talk but Miss Reynolds wasn't able to understand either of them. She eventually concluded that they wanted to enroll their children in the school. Before leaving, the two Ukrainian mothers burst into tears, thrust a child's hand into the teacher's and in sorrowful and pleading tones mumbled, "bud dobborah", "bud dobborah" (be good). This was how Slovka and Peter were first registered in the Big Coulee School.

Emergencies sometimes arose to test the teacher's mettle, as well as bring a break in the usual school routine. It is one thing to pick up a telephone today, contact a doctor and the parents, and have the injured child whisked immediately to the hospital by car and an entirely different situation to have had the same accident occur in a rural school, say in 1912, with no telephone, with the nearest doctor or hospital thirty or

fifty miles away, and walking or riding a horse the only means of transporting the patient. The four accidents described below show that, in
spite of the many attending difficulties, most rural teachers were able
to cope with any exigencies that occurred in their schools.

One day in No. 5 Shenston, a school in the Rainy River Valley
of Ontario, Jimmy cut his foot with the axe in the woodshed. It was his
own fault because nobody below grade seven was supposed to use the
axe. It was a bad cut and the teacher looked very pale and nervous as
she examined it. For once she did not scold. There was no first-aid kit
in the school but the teacher fortunately located a clean cotton sack
in which seeds for the school fair had come. She ripped it up and used
it to bandage the injured foot. Jimmy lived three miles from the school
and had to be carried home, partly piggyback and partly in a chair
fashioned by clasping wrists. His older brother and sister did the carrying.

In another rural school near Irvine, Alta., a large steer had wandered
into the yard and eventually found its way into the barn. A boy who had
noticed the animal, raised his hand to be excused, and then stealthily
crept to the stable and shut the door. During recess the boys cornered
the steer and as many as possible climbed aboard. By this time the steer
became frantic and when it bucked the air was filled with flying boys,
some were propelled, while others jumped to save themselves. Someone
finally opened the stable door and the annoyed beast dashed for its
freedom spilling the remaining two or three youngsters in the process.
Soon a boy ran into the school and excitedly yelled to the teacher, "We
need your help in the barn!"

"What for?" she asked.

"Well, one of the boys is hung up on a big spike. It went in at his
mouth and came through his cheek. We're having trouble getting him
unhooked."

Twin sisters were riding to the Ribstone S.D. 2861 (Coronation, Alta.)
one morning in 1931 when the horse bucked them off. The girls arrived
at school covered with blood and dirt. One was dazed and had a bad
bruise on her head. She didn't seem to understand what was being said
to her and merely answered "yes" or "no" in a monotonous voice. The
teacher didn't know what to do as a saddle horse was the only mode of
transportation available and she was certain that the girl couldn't ride
home. The worried teacher sent an older pupil about a mile to a neighbor
who happened to own a car. He took the dazed youngster home. It was
several days before the child regained full consciousness. The parents
concluded the horse must have kicked her as she fell, but the girl herself
could never remember anything about the accident.

No experience was more distasteful to a rural child then that associated
with the first visit of a dentist to the area. In the Shining Bank S.D. 4034

(Edson, Alta.) for instance, the teacher accompanied the children in a lumber wagon that took them to the Neighboring S.D., some ten miles away, where the dental clinic was to be held. There were no facilities available in a newly-settled district so each teacher was required to hold her own pupils as they sat perched on top of a desk while the dentist worked on their teeth. Since this was the first visit to a dentist for the majority of the pupils many required several extractions and fillings. The ordeal was just as trying for the teachers as it was for the pupils. More than one pedagogue, after serving in the capacity of a dental assistant for his students found the task so exhausting that he collapsed from nervous strain. No one was able to figure out exactly who suffered the most, the children from physical pain or the teacher from mental torture.

Going barefoot could have its disadvantages. One noon hour in the May Hall S.D. 3299 (Schuler, Alta.) while the children were playing tag on the rough-wood floor one of them picked up a four-inch splinter in his foot. It took six boys to carry him home. Then they had to forcibly hold him down while his father removed it with his straight-edge razor. Ben Weisgerber, one of the boys assisting in the operation said, "I can still hear him scream. We didn't know what a doctor looked like in those days for we never saw one."

The majority of students brought lunches to school. According to today's standard they should have suffered from diet deficiencies but they were a healthy lot. School lunches were prosaic affairs. Sandwiches of jam, a hard-boiled egg, a piece of cake and in winter an apple was the more or less standard fare. When meat was to be had they got it but this was not too often. An orange was a luxury. The Russian immigrants who took up land in the Rush Centre S.D. (Esther, Alta.) around 1913 grew many sunflowers. Their children brought sunflower seeds as a part of the school lunch. The rest of the community thought it was an appalling thing to do. In England sunflower seeds were fed only to parrots.

During the Thirties the lunches were even less substantial. Not many people today could stomach a diet of bread buttered with lard and garlic dill pickles for weeks on end. Many boys and girls of that era did.

The mother or the oldest girl had the responsibility of making up the lunches every morning. This was no light task especially if there were six or seven children attending school. The lunches were carried to school in tin pails. The students who rode horseback safeguarded their packet of lunch by placing it in a schoolbag. It shook to pieces in a pail.

What happened if a child forgot his lunch, or latched onto a pail of honey or lard instead of his lunch bucket? There were schoolmates always ready to share their lunches with him; a passing neighbor could bring the forgotten lunch; the kind people living across from the school

Lunch time in the Newell
S. D. 3005 (Coronation,
              Alta.)

—Mrs. C. Talmage

often sent over a makeshift repast. Of course all these considerations
made it easier to forget the occasional lunch pail.

A mother in the Fairlight S.D. 2191 (Winnifred, Alta.) had the
custom of including a special treat in her daughter's pail. The girl
always looked forward to these little surprises. One day while the
children were sitting in the shade eating their lunches the usually fortunate lass happened to notice one of her classmates eating candy just like
she was supposed to have. She frantically searched through her lunch
bucket looking for hers but did not find it. It was easy to get lunches
mixed, as many were put up in Roger's Golden Syrup pails. The innocent recipient of the delicacy really felt badly but since the candy was
all gone there was very little she could do except feel sorry.

Just as soon as the students arrived at school they stacked their
lunch cans on a designated shelf in the anteroom. This comprehensive array of pails added a bit of color to the drab appearance of the
cloakroom. They came in a variety of sizes, shapes and colors. There

were lard pails, honey pails, square tobacco tins, jam cans, syrup pails, peanut butter containers and molasses receptacles. No thermos bottles were evident as they still were luxuries. Very few children considered drinking anything else but water with their lunches. A number of diet-conscious teachers went to the trouble of preparing hot soup or cocoa for their students during the cold weather but this was an exception rather than a general practice in rural schools. A teacher in the Red Willow S.D. 1428 (Red Willow, Alta.) encouraged the students to bring milk. One boy brought his in an oil can and drank it out of the long spout!

If the teacher insisted on neatness, the lunch pails were systematically stowed on the shelf, otherwise they were dumped on the floor in mingled disorder. The lunch pails had an uncanny habit of increasing in number as the school term drew to a close. Any time a student forgot to take his pail home, he returned the next morning carrying another. By the end of the year the cloakroom resembled a general store.

The life expectancy of a pail could be counted in weeks. They received anything but a gentle treatment from their youthful owners. The lunch buckets fell out of the buggy and came in contact with the horse's hoofs or the carriage wheels. Children often volunteered their pails for bases in an impromptu game of ball, or even as the "can" in kick-the-can. It was remarkable the punishment they absorbed and still survived to hold the lunch for another day or so.

Pilfering tasty morsels from lunch boxes was a problem common to most rural schools. It was easy to do. Whenever the teacher permitted a child to leave the room it was no trick for him to help himself to any delicacy to which his palate responded. Once in the outhouse he was free to enjoy it without the fear of being noticed. Lunches packed by mothers who had the reputation of being good cooks suffered the most casualties. The only practical way of trapping these gourmands was to season some specially-prepared food with red pepper, castor oil or hot mustard. The resulting effects upon the culprit soon revealed his identity.

Purloining lunches was not always an "inside" job. A preschool lad who lived on a farm just across from the Jumbo Valley school (Granum, Alta.) had fallen into the habit of crossing the road and dipping his hand into the various lunch pails. His mother, not aware that her little darling was feasting on the best foods that the school could provide, worried over his lack of appetite. The teacher was also concerned but for a different reason. She was unable to catch the thief, who, she presumed, was one of the students in the school. What a surprise for both the mother and the teacher when the little fellow was eventually caught right in the middle of a raid!

Humans were not the only ones who filched lunches. Such animals as horses, dogs, chipmunks, squirrels and gophers soon learned that the tin pails contained food and they were quite capable of prying the lid off and helping themselves. The children were careful not to leave their lunches around where these creatures could get at them. Gophers in particular were a nuisance. Any time they found the door to the school open they sneaked unnoticed into the cloakroom, wrestled the lid off a lunch pail, and proceeded to eat some of the food and ruin the rest.

For the most part, the students ate their lunches at their desks. In winter they huddled about the stove, while on a hot summer day they gathered outside and sat in the grass on the shady side of the school or barn.

The lunch period had all the earmarks of a picnic for kidding, chattering and general good humor prevailed. Trading of lunches was common. In the Mount Hecla S.D. (Leslie, Sask.) everyone liked to swap with the Icelandic children for some of their sweet rolls, while in the University S.D. (Sibbald, Alta.) the Jewish youngsters used to exchange their matzoth (unleavened bread patties) for pork sandwiches. Hard-boiled eggs were favorite articles of barter almost anywhere. They enabled the more hardy souls to show off by cracking them against their foreheads. Once in a while some child found a surprise in his lunch pail—a chicken leg, a piece of saskatoon pie, or store-bought cookies. If the children ate outside they shared their lunches with the animals just for the antics that accompanied the feeding. In the Larcombe S.D. (Stewart Lake, Man.) it was a chipmunk that provided all the amusement. He taught the children to wash their hands as he did in an elaborate ceremony after he ate each morsel of food. Then in some schools there was the fun of making cocoa by suspending a large kettle by the handle on a poker over the red coals in the stove. Now and then a teacher permitted the students to toast their sandwiches more for the diversion that it offered than for any other reason. The students of the Ridgeway School discovered that they could bake potatoes by placing them on the metal ring that surrounded the stove just above the fire-box. For the entire winter the youngsters appeared to thrive on a diet of baked potatoes, butter and salt. If left on the stove too long the potatoes burst open with a sudden "Poof!" The children enjoyed the surprising deflationary sound but not the teacher.

Winter brought an added problem to the rural children. By the time they reached school in the below-zero temperature their lunches had frozen solid. Hence during this season of the year the pails were brought right into the classroom and placed around the stove. This gave the food inside the bucket a chance to thaw out. The sandwiches turned soggy but were still edible.

The lunch pail was a symbol of the Little White Schoolhouse. Not many people of that day will ever forget how the shiny dinner pail caught the sun's rays as it swung energetically in its owner's hand; how wars were

—S. B. Smith

Three little girls homeward bound from the Poplar Dale School (Dapp, Alberta), with lunch pails gleaming in the sun.

waged with these weapons; how the dented pails came home with no excuses for their many shapes; how sometimes their contents became sadly depleted before noon; how during the warm barefoot days the youngsters removed their shoes and stockings and carried them home in their lunch pails; and finally, how the teacher's attempt to encourage better lunches and more gracious lunch-time habits always met with defeat.

The libraries of the one-room school were inadequate. An auspicious beginning was made in 1912 when the Alberta Government gave an annual grant of new books to each school. As a result every district had the nucleus of a good library. However the policy was discontinued by the Farmers' Government in 1922 and most schools found themselves with inadequate libraries. Very few volumes were added as a good number of pioneer parents, including trustees, did not approve of the children reading too many books. "Just filling their heads with trash!" some remarked. The school that managed a collection of one hundred books or more was considered fortunate. British teachers, in particular, encouraged the students to read, and influenced school boards to build up splendid libraries. The standard rural library contained many of the old classics, a few modern books of the day and a sprinkling of reference materials. There was a decided lack of books suitable for small children.

Since the children spent most of their school day working by themselves, reading became a pet diversion. Of course a few boys and girls were not a bit interested in reading but a goodly number became bookworms. If the libraries had been adequate, and some were, the rural schools would have offered better educational opportunities for their students than the spoon-feeding centralized institutions. As it was, the rural child learned as much from the books that he read as he did from his teacher. A casual inspection of the school library indicated that the books were being used. They were dirty, marked, dog-eared and well-worn. No wonder—some of the students had read and reread each one two or three times.

Books were prized. They were given as awards and as Christmas or birthday presents in those days, rather than toys. Teachers made their own books available to the children or even went so far as to donate books to the library. The same was true of parents who were fortunate in owning a few books. The Eaton's or Simpson's catalogue was the only book to be found in some homes. It was not unusual for schools to sponsor money-raising activities to buy books for their library. The boys in the Social Plains S.D. made an assortment of bird-houses out of apple-boxes and tin-cans while the girls sewed a few simple articles of clothing out of flour-sacks. The proceeds from the sale of these items enabled the school to purchase many needed books for the library. A number of rural schools supplemented their meagre libraries by soliciting city public libraries for their discarded volumes. All the schools had to do was to pay the express charges. The Ensleaf S.D. (Buffalo, Alta.) once received a shipment of thirty-three books from the Calgary Public Library after directing an appeal to the proper city authorities.

Some students made excellent use of these rural school libraries. Read what two former pupils had to say about their experiences with books. First, Irma, who attended the Jordon S.D. 3431 (Ravenscrag, Sask.):

"I trace my love of good books back to my early school days in the Jordon School and to the top shelf of its glass-doored library. On that top shelf were twenty red-bound volumes of the Books of Knowledge. My eager mind reached for that knowledge like a hungry child gobbling a plate of various foods—taking a taste of each kind in case it should be snatched away before he had sampled all of them.

"I remember so many of the divisions of those books—The Book of Golden Deeds, The Book of All Countries, The Book of Famous Stories and The Book of Poetry. I remember as clearly as if it was yesterday the full-page colored illustrations of Marley's Ghost, Fezziwigg's Ball and of Robinson Crusoe in his goatskin garments. I remember the black-and-white pictures of the unfortunate Little Princes in the Tower, the rich Inca Rulers of the Andes and of the hideous but fascinating Boa Constrictor strangling his prey. Truly those volumes contained a feast for the mind!

"About the time of the first snowfall each year Jordon School was closed for the winter. We took our arithmetic books home and struggled away as best we could over the long dreary holidays. I think my father loved books, too, for somehow, either legally or illegally, he managed to gain custody of the dearly beloved Books of Knowledge while the school was closed. No one could have taken better care of them! Our hands were washed, the table cleared, and the youngsters sent off to bed for the night, before father and I shared the books around the coal-oil lamp with a feeling almost akin to reverence. The times I liked best were when we came to the Book of Things to Make and Do. At home we could actually try these things; in my spare time at school I had only been able to read about them.

"Now most children have access to a paid-by-the-month encyclopedia in their own homes, supplemented by several sets at school and more at the public library. Perhaps the very surfeit makes them less attractive. I think that few of our modern young people get the pleasure that I did from the right to share that single top shelf."

Caroline gives an enlightening description of a typical rural school library, while she reminisces about the one in the Moose Hill S.D. 2727 (Thorhild, Alta.).

"I am so thankful to the person who chose the books for that first library. There was a huge Webster's dictionary and two or three pocket editions. There was an encyclopedia but as I remember there was only one volume of it. We found it too large to carry home for research or anywhere for that matter except to the nearest desk.

"All the classics prescribed for reading were there and I spent years travelling the byways of the world with their people. Also there was a volume of Swiss Family Robinson. Never since have I seen one and how I long to read it again. There were others like Uncle Tom's Cabin, Black Beauty, Robinson Crusoe, Tale of Two Cities, The Talisman, Lorna Doone, Gulliver's Travels, Tom Brown's School Days, Grimm's Fairy Tales, Christmas Carol, Hiawatha and Evangeline and The Story of Little Nell. Name the book and it could be found in our library.

"We could take the books home to read, which I often did. Our family spent many cozy winter evenings around the glowing heater while dad read aloud in his lovely tenor voice the poems and stories which I had picked for us.

"No Horatio Alger stories were to be found nor girls' or boys' books for which I am glad, much as I loved Little Women. The volumes on our shelves were citizen's books, character-building and vision-giving. Thank you very much, our pioneers!"

Generally speaking the children in the rural schools took infinitely more care of their library books than youngsters are wont to do today. A bright boy who lived alone with his father in a tiny one-room log shack in the Hillman S.D. 3077 (Dapp, Alta.) in 1936 illustrates this point neatly. The lad read everything he could and used to ask his teacher each Friday for permission to take home some of the reference books in the library or a few of the teacher's books, particularly the Books of

Knowledge. These he wrapped carefully in protective paper and carried them home as if they were made of china.

A favorite plea of children was, "Read me a story!" Rural teachers did just that. On Friday afternoons, or whenever the work was completed on the other days of the week, she read aloud to the whole school from a book such as Treasure Island, Black Beauty, or Beautiful Joe. The teacher's ability to read it dramatically added much to the children's enjoyment of the story. Sometimes the interest reached such a pitch that students begged the teacher to continue reading during the recesses or the noon hour. "Please teacher! Read just one more chapter. Please!" they pleaded. It was a touching scene to see a group of attentive youngsters crowded about the teacher's desk following the story word by word. The smaller students stood so close to the teacher that at times they touched, or even placed a loving hand on her. If she had permitted them some most certainly would have crawled onto her lap. Quite often the teacher stopped reading at a crucial point in the story and this created some dismay. If this happened, the pupils discussed the incidents that led up to the climax and attempted to guess the outcome. As the plot in the story unfolded the children smiled and displayed happiness if everything was going well with their heroes, but it was not uncommon to see a tear or two if misfortune overtook them. The children lived the story vicariously.

Educationalists might shudder at the thought of a grade one pupil attempting to get something from a reading of "The Lady of the Lake" along with the grade nines. But maybe the idea is not as preposterous as it sounds after reading about Edna Edler's experience in the Broadview S.D. (Broadview, Sask.).

> "On Friday afternoons the teacher read to us from Scott's 'The Lady of the Lake'. Such enthralling moments those were.
>
> "I can't recall that I had ever seen a deer at that time, yet under the hypnotism cast about in that little schoolroom by the voice of our teacher, I sat spellbound while the noble stag 'tossed his beamed frontlets to the sky' and quivered with anticipation as he 'gazed down the dale, sniffed the tainted gale and listened to the cry that thickened as the chase drew nigh.'
>
> "Years later, when I studied 'The Lady of the Lake' as literature in high school, fellow students were inclined to raise their eyebrows when I told them I had already taken the poem in grade one."

Reading of a story by the teacher was considered to be a privilege so if the children misbehaved the favor was withdrawn. On the other hand if their deportment was above-average the teacher read an extra chapter or so. It was surprising what an exciting story and good reader could do for the discipline of the school.

Friday afternoons were reserved for a variety of special activities. If the teacher had a fair voice, or the ability to coax a tune from a piano or organ, she taught the class many of the favorite songs. Sometimes a tuning fork was the only instrument available so at least it gave the would-be singers the correct note. The children loved a sing-song. No one held back. They all joined in, including the monotones and those whose voices were changing, singing lustily and sincerely although probably not too tunefully. Who cared? Nobody was listening and they were happy making a joyful sound. They sang songs like: Goodby My Bluebird, Tipperary, We'll Never Let the Old Flag Fall, There's a Long Long Trail, Keep the Homefires Burning, Clementine and so on. Each child had his special songs and volunteered, if cajoled sufficiently or even shoved physically forward by his classmates, to sing a solo. Some preferred to sing in duets as it gave them an added sense of security to have a friend accompany them to the front. Those who felt that their ability did not extend to music offered to recite, give a reading, or put on an act. Soon an impromptu program began to unfold. It gathered momentum as the afternoon slipped by but mysteriously stopped just before three-thirty.

Now and then these Friday afternoon activities proved disappointing. Since the children enjoyed and anticipated these periods a few went so far as to prepare special numbers for the program. Their chagrin was obvious if the teacher cancelled the Friday performance after an "incident". The guilty ones and the potential performers sat through the entire miserable afternoon with lowered eyes, damaged pride, and depressed emotions. The lowered morale often prompted the teacher to alter her decision. "All right! since you feel that badly about it. You can have your concert!" The prevailing mood swiftly changed to one of relief and pleasure accompanied by a whit of reservation. The program that followed consistently lacked the spirit of good fellowship that had characterized all of the other ones. The trespassing students and the punishing and forgiving teacher had in some mysterious manner detracted from the gaiety of the occasion.

Not all Friday afternoons were devoted to this particular type of pastime. There were contests of all types including spelling, geography, charades and softball. Students were permitted to spend some time on their supplementary reading or painting exercises. Painting with water-colors was such a time-consuming enterprise that many teachers preferred to teach the whole school on Friday afternoons. In this way it became an enjoyable and unhurried art lesson. Friday afternoon was also the time to go beyond the school yard and study nature at firsthand whether it was a visit to a hawk's nest high on a neighboring hill or an excursion to a valley to see a newly-discovered snake pit. Skating or just sliding on the ice of a frozen slough was a treat for the youngsters, both old and young alike. So were the jaunts to the snowcovered slopes for sleighing, tobogganing or skiing. True their vehicles were only the backs of broken desks, ends of boxes, or sheets of tin, but the boys and girls had as much fun as if they were using the real things. There was no end to the number, or nature of these Friday afternoon diversions. Furthermore, no matter what sphere of action was followed the teacher and students enjoyed the relaxation and the close association that it permitted.

This spirit of the Little White Schoolhouse continues to live among the yellow and well-worn pages of the odd school yearbook or diary still in existence today. The students of the Wiese S.D. 3089 (Scapa, Alta.) began such a document in 1934 and continued it until 1954 the year the school was closed. Mrs. Freda Viste, a former student, has carefully preserved these historical records. So turn back the calendar to 1934 and follow the students of the Wiese School in their day-to-day activities for the months of January and June.

January   9—Started making a ski slide.
January 10—Finished the ski slide.
January 11—The weather was fine when we came but we went home in a
            blizzard.
January 14—Annie was sick today.
January 15—Frank and Joseph stayed home.
January 16—Dick went home with a gunny sack around his face.
January 17—Gauglers went home in a hay rack.
January 18—Sleigh bells heard again. Roads are open.
January 21—Weather recovering after 50° below.
January 22—We are all expecting a chinook.
January 23—Our chinook died out at Calgary.
January 24—Another struggle with geometry.
January 25—Lucy and Donald taught Frank and Annie some manners in
            a small play this afternoon.
January 28—Played coyote and dog in the deep snow.
January 29—We took pictures for our annual book.
January 30—Exams start. We took pictures of the ski slide.
January 31—We were all out rolling balls for the snow forts.
June   3—We examined the new readers.
June   4—Gwyneth came back to school.
June   5—Lucy took her music lessons at noon and recess.
June   6—Today was the last composition period before exams.
June   7—Losers in the health chart brought candy.
June   10—We got some tennis balls.
June   11—Took pictures under the trees.
June   12—Bugs are coming from all directions.
June   13—It was very rainy this morning and children got to school at
            all hours of the day.
June   14—We heard Frank Brunners had a new brother.
June   17—First final examination.
June   18—Mr. Williams and Mr. Haessel were very busy cultivating the
            school trees. There was a Social Credit meeting that night.
June   19—There was a strong smell of smoke in the school.
June   20—A strong wind was blowing all day.

June 21—We had a ball game in the evening. We took up a collection for prizes for June 28.

June 24—Frank brought five bees for the insect collection for the fair.

June 25—We had sun, wind, rain and dust today.

June 26—All examinations were finished for the year.

June 27—Phyllis and Jean took their last look at the school.

June 28—We had a picnic with ice cream and fine lunch.

The Little White Schoolhouse had its bad days too. Take the years when dust storms swept across the prairies. Black blizzards, some people called them. They devastated the fields and ruined the crops. Farms lost from a hundred to a thousand tons of earth per acre. Ditches disappeared under shifting hills of soil, while mounds of sand appeared along road allowances covering fences and machinery. Buildings became grey with the dry pulverized particles of earth. Meals not immediately eaten became covered with dust in minutes. In the Thirties, especially in 1932, 1934, and 1937 all records were broken for drought, dust and poverty. Sloughs and wells went dry. Many young children never knew what rain was like. The sun beat down relentlessly day after day searing the last traces of green and turning the prairies into miniature deserts. The boys and girls had to learn to study, play and grow in the stifling heat and the persistent dust. When one of the many storms whined and groaned as it whipped its precious black cargo around the corners of the schoolhouse the teachers knew what to do. They kept the students working harder than ever. The youngsters stopped frequently in their labors to blow away the accumulation of sand on their scribblers. If this wasn't done the grit lodged between the paper and the point of the pencil and made writing an impossibility. It required an unflagging pioneer spirit to study under such depressing and uncertain conditions. Education had to go on in spite of the economic and agricultural destruction being wrought by nature on the outside. The dustbowl days were not to be in vain.

Experiences with dust storms were never pleasant. Two schools in the Fort MacLeod area of Alberta illustrate this fact.

In the Parkerville S.D. 2903 the sand storms became so severe in 1919 that the teacher waited until the black blizzard subsided somewhat before dismissing school. When she considered it safe she instructed the children to walk hand-in-hand down the centre of the road allowance. This precaution was necessary to prevent the smaller tots from being blown against the barbed wire fence and injured.

The Burmis S.D. had a different problem. A severe dust storm stripped off all the paint on one side of the school. It was repainted. But three days later another storm blew up and completely sanded the new paint job. After these experiences the trustees decided to forego, for the time being, their attempts to improve the outside appearance of the school.

—Mrs. J. P. Mitchell

The children of Clover Bar S.D. 212 (Bremner, Alta.) homeward bound.
(Winter of 1938).

Usually the rural school that started the day with the Lord's prayer also had a fitting closing exercise. The students who attended the school at Lake Louise between 1912 and 1920 will never forget the words of the song they used to sing at dismissal time.

> "Now the day is over
> Night is drawing nigh
> Shadows of the evening
> Steal across the sky.
>
> Now the darkness gathers
> Stars begin to peep,
> Birds and beasts and flowers
> Soon will be asleep."

No sound can be more pleasing to a child's ear than the tinkling of the desk-bell at 3:30. Instantly the youngsters surge to the back of the room to prepare for the trip home. The big boys took very little time in dressing and almost in one motion were on their way to the barn to harness the horses. In the meantime the teacher and some of the older girls began stuffing the little people into their heavy coats and wrapping their heads with scarves. Overshoes were always a bugbear. First it required some searching before the right pair could be found and secondly it took patience and dexterity to be able to pull a size three overshoe over a size four shoe. After a few hectic minutes it was always a comforting sight to be able to gaze on five or six small students bundled up to their very

No. 3 Russell Scho.

MONTHLY REPORT

of Georgina Britt

for month of March 1878

Third Class Jr. Section.

Perfect Recitations.	Imperfect Recitations.	Total No. in Class.	Standing in Class.	Times late.	Days absent.	Marks of Good Conduct.	Marks of Bad Conduct.	Total marks of Credit.	Total marks of Discredit.
53		9	1	0	1	18	2	71	3

The greatest number of CREDIT MARKS given to any member of this Class was 71

given to Georgina Britt

The greatest number of DISCREDIT MARKS given to any member of this Class was 22

WHlearoon Teacher.

N.B.—Parents will please examine, sign, and return this Report without delay.

J. Britt Parent's Signature.

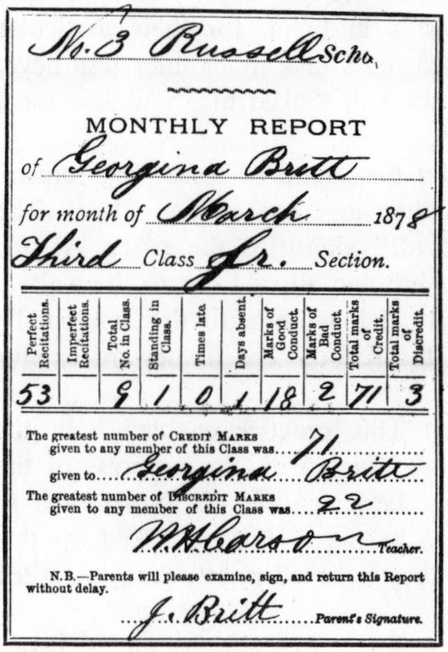

A REPORT CARD OF 1878

An examination of the type of report cards used in 1878 by Public School No. 3 in the Russell Township of Ontario reveals that teachers taught "students" rather than "subject-matter". No mention was made of whether a student was good, bad or indifferent in a particular area of study like arithmetic or grammar, but rather emphasis was placed on the development of such personal attributes as deportment, punctuality, good study habits, and discipline.

—L. E. Helmer

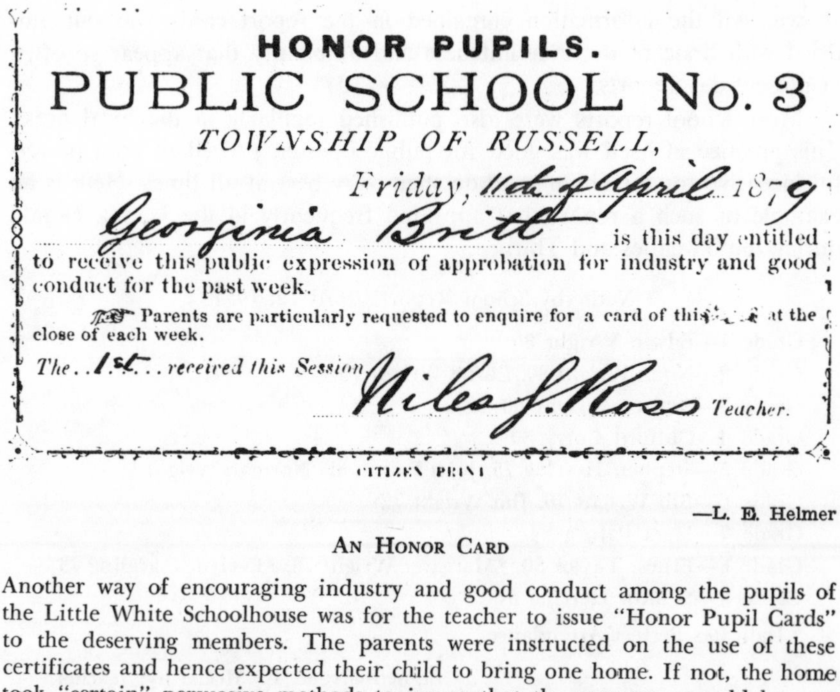

HONOR PUPILS.

PUBLIC SCHOOL No. 3

TOWNSHIP OF RUSSELL,

Friday, 11th of April 1879

Georginia Britt is this day entitled to receive this public expression of approbation for industry and good conduct for the past week.

☞ Parents are particularly requested to enquire for a card of this kind at the close of each week.

The 1st *received this Session.*

Niles J. Ross *Teacher.*

CITIZEN PRINT

—L. E. Helmer

AN HONOR CARD

Another way of encouraging industry and good conduct among the pupils of the Little White Schoolhouse was for the teacher to issue "Honor Pupil Cards" to the deserving members. The parents were instructed on the use of these certificates and hence expected their child to bring one home. If not, the home took "certain" persuasive methods to insure that the youngster would be sure to earn one the following week.

eyes in warm clothing. They looked like stuffed teddy bears as they patiently and silently waited, lunch pails in hand, for their particular rig to drive up from the stable. The teacher's task as clothier was never quite finished. Up to the last moment she still looked high and low for a missing mitt, or scarf.

The sharp clatter of horse hoofs and the sound of screeching runners heralded the arrival of somebody's cutter in front of the school. The shout "Are you ready?" or "All aboard!" identified the party. At this bidding one or two youngsters came to life and slipped out to the waiting sleigh. This routine was repeated again and again until the last bundle of humanity had taken its leave from the school. The homeward exodus had begun.

Report cards were issued monthly. This practice enabled both the teacher and the parents to keep in close touch with the progress of the child. If something was amiss it could be diagnosed in ample time to permit some form of remedial action to be taken. Parents asked for this frequency of receiving report cards for they believed rightly that, "A stitch in time saves nine."

The student's progress in each subject was rated by a percentage mark. Even subjects like writing, drawing, music, handwork and memory work were assigned marks based on 100. The student's rank in class was also shown. All the information contained in the report cards was cut-and-dried with none of the indefiniteness and ambiguity that appear so often in present-day reports.

Most school reports were also published regularly in the local press. This practice in itself was good for public opinion proved to be a powerful incentive for the children to do their very best at all times. Here is an example of such a report that appeared frequently in the Hanna Herald during the Twenties and Thirties.

Netherby School Report, April 12, 1934

Grade 1—Edwin Wright 85
Grade 2—Nona Wright 80, Lorne Wright 70
Grade 3—Audrey Wright 80
Grade 4—Clifford Corry 80
Grade 5—Stephen Herring 75, Joan Patton 65, Norman Wright 55
Grade 6—Bill Wright 76, Jim Wright 72
Grade 7—Meta Patton 84
Grade 8—Ernest Taylor 80, *Margaret Wright 78, *Evelyne Standing 73
Grade 9—*Philip Herring 81

* Indicates Perfect Attendance.

Signed—Irene E. McCarthy, teacher,
Netherby S.D. 2348.

MARKING

100% = Perfect = PP
Over 90% = E   Over 80% = VG
" 70% = G   " 60% = FG
" 50% = I   " 40% = P
Fail = F. 40 and Under

PARENTS and GUARDIANS

are cordially invited to co-operate with the teacher for the better advancement of the child.

Please examine this report carefully and note pupil's progress. This report should be properly signed and returned to the teacher.

....
Principal.

TEACHER'S REPORT

On ......Bernard...Smith.........
Month...June...1931...Grade....I.A.....
School....Rosy Lynn #350.....
Teacher....Mb.A.Park.....

Subject	Possible Mark	Pupil's Mark	Subject	Possible Mark	Pupil's Mark
Reading		V.G.	Writing		70.
Literature			Drawing		85.
Composition			Handwork		80.
Grammar			Nat. Study & Agric.		
Spelling		G.	Music		
Geography			Mem. Gems		V.G.
Hygiene			French		
Civics			Ancient History		
Can. History			Science		
Eng. History					
Arithmetic		95.			
Geometry			Attendance		
Algebra			Punctuality		
No. in Class		2.	Total		
Rank in Class		1st	Average		85%.
Attitude to work		V.G.	Times Late		
Progress		V.G.	Days School Open		57.
Conduct		G.	Half Days Absent		0.

Teacher's Remarks: .....Bernard..is..a........
....very..good..pupil.........
....Mary..A..Smith
Parent's Signature

—Mrs. David B. Smith

A sample page from a type of report card that was used in the days of the rural school.

The highlight of any school year was undoubtedly the writing of the Department of Education Entrance Examinations. For a good many students it meant the end of their school education. They often worked at home until it became feasible for them to rent or buy a farm of their own. Land was cheap and it was possible for a young man to start farming with a minimum of equipment. The girls helped at home until one of the many bachelors in the district decided that he needed a help-mate. Many young farm people were also lured to the cities by prospects of jobs, independence and adventure.

All rural teachers were apprehensive of the Departmental Final Examinations. They meant so much! Teachers have been known to leave a particular school when the potential grade eight students appeared to be weak. The alternative was to hold back the dull ones in grade seven and only promote the bright pupils. New teachers always took cognizance of this situation and the backward youngsters in the entrance class could expect a hard and unpleasant year. The worship of this grade-eight or nine fetish in the rural schools amounted to an evil. The teachers often neglected to a greater or lesser degree the other students in the school in their attempt to achieve a good pass record on the final examinations. The entrance class received special lessons before nine o'clock, during the noon hour, after school and on Saturdays. It was work, work, work and more work. During this period of intense preparation the teachers became adamant, irritable and seemingly very unfriendly. Students struggled and suffered, but little did they realize that the teachers were also going through torments of their own. The poor students were apparently getting poorer and the average ones were having a struggle to retain what little they had learned. Cramming for examinations was both unpleasant and nerve-wracking. In fact the start of the final examinations was greeted with a sense of relief after the ordeals of reviewing.

The grade eights used to write five examinations during the last week in the month of June. These included: Arithmetic and Rapid Calculation; Literature and Spelling; History; Geography and Civics; Composition and Grammar; Agriculture; Hygiene and Art. These examinations were all of three-hours duration scheduled either between 9:00 and 12:00 in the morning, or between 2:00 and 5:00 in the afternoon. When the grade nine entrance examinations were introduced in 1936 they consisted of papers in: Reading, a General Ability Test, Language, Social Studies, Literature, Science, Mathematics.

The examination papers were sent from the Department by registered mail to the secretary-treasurer of the school district. It was his or her responsibility to safeguard the papers and deliver to the teacher each day the envelope containing the proper examination. In the early days before school secretaries became acquainted with examination practices the papers were delivered directly to the teacher. The local teacher presided during the writing of the examinations and in the end was required to make a declaration before a justice of the peace, or a commissioner of oaths, that every detail of the regulations governing the examinations had been observed.

Things happened during examination time.

An outbreak of scarlet fever occurred in the East Kleskun S.D. 3635 in the Peace River Country at the close of the school year. The six grade nine students were unable to write their final examinations, some of them as a result of being ill with scarlet fever and others being quarantined as contacts. The entire district was upset for they feared that the ailing students would have to repeat their year. Such was not the case. As it happened all the grade nines were recommended by the superintendent on the basis of their year's work. Sadness quickly changed to joy in the East Kleskun district.

The first time the grade eight examinations were held in the McCann S.D. 2562 (Hanna, Alta.) everyone evinced an interest. The school had now attained a certain status in the educational world. The trustees felt that the majority of students would be deprived of several days of education if they dismissed the rest of the school in order to permit the two grade eight girls to write the finals undisturbed. Frank McCann, the sixty-year-old bachelor and chairman of the school board, had a solution. Since his farmyard was just across from the school, he moved two granaries into the schoolyard and placed them side by side near the school. Each girl had a private examination room to herself. While the regular teacher taught in the schoolhouse, Mr. McCann paced back and forth in front of the two granaries overseeing the two grade eights inside. Without a doubt this was the best supervised class in the history of Departmental Examinations. However the teacher, being a truthful and conscientious girl, refused to sign the examiner's declaration. After all she did not supervise the examinations. The Department officials notified Mr. McCann that unless the declaration was forthcoming the results of the grade eight examinations of the McCann students would be withheld. Delay followed delay but the teacher maintained her original stand and refused to sign. Finally Mr. L. H. Thurber, the school inspector, visited the district and settled the matter with the chairman. The McCann School returned to the standard practice of supervising Departmental Examinations.

Examinations are still examinations no matter when or where they are written. But in the rural school they appeared to carry just a trace more significance. All the other children in the school would be dismissed for their summer holidays and this in itself left the school as quiet as a tomb. The students writing the examinations arrived at the school much earlier than had been their custom, dressed in their best clothes. They crowded together like people who were anticipating some imminent tragedy but didn't quite know what it was likely to be. The children tried to be brave but nobody was fooled. The nervous laughter, the attempt to be witty, the fidgety hands and the constant pacing all pointed out the tenseness of the moment. The teacher was no different. She darted about the room like a sheep-dog tending her flock, doing useless errands. Soon the students, as if going to their doom, moved silently to their assigned seats. Several empty desks on either side isolated each youngster from the rest. They were caught. They waited with pounding hearts and breathless expectation as the teacher tore open the huge official brown envelope and distributed copies of the examination to each one. The examination was about to start.

As if in a dream each child glanced through the questions on the paper. They appeared to be reading and yet not reading. A number always just sat there and gazed into space or tried to collect their scattered thoughts. These leisurely and time-consuming preliminaries exasperated the anxious teacher. One by one, in their own good time, they eventually turned to the task at hand. After that the scratching of pens, the lazy drone of blow flies and the steady ticking of the school clock were the only sounds heard. The odd squirrel or gopher sometimes stole into the quiet examination room, caught sight of the hard-working children, and quickly scampered out again. Periodically the rumble of a wagon, or the beat of horse hoofs, indicated that someone was passing by the school. But for once the students did not look out to see who it could be.

Soon, all too soon, the teacher announced in a nervous, high-pitched voice, "Time is up. Everyone stop writing."

There is no feeling more frustrating than the one that follows turning in the paper. Yes, the students were very elated that the examination was finished, but the uncertainty of passing, acted as a damper on any levity. Some just knew that they had failed. Horses were understanding creatures, so more than one child wrapped an arm about the horse's neck and cried in its mane. It turned out to be a long and sad ride home that day. The horse appeared to comprehend the mood of his rider. He frequently turned and craned his neck to have a better look at the forlorn and unhappy youngster.

The last day of examination in the one-room school was the most depressing. Once the horses were saddled the individual youngsters started slowly and unwillingly for home. Each went his way. When the students looked back the schoolhouse appeared so desolate and insignificant basking in the hot sun with no children, no horses, and no buggies around it. Eight years was a long time to attend the same rural school yet there were many sad and happy memories to take away. It had been worth it. Time and again deep in meditation the boys and girls turned to wave to each other until eventually all were out of sight. It seemed as if a curtain had been wrung down unceremoniously to end an interesting play. A school term had come to an end.

Educators of today are resolved that the standards of education are steadily improving. But that is only an opinion! Why not find out experimentally how students of today would fare on a series of final examinations prepared originally for the grade eights of 1915?

Mrs. C. Nordstrum, a rural teacher from Wildwood, Alta., acquired a good collection of these examinations down through the years and she also put them to good use. Every May and June she prepared her students for the Entrance or Grade Eight Departmental Examinations by giving them the practice of working typical questions from these old examination papers.

Below are two examination papers taken from her collection, one in Grammar and the other in Arithmetic. It will be seen that the students who attended the "Little White Schoolhouse" must have been taught well to be able to pass such formidable tests.

DEPARTMENT OF EDUCATION
MANITOBA

*   *   *

ENTRANCE EXAMINATION, 1915

*   *   *

GRAMMAR

WEDNESDAY, JUNE 16, 14.00 TO 16.00 O'CLOCK

*   *   *

VALUES

16   1. Write:
  (a) The possessive case, singular and plural, of man, thief, child, heiress.
  (b) The comparative form of many, sweet, well, widely.
  (c) The objective case of I, he, they, who.
  (d) The past tense (1st pers. sing.) and past participle of dig, lie, bid, fly.

12   2. Define tense and voice. Name the tenses here illustrated and state the voice of the verb in each: I am praising; I am praised; I praised; I had been praised; I shall have praised; I shall be praised.

12   3. (a) State whether the present participle is used correctly or incorrectly in each of the following sentences, giving a reason for your answer in each case:
  Riding along the road, my hat was blown off.
  Hearing the noise, the people left their houses.
  The stable door being open, the horse was stolen.
  The hunters saw a number of dead wolves riding across the prairie.
  (b) Parse the words ending in "ing" in the following sentences:
  He earns his living by driving a motor.
  Driving carelessly around a corner one day, he ran into a working man who was crossing the street.

30   4. Analyse fully:
  When Columbus crossed the ocean to *America* in 1492, he *discovered* the *existence* of the current *which* enters the Caribbean Sea and helps *form* our Gulf Stream. All the old Spanish navigators noticed *this* current *and* wondered what could be its cause.

20   5. Parse fully the words italicized in the selection to be analysed.

10   6. Make corrections where necessary in the following sentences, giving a reason for each correction made:
  1. We will lose the train if we do not hurry.
  2. Neither he nor his brother are good writers.
  3. Between you and I there must always be friendship.
  4. This is the best of the two.
  5. John can write better than me.

DEPARTMENT OF EDUCATION
MANITOBA

* * *

ENTRANCE EXAMINATION, 1915

* * *

ARITHMETIC

FRIDAY, JUNE 18, 9.30 TO 11.30 O'CLOCK

* * *

VALUES

12   1. To the difference between 10.2 and 2.345 add the product of 0.2 and 43.68 and divide the sum by 2.5.

13   2. Find the amount, when due, of the following note:
      $272.50   Winnipeg, May 7th, 1915

      Three months after date I promise to pay to Charles Armstrong or Order, two hundred and seventy-two dollars and fifty cents with interest at eight per cent. per annum, value received.

J. H. Warner.

13   3. If a gallon of water weighs 10 lbs., and a cubic foot of water weighs 1,000 ozs., and a barrel holds 31½ gallons, how many barrels of water will be contained in a cylindrical cistern 14 feet in diameter and 9 feet deep?

13   4. A man bought a lot 120 feet long and 100 feet wide. He had it fenced at $7.50 a rod; and he had a cement walk 4 feet wide made around the lot inside the fence at 75c a square yard. How much did the fence and walk cost him?

12   5. At 85c a rod, how much will it cost to fence a square field containing 11 acres, 89 square rods?

12   6. From a school district assessed at $180,000 it is desired to collect by special tax $2,340. How much special tax will I have to pay on a half section of land in this district worth $43 an acre, and assessed at ¼ of its value?

12   7. A steer on foot weighed 1,325 pounds; when dressed it weighed 768½ pounds. The dressed beef was what per cent. of its live weight?

13   8. What would be the cost per acre of growing wheat, allowing for plowing at 3 acres per day, 2 harrowings at 15 acres per day, seeding at 15 acres per day, 6 pecks of seeds per acre at $1.00 per bushel, cutting at 75c per acre, shocking at 4 acres a day to each man, and a threshing expense of 7 cents per bushel on a yield of 24 bushels per acre. (Allow $2.00 a day per man; $4.50 per day for man and team.)

Many rural grade eight students were forced to go to an examination centre in some nearby town school to write their final examinations. This was a novel experience. The parents took them into town a day or two prior to the starting date and found a place to stay.

The five or so days spent in town was something the student never forgot. No matter how small the village or town was, to the children who had spent all, or most of their lives on farms, the streets seemed to teem with people. Excitement, color and adventure abounded everywhere. The youngsters felt sophisticated to be a part of this commotion. For once they felt they were "living it up". Even the opportunity to partake of such delicacies as bananas, store-bought cookies and soda added to the novelty of living in town. It was difficult to study for the examinations in such an unfamiliar and pulsating environment but most of the rural students managed nobly.

Throughout the summer holidays the students were haunted by the examinations. Did they pass, or did they fail? Their mood appeared to range between two extremes. On days when the youngster thought he had passed, his joy knew no bounds and he smiled, laughed, whistled and radiated goodwill everywhere. But on occasions when he foresaw failure a sense of gloom pervaded all his activities. Meals were half-eaten, favorite animals mistreated, harsh words spoken, chores shirked and all friends and relatives shunned. The day of judgment arrived in mid-August. Every daily newspaper published a list of successful candidates and the weeklies copied the names that concerned the people in their areas. It necessitated many closely-printed pages to do this but the editors believed that the examination results were important and had news value. They were right. Thousands upon thousands of children, parents and teachers carefully scanned the newspaper lists for certain all-important names. No sensation could quite compare to seeing them in print. They had passed their entrance examinations. What a relief after weeks of tension! It was incredible to believe. Yet there was the name in the paper. The youngsters gloated for days after the results were announced.

Some failed and did not see their names in print. They lived in depths of despondency for a while but soon realized that the world had not been shattered by their failure. Examinations did not prove to be the bugaboo that they had originally thought they were. Birds still sang, the hustle and bustle of harvest time were still there, the savory scent of new-mown hay was still there, the sun still rose and friends and relatives were still warm as ever. They discovered, much to their surprise, that they didn't have to pass examinations to enjoy life in the country. Soon these youngsters took up the thread of everyday living again. The student who finished grade eight and successfully wrote the Departmental Examinations in those days was much more of a phenomenon than the grade twelve matriculant is today.

Later on the successful student received his grade eight diploma from the Department of Education. It was an imposing-looking document bearing the student's name in script across the face of it and signed by the Minister of Education. It made one feel important to be officially recognized. There was no doubt any longer that the student had passed. But there were still worries. The big question now was what to do next. Continue on into high school, or what? Nevertheless the Little White Schoolhouse had demonstrated its ability to further the education of a future citizen of our land.

END OF VOLUME 1

INDEX